J. E. SPINGARN
AND THE RISE OF
THE NAACP,
1911 – 1939

B. JOYCE ROSS has taught at South Carolina State College, Howard University, and Kent State University and is now in the Department of History at Stanford University.

J. E. SPINGARN
AND THE RISE OF
THE NAACP,
1911 – 1939

B. Joyce Ross

STUDIES IN AMERICAN NEGRO LIFE
August Meier, General Editor

New York

ATHENEUM

1972

To my mother and father

Preface

I T IS a basic part of the liberal credo that a man need not
be black in order to become sincerely indignant about the
second-class citizenship status which is afforded his black neighbor. The twentieth-century civil rights movement, as manifested through large-scale organizations like the National
Association for the Advancement of Colored People and the
National Urban League, has been biracial in both administrative
leadership and membership. Indeed, whites were prominent in
the founding of both organizations.

This study seeks a deeper understanding of the role, motiva-
tions, strengths, and shortcomings of the white liberal leadership of minority-group organizations, by focusing in depth
upon one such white liberal, Joel Elias Spingarn, who served as
an incorporator of the NAACP, Chairman of its Board of
Directors, Treasurer, and President. Spingarn is an ideal choice
for a study of this nature, for his active participation in the
NAACP spanned, almost without interruption, twenty-eight

of the first thirty years of the organization's history. More significantly, he as an individual was sufficiently complex and his interests so varied that by looking through his eyes and seeing the organization's rise as he saw it, much light is shed upon such pertinent questions as the nature of the interpersonal relationships between whites like Spingarn and their black co-workers; the relationships which white administrators shared with each other; the extent to which the economic and social philosophy of a white liberal like Spingarn complemented or differed from that of his black counterparts; the influence of whites' philosophy in shaping the organization's tactical approach to the race problem; and, conversely, the impact of shifting currents of black thought and changing times on Spingarn's personal philosophy and outlook on the race problem. Although the study focuses upon Spingarn, his role is not presented in a vacuum. Through the use of brief syntheses, highlights of the organization's program and the activities of other key administrators are projected as a backdrop for his individual movements within the larger structure.

This study seeks neither to praise nor to blame Spingarn for what he was and what he did. Rather, its aim is to present the problems which confronted him, the alternatives available to him, the reasoning which governed his choices, and the consequences of his decisions upon the development of the organization and upon those closely associated with him. To do otherwise would amount to little more than an expression of the author's personal opinion, for as the study progressed it became quite clear that in the decade of the 1970's, as was the case in his own times, thousands of blacks would support his views while other thousands would be numbered among his most severe critics.

The study often sacrifices chronology in the interest of continuity of themes. Two simultaneous yet distinct processes were continually evident in the Association's rise: the interpersonal relationships attending its internal administration and the broader tactical program through which it seeks to realize its goals. Though Spingarn's dual roles of tactician and administrator progressed simultaneously, in this study they are often treated separately in the interest of clarity and completeness of thought.

Even with the aid of the most modern research equipment, the sheer vastness of the manuscript collections associated with a study of a large-scale organization like the NAACP presents a major problem (the Archives of the Association consist of some 800 boxes of material for the period to 1939 alone). One must somehow find a familiarity with the Archives which will permit sweeping yet valid statements regarding, for example, Board attendance over an extended period, or participation in the annual business meetings of the corporation. It is only with a prior understanding of how the democratization of the corporation in the 1930's brought about the twilight of white liberalism that the closing of the corporation during the formative years assumes real meaning.

Several of the key administrators during the organization's formative years have no collected papers, a factor which is particularly damaging to a study of Spingarn, since he rarely retained copies of his personal correspondence. Especially conspicuous for their absence are the papers of Mary White Ovington and May Childs Nerney. This same problem arises in regard to such key Board members as Paul Kennaday, Isadore Martin, and William A. Sinclair. The absence of collected correspondence of the overwhelming majority of early Board members partially obscures the precise nature of the interpersonal relationships within the administrative hierarchy during the early period.

B. J. R.

Acknowledgments

I WISH to express my appreciation to all who have aided in the preparation of this work. Mrs. J. E. Spingarn not only provided valuable insights into the period through personal recollections of the activities of her husband and his associates but also gave me access to her husband's papers and made available family records in her possession. Though plagued with ill-health and advanced age, Arthur Barnett Spingarn shared with me his personal recollections of the early evolution of the Association's legal department, providing data which otherwise would not have been available. Mrs. James Weldon Johnson generously permitted me access to her husband's papers, and Herbert Aptheker placed at my disposal the W. E. B. Du Bois Papers, transporting the manuscripts daily by subway to and from his home, at what must have been considerable inconvenience to him. Preparation of the first draft of the manuscript was facilitated by a generous research grant from Howard University.

I am most of all indebted to August Meier and Elliott Rudwick, whose criticisms and suggestions proved invaluable and
whose friendship and encouragement have been more decisive
than I can fully express or than they perhaps can ever fully
realize. I have also benefited immeasurably from the suggestions of Robert Beisner, Robert Zangrando, Roger Brown, and
Thomas V. DiBacco, who served as dissertation committee
members when the manuscript was submitted in partial fulfillment of the Ph.D. degree at American University. Two
personal friends, Elois H. J. King and Stella Jones McLain,
shared with me both their insightful criticisms of the manuscript and the sustaining warmth and patience which only true
friends can provide.

Last but certainly not least, I am indebted to the numerous
librarians and library staff members who saved me countless
research hours by generously sharing their vast, firsthand
knowledge of the holdings of their respective facilities. I am
especially appreciative of the efforts of the staffs of the Howard
University Library, the Yale University Library, the Houghton Library of Harvard University, the Amistad Research
Center at Fisk University, the New York Public Library, the
Library of Congress, and the Morgan State College Library.
Needless to say, although many have contributed to the positive aspects of the volume, all faults and errors are solely my
own.

Contents

J. E. SPINGARN
AND THE RISE OF
THE NAACP,

1911 – 1939

I

RENAISSANCE MAN

LIKE SOME latter-day Renaissance man, J. E. Spingarn immersed himself in an endless variety of pursuits, both intellectual and practical. Enamored by the concept of the scholar as man of action, he encompassed within his lifetime the careers of teacher, writer, poet, publisher, horticulturalist, progressive politician, soldier, and humanitarian reformer. Indeed, before becoming affiliated with the NAACP in 1910, he already had attained national recognition as a foremost scholar in the field of literary criticism. That Spingarn undertook so many pursuits was perhaps neither uncommon nor phenomenal. But that he excelled in all of them would have made him an extraordinary man in any age.

Elias Spingarn—the surname is a derivation of "spinners of yarn"—migrated with his brother from their native home on the outskirts of Vienna to New York City in the late 1840's. Endowed with little material wealth, Elias, like thousands of other immigrants, sought to make a new start, later specializing in the wholesale tobacco trade. Presently he married Sarah Barnett, a native of Hull, England, and, like himself, of Jewish lineage. Joel Elias, the first of four sons, was born in May 1875.

Arthur Barnett Spingarn, whose career in the NAACP was to parallel and extend beyond that of his brother, was born three years later in 1878.[1]

There was little in J. E. Spingarn's background to foreshadow his emergence as the most flamboyant of the twentieth-century Abolitionists. Unlike some of his white counterparts in the NAACP, he could boast no Abolitionist heritage. Even Abraham Lincoln had not received Elias Spingarn's political support. According to family legend, the elder Spingarn had seen and heard Lincoln for the first time when he delivered the famous Cooper Union speech, but he considered the Illinoisan so unimpressive in terms of both physical appearance and doctrine that he later cast his lot with the Democrats. By the turn of the century, Elias Spingarn, who remained a staunch Democrat throughout the post-Civil War period, had built a thriving wholesale tobacco business, and enjoyed the enviable status of senior member of the New York State Chamber of Commerce. There is no indication that he manifested any active interest in the race problem.[2]

Both his training and his talents peculiarly suited the young J. E. Spingarn for predominantly intellectual pursuits. Upon completion of his secondary education (Elias Spingarn enrolled his sons in the public school system so that they might be exposed to classmates from a variety of backgrounds), he briefly matriculated at the Collegiate Institute of New York City and the City College of New York, then entered Columbia College, where he majored in literature. During his senior year he came under the influence of George E. Woodberry, one of the nation's foremost authorities in the field of literature and the favorite student of James Russell Lowell and of Charles Eliot Norton, the translator of Dante. In later years Spingarn credited Woodberry, whom he termed "the greatest teacher our country has ever known," with having introduced him to a finer humanism than any of his contemporaries of the 1930's could boast. Immediately upon the completion of his undergraduate studies at Columbia in 1895, Spingarn enrolled at Harvard University for a year of postgraduate study. The following year he returned to Columbia for doctoral study, graduating as the youngest man (twenty-four years old) in his class in 1899.[3]

The first decade of Spingarn's professional career seemed further to portend a long and distinguished career in the world of academe. In 1899 he accepted an opportunity to work with George Woodberry as an assistant professor in Columbia's Department of Comparative Literature, quickly gaining a reputation as *the* brilliant young man on the faculty, and publishing his doctoral dissertation, *History of Literary Criticism in the Renaissance*, before the end of his first year of teaching. Spingarn's simplicity of style, coupled with the mastery and critical discernment which he brought to his subject, won him international acclaim and established the volume as a classic in its field. A relatively prolific man of letters, Spingarn buttressed the acclaim accruing from the impressive *History* with nearly a score of additional publications by the mid-1920's, the most important in terms of their impact upon the academic community being *New Criticism* (1911) and *Creative Criticism* (1917). In addition, he was given to dashing off poetry— one of his best-known verses was begun during a train ride— encompassing an endless variety of subjects and moods. His first volume of verse, *New Hesperides and Other Poems*, appeared in 1911 and a second, *Poems*, in 1924. His commanding status within the academic community was reflected in his personal acquaintance and friendship with many of the nation's most illustrious literati—including Carl Sandburg, H. L. Mencken, Upton Sinclair, and Ludwig Lewisohn—some of whom solicited his critical advice in the preparation of their manuscripts.[4]

Yet, as if fate had played some cruel joke, Spingarn, as an academician, was to be the proverbial prophet without honor in his own time. By 1908 he had begun utilizing his major publications, most notably *New Criticism* and *Creative Criticism*, to expand on a revolutionary thesis which he had partially imbibed from Woodberry: that the impact of a work of art upon the viewer was not the determinant of its value; rather, that every work possessed an intrinsic value, "something that in itself is a life and a full life." Spingarn was the

6

first to introduce in America the works of the Italian philosopher Benedetto Croce, one of the foremost European exponents of the new concept of criticism, and he actively sought to revive interest in other writers of the pan-European tradition of scholarship, including De Sanctis, Gentile, Borgese, and Pareto.[5]

But Croce and Spingarn's thesis was squarely opposed to the dominant contemporary trend in American literary criticism, which had been greatly influenced by John Dewey's pragmatism. Instead of appraising a work as having an inherent value, critics were prone to subject the poem, the play, or the essay to the pragmatic test of its effectiveness in terms of critical public acceptance, its fulfillment of the author's objectives, or the motivation which had called it forth. One professor at Urbana, Illinois, termed Spingarn's thesis un-American, although Spingarn explained that Ralph Waldo Emerson and James Russell Lowell had espoused a similar view. A Harvard humanist denounced the thesis as a romantic denial of the moral obligation of the artist, and some of Spingarn's colleagues at Columbia so vehemently opposed his doctrine that on occasion he refrained from discussing points of literary criticism in order to avoid conflict. Yet, like some latter-day prophet, Spingarn was merely ahead of his times. By the mid-1920's a new school of critics, led by Ludwig Lewisohn and Isaac Goldberg, were pioneering in the application of the controversial concept, and they were joined by such writers as T. S. Eliot, John Crowe Ransom, and Allen Tate. By the end of the 1930's Spingarn's thesis generally was accepted as a truism, but long before then he had retired from university life without having been wholly vindicated.[6]

Indeed, by 1910 a confluence of forces had cast a shadow over Spingarn's once promising career at Columbia. The opposition which his controversial thesis occasioned among his colleagues already has been noted. More importantly, he, like a host of other middle-class Americans of the progressive era, experienced firsthand what he believed to be a loss of status within his profession, a phenomenon which he largely attributed to the invasion of university affairs by a new economic plutocracy. Hofstadter and Metzger [7] have indicated that members of the *nouveau riche* business class of the post-Civil War era, whose financial contributions often facilitated the advent of the modern university with its superior equipment, research facilities, and professional standards, were frequently repaid by being awarded positions on university boards of trustees, thereby usurping some of the control of university affairs previously enjoyed by the professoriat. It was this phenomenon which proved so disturbing to Spingarn. In contrast to European universities, he lamented, "our own institutions are governed by self-perpetuating boards of trustees, consisting of financiers, engineers, lawyers . . . , not one of whom is a scholar by profession. . . ." The modern university was designed "to make scholars and specialists of their students [rather] than to give them that broad culture and high training which in former days made their influence so potent and so deep"; the professors were fast becoming "scholarly automata" whose hold on undergraduate life was being decreased by pedagogic methods. [8]

Spingarn's decision to challenge, often single-handed, the seemingly all-pervading impersonalization at Columbia was one of the first indications of the idealism and receptiveness to practical struggle which were to characterize his later career in the NAACP. Although eminently qualified to teach graduate students, he insisted upon instructing undergraduates, undoubtedly because he felt that a professor's influence would have a greater impact upon younger minds. In the wake of advancing science, he sought to encourage interest in the humanities by inaugurating annual prizes for the best undergraduate entries in belles-lettres. He received widespread publicity in the New York press by refusing to conduct his classes in a new $500,000 lecture hall, on the grounds that pure white plaster and shining new blackboards were incompatible with such a romantic subject as comparative literature. When the administration merged the Comparative Literature and English departments in November 1910, Spingarn refused to recognize the merger, later recalling that "to me it seemed like putting a professor of the history of religion in the department of biology and telling him it was only an administrative matter and would not affect his teaching." An open confrontation with President Nicholas Murray Butler (whom the Boston *Evening Transcript* characterized as being better suited to the cutthroat-competition milieu of the corporation executive) was narrowly averted when, in January 1911, the administration appointed Spingarn chairman of a newly created Department of Comparative Languages and Literature.[9]

This rapprochement was short-lived. In early 1911 the trustees fired Harry Thurston Peck, an internationally acclaimed authority on Latin languages and a professor at Columbia for twenty-two years, when he became the defendant in a widely publicized breach-of-promise suit. In the resolution of dismissal, no mention was made of Peck's academic laurels or his many years of service. The Peck case provided the rallying point for a group of insurgent professors, led by Spingarn, to probe the broader issue of faculty-administration relations. On behalf of the faculty of philosophy, Spingarn drafted a resolution declaring that the law of the land must decide Peck's guilt or innocence lest truth be lent to the theory that the trustees' pleasure in determining the tenure of professorships "is not so much their just pleasure as their whim." In the wake of this and other more caustic utterances, Butler warned Spingarn that he was overstepping his jurisdiction, and when Spingarn refused to be silenced, he too was relieved of academic duties, on March 6, 1911. Spingarn countered by releasing to the press vehement denunciations of the "absolutely unmanly timidity" into which Columbia's professors had been "cowed by Dr. Butler," and by continuing to conduct his comparative literature class at his home. At the same time, Professors John Dewey and J. M. Cattell led an insurgent revolt on Spingarn's behalf among the faculty of philosophy, drafting a resolution (defeated by a vote of 16 to 12) demanding that Columbia's entire dismissal procedure be "rigidly investigated." The heated controversy raged in the press and on the campus for several months, but neither Spingarn nor Peck was reinstated at Columbia.[10]

Although Spingarn published the influential *Creative Criticism* and several other books after 1911, his dismissal from Columbia marked his retirement from active participation in university life. He never sought another teaching position, although he undoubtedly could have secured a professorship at any number of first-rate institutions. In fact, after an initial period of bitterness he expressed relief at having been freed from the narrow confines of the university. "How like Héloïse in her nunnery," he quipped, "is any man who is locked up with seven hundred professors." Nor did time bring regret; in 1936 he held a cocktail party in his New York apartment to celebrate the twenty-fifth anniversary of his departure from the university.[11]

Yet to view Spingarn solely as a scholar, even during his early adult life, is to miss much of the complexity and the essence of the whole man. Once, in commenting upon a biography of Edgar Allan Poe, he observed, "I distrust the books that attempt to sum up a life in terms of a single theory, however good the theory; they are the equivalents of what I call the panaceists in the world of action." [12] Even as a boy he had been partial to poetry and prose which emphasized man's duty to struggle against even the most impossible odds in order to uphold a principle in which he believed. Near the end of his life, he recalled that in his boyhood he had been "profoundly thrilled" by a stanza from Spenser's *Faerie Queene* in which the Renaissance poet had equated honor with effort, whether intellectual or practical effort. Referring to honor, Spenser had written:

> In woods, in waves, in wars she wonts to dwell
> And will be found with peril and with pain.
> Nor can the man that moulds in idle cell
> Unto her happy mansion attain.[13]

Spingarn recalled that "all of my life these lines have in some way consciously or unconsciously influenced me, perhaps sent me out on many quests for which I was unfitted." [14]

While it is impossible to chronicle either the specific time or the immediate circumstances which launched Spingarn's career of practical struggle, there are indications that a speech delivered by Theodore Roosevelt to Spingarn's graduating class at Columbia University in 1899 was influential, if not decisive, in directing him toward a career in public service. Roosevelt emphasized the need for men of action who would struggle to eradicate society's ills, insisting that it was not sufficient for man to be merely a thinker. Politics, taken in the broadest context of struggle, was the noblest occupation of man, contended Roosevelt, and he admonished his young listeners to apply their knowledge in practical pursuits. Spingarn pleaded for a chance to serve under the Rough Rider during the Spanish-American War, but was rejected by the military because of extremely poor eyesight, a disability that almost prevented his serving in World War I as well.[15]

Nevertheless, the division of his time and energies between the intellectual and the practical—between thinking and doing—was to characterize the remainder of Spingarn's life. For man to permit his life to be guided only by reality would circumscribe the free range of his intellect and will, Spingarn believed. Yet for man to give himself over totally to theory would rob him of that strength and determination which only practical struggle and even failure afforded. "Virtue is never solitary," he once wrote, "it takes part in the conflicts of the world." To think *and* to do; to effect a balance between the cloistered study and the arena of practical struggle—such was the essence of man,[16] insisted Spingarn.

Undoubtedly it was this philosophy which led Spingarn to struggle to eradicate the grievances which personally affected him at Columbia. But simultaneous with the internal struggles at the university came the development of a social conscience, a compelling desire to realize some spiritual ideal of justice and equality in the larger community. On one occasion he observed that people were beginning to realize that life was more important than things, and the spirit more than mere form. A new "American Movement" (a reference to Rooseveltian progressivism) was upon the land, he insisted, representing a realization of the spiritual and social ideal which would make the community a better place in which to work, to live, and to have being. The intellectual, together with other privileged elements in society, must be able to comprehend both this larger ideal and the rising expectations of the masses, for scholarship without action and intellect without application served little purpose. In writing of one of his recently deceased associates in the academic community, Spingarn noted that his friend's major short-coming had been his inability to "understand the new spirit of our democracy, the hope of teeming millions." [17]

As early as 1901, before his place in the academic commu-nity had been assured, Spingarn was paralleling his academic career with the first of what was to become an unbeliev-able array of nonacademic endeavors. In that year he was elected president of the Civic Club of New York City, an organization devoted to curtailing the Tammany machine by promoting fusion tickets comprised of candidates who, regardless of party affiliations, displayed a willingness to support reform measures. As an adjunct to its political activi-ties, the club sought to foster civic responsibility and the "social idea" among the electorate.[18] By 1908 he had become a major political figure in New York State, serving in that year as the Republican candidate for the United States Con-gress from New York's eighteenth district, the largest con-gressional district in the country. Although he lost the elec-tion by a narrow margin to his Democratic opponent, Spingarn's showing was the strongest thus far of any Repub-lican candidate in the traditionally Democratic district.[19] By 1914 he had become deeply involved in the work of the NAACP, having been elected Chairman of the Board of Directors in that year and, in addition to administrative duties, having undertaken three transcontinental speaking tours on the organization's behalf by 1915.[20] Even as his *Creative Criticism* was appearing in 1917, he was preparing to enter officers' training camp, from which he was to emerge with the highest rank in his class of 2,500 and to return from World War I as a military hero.[21]

Meanwhile, with the purchase in 1910 of Troutbeck, an

historic country estate in Amenia (Dutchess County), New
York, Spingarn added the roles of country gentleman and
patrician reformer to his already multiple roles of teacher,
scholar, and progressive politician. In what appears to have
been his first substantial gesture on behalf of black people,
he purchased the Heart of Hope Club, which was designed
to provide free hot meals and recreational facilities for
Amenia's destitute blacks. Apparently Spingarn's compassion
had far outstripped his practical knowledge, for he later recalled that he "didn't know what to do in the Club." In seeking advice as to how to operate and organize the club, he
wrote W. E. B. Du Bois, newly appointed editor of the infant
NAACP's official organ, the *Crisis*, who was destined to become Spingarn's lifelong friend and antagonist in the
NAACP.[22] In later years, as Spingarn's active interest in the
Negro problem intensified, two conferences of black leaders
would be hosted at Troutbeck, and its doors always would
be open to his many black friends at a time when blacks had
reached the nadir in American life and thought.

Nor were Spingarn's efforts in the Amenia community confined to blacks. His sponsorship of the Amenia Field Days—
admission-free annual festivals of games and sports to which
the entire countryside was invited—won him the title of
"father of rural cooperative recreation." [23] He published a
reformist paper, the Amenia *Times* (1911–26), and was a
leading activist in the Dutchess County women's suffrage
movement, attempting unsuccessfully to convert Theodore
Roosevelt to the suffragettes' cause.[24] As if to dispel any lingering doubts as to his consummate versatility, Spingarn
somehow found time to devote countless hours to the cultiva-
tion of more than 250 different varieties of a humble vine,
the clematis, surpassing even the prized collection of the
British Botanical Society. By the time of his death in
1939, Spingarn had published a monograph on the clematis,
won more than half a dozen medals and awards from the nation's most prestigious garden clubs, and earned recognition
as the world's foremost authority on the flower and its culti-
vation.[25] Reflecting upon the sundry activities he had under-

taken prior to 1919, Spingarn modestly termed the period "Some Busy Years."

Thus, by 1911, on the eve of his affiliation with the NAACP, Spingarn had virtually completed the first of two major phases of his life. At the age of thirty-six, when the average individual is just beginning to approach the peak of his career, Spingarn already could boast the chairmanship of a department in one of the nation's major universities; national recognition as an eminent though controversial author in the field of literary criticism; statewide recognition as a progressive politician; a position of social and political leadership in Dutchess County; and growing acclaim as the world's foremost authority on a humble vine.

More significantly, Spingarn's approach to the problems which confronted him during the first phase of his life provided a clue to the attitude and philosophy that were later to undergird his outlook on the race problem. The programs he advocated both as a politician and as a social crusader fitted well within the framework of what political scientists term "noneconomic liberalism"—strong reformist impulses in the realms of civil liberties, race relations, and foreign affairs but not in the basic distribution of wealth and power. The major determinants of noneconomic liberalism appear to be level of education, psychic security, and over-all sophistication. Evidence from several studies indicates that educated, cosmopolitan individuals are more likely to be tolerant toward social democracy and its adjuncts than people of less education and more limited experience. Conversely, persons who are poorly informed on public issues or who are provincial in outlook are more likely to be conservative on noneconomic issues but relatively liberal on economic ones—welfare-state measures, support of trade unions, graduated income taxes, etc. Although education, sophistication, and psychic security seem more important than social status in determining who will be a noneconomic liberal, these factors are so closely associated with the wealthy or upper classes that it is safe to assume that members of these classes are more likely to be noneconomic liberals, while economic liberalism is likely to be more prevalent among the poor or lower classes.[26]

Undoubtedly the adherents of noneconomic liberalism shied away from appreciable change in the economic sphere largely because they themselves, much like Spingarn, had attained a measure of prosperity and social status under the existing economic system. Yet, despite the security which their wealth and status ostensibly afforded, the upper classes liberally supported various reform movements ranging from nineteenth-century Abolitionism to twentieth-century Progressivism. To a great extent their motives were selfish. Much of their attack was leveled against professional politicians, *nouveaux riches* businessmen, and other groups which threatened to usurp the social and professional leadership which the old upper classes traditionally had enjoyed.[27] Spingarn's denunciation of the business interests which were gaining ascendancy over university policy, and his crusades against "low-brow" politicians, demonstrated how deeply and personally the new phenomenon touched and disturbed him.

But the viability and practicality of noneconomic liberalism as a social philosophy was to receive its greatest test when applied to the race problem. As Spingarn's tactical approach to the problem of racial adjustment unfolded over the years after his affiliation with the NAACP, it was to become apparent that this all-important problem was to be governed by the tenets of noneconomic liberalism; more specifically, that the black man's struggle for full civil and political rights must take precedence over any program of economic advancement, for once color discrimination had been swept away, the black man would be able to compete successfully with his white counterpart in jobs, education, and other avenues to economic stability. Inherent in this philosophy was the belief that the existing economic system was capable of providing economic uplift to all of those allowed to freely partake of it. It was this staunch philosophy of noneconomic liberalism which was to be adhered to not only by Spingarn but also by the majority of his black and white associates in the NAACP administrative hierarchy and which was to determine the organization's tactical approach to the race problem for the first twenty-five years of its history and precipitate during the 1930's the most serious challenge to the organization's survival.

Finally, the first phase of Spingarn's life demonstrated that he was indeed a totally independent spirit—"my lonely warrior mood," he once termed it—who, when personally convinced of the righteousness of the cause at hand, proceeded at full speed, regardless of the opposition and often to the consternation of his closest colleagues. On one occasion he angrily proclaimed that he would never submit to the dictates of any man. "Why should I?"[28] he asked rhetorically. But, as he all too vividly discovered from the criticism his colleagues leveled at his controversial thesis and his battles with Columbia's administration, the academic community was not always the best showcase for such independence. On the other hand, he undoubtedly saw the NAACP as the perfect arena for venting his penchants for both idealism and practical struggle within the broadest context of politics. It was Spingarn's friend and admirer Lewis Mumford who perhaps best summarized the triumphs and tragedies of Spingarn's career. Depicting the master of literary criticism near the end of Spingarn's life, Mumford wrote:

The reader must picture the man himself, nearing sixty, slim, erect, austere, with dark brown eyes that would ignite under the first spark of thought: a man impetuous and intense, proud as Dante and somehow looking as one feels Dante must have looked. A poet who had known the life of action; an active man who had known pain, solitude, deprivation, isolation; a philosopher who, like Socrates or Descartes, could still lead an army and who was capable of advancing resolutely in the face of the enemy, without faltering because no one followed: such a man was J. E. Spingarn.[29]

2

REINCARNATION OF THE
ABOLITIONISTS

As IF BY some star-crossed destiny, Spingarn's dismissal
from Columbia coincided with the formative period of
the National Association for the Advancement of Colored
People. The peculiar administrative structure of the Association, the intensity of interest which Spingarn devoted to its
work, and his prowess as an interpersonal leader catapulted
him to the status of a key member of the NAACP's administrative hierarchy by 1914.

THE SECOND GENESIS

The facts surrounding the formation of the NAACP have
been told too often elsewhere to warrant detailed repetition.[1]
The Progressivism that permeated American life during the
period 1900 to 1914 harbored few benefits for blacks, either
above or below the Mason-Dixon line. In 1910 Baltimore en-

acted the nation's first residential segregation ordinance, and by 1914 similar laws were in effect in the cities of at least five Southern and border states. By 1911 ten Southern states required the segregation of blacks and whites in the use of public transportation facilities. Around the turn of the century, Wilmington, North Carolina, New Orleans, and Atlanta were the scenes of violent strife between the races while lynching was emerging as a distinctly racial custom.[2]

Nor was the wave of anti-Negro sentiment confined to the South. In more subtle but equally effective ways, the North also practiced discrimination, as in the tacit exclusion of blacks from universities and professional groups, and the exclusion or segregation of blacks in the use of theaters, hotels, common carriers, and other public facilities. Between 1911 and 1915 anti-intermarriage bills were introduced in the legislatures of New York, Massachusetts, Michigan, Kansas, and other Northern states. Shortly after the turn of the century, Akron, Ohio, New York City, and even Springfield, Illinois— the home of Abraham Lincoln—witnessed bloody race riots.[3]

The national political climate abetted the anti-Negro sentiment that pervaded the nation. The powerful Southern bloc in Congress either effected a holding action on legislation favorable to blacks or assumed the initiative in advancing legislation to enhance the trend toward separation of the races. The Wilson administration had barely got under way when the segregation of black civil service workers in federal government departments in the District of Columbia reached unprecedented proportions. It was also the Wilson administration which witnessed, and did little to thwart, the introduction of Congressional bills designed to nullify the District of Columbia Civil Rights Act and to prohibit intermarriage in the nation's capital.[4] In short, for a progressive with strong Negrophile sentiments, there was no wholly satisfactory place to go within the contemporary reform movement.

Progressivism's rejection of the Negro's cause was paralleled by an even more bizarre phenomenon in the black community. In the wake of the white world's rising hostility toward the Negro, Booker T. Washington, the most influential black leader of the early twentieth century, counseled members of his race to adopt a gradualist racial philosophy. Washington condoned the social separation of the races, advised the Negro to be patient in the wake of prejudice and discrimination, and assured whites that blacks were more interested in economic opportunity and industrial education than in political rights. Outright opposition to Washington's philosophy by Negro "radicals," including W. E. B. Du Bois and William Monroe Trotter, editor of the Boston *Guardian*, had appeared as early as 1903, but as late as 1909 Washington's opponents remained scattered and relatively unorganized.[5]

It was in the midst of this rising white hostility—especially the 1908 riot which symbolically occurred in Springfield, Lincoln's home—and Washington's gradualism that a small band of white liberals vowed to take positive action on behalf of equal rights and fair treatment for black Americans. The members of this tiny group—William English Walling, Mary White Ovington, Charles Edward Russell, and Oswald Garrison Villard—derived from diversified backgrounds and were attracted to America's most unpopular cause by a variety of personal motives. It was perhaps natural that Ovington, Russell, and Villard should have taken an active interest in the problems of black Americans, for each was the descendant of an Abolitionist. Indeed, Villard was the grandson of the famous William Lloyd Garrison. On the other hand, Walling was a Southerner and the descendant of a slave-owning family; but he had traveled extensively in the North and abroad and had manifested a deep interest in a variety of social and humanitarian causes before 1908.[6]

Russell, Walling, and Ovington were avowed economic liberals, specifically socialists. In fact, had Miss Ovington not feared ostracism by her friends and family, she would have devoted her life to active participation in the socialist movement. But despite the strong socialist leanings of some of the founders of the NAACP, the program they formulated for blacks emphasized the attainment of full civil and political rights under the existing socioeconomic system, to the virtual exclusion of a program of black economic uplift. Recognition of the overwhelming "color factor" caused even a staunch socialist like Mary White Ovington to divorce the cause of the Negro from that of Socialism on the grounds that the Negro must develop priorities in his struggle for uplift; that he must free himself from the last vestiges of chattel slavery before engaging in any movement for revolutionary change. Similarly, Charles Edward Russell vehemently opposed blacks' participation in any "radical" movements.[7] Miss Ovington's strict noneconomic philosophy in regard to the race issue was to prove an especially crucial factor during the 1930's, when she would adamantly oppose black insurgents who were seeking to have the Association adopt an economic program of black uplift.

Thus a potential division among the founders as to whether the NAACP should adopt an economic or a noneconomic program of black advancement was averted. The NAACP would be able to boast the representation of strong economic liberalism within its leadership while, paradoxically, attaining almost perfect accord within its administrative hierarchy on a predominantly noneconomic program.

Other factors further entrenched the infant NAACP in its noneconomic program. As early as the Association's first year, 1909, the founders had contemplated adopting as an auxiliary goal the linking of the Negro's cause with the labor movement, but this plan was abandoned because it was feared (with good cause as events were to prove) that few, if any, labor leaders would champion the aspirations of black workers. Equally important, in 1910 the National League on Urban Conditions Among Negroes (Urban League) was founded with the avowed primary goal of effecting blacks' economic uplift. In 1911 the two organizations tacitly agreed that each would largely confine its activities to its avowed role. Indeed, whenever two or more organizations are seeking to fulfill the same purpose—in this case, the general uplift of blacks—each must carefully define its specific activities in relationship to those of its rivals. Failure to do so may result in highly detrimental competition for membership, income, and resources. Even during the 1930's, when the Depression fostered tremendous internal and external pressures for the NAACP's adoption of a strong economic program, fear of encroachment upon the League's activities was to give the NAACP leadership serious pause.[8]

Joel and Arthur Spingarn were attracted to the NAACP almost accidentally and were latecomers in comparison to Ovington, Villard, and the other founders. A 1909 "call" for a conference on the Negro problem had been issued, a committee consisting of founders and other interested persons had convened several times to implement the tenets of the "call," and the organization's first conference on the Negro problem had been held[9] when, in the fall of 1910, Spingarn's attention was captured by a newspaper item which was destined to launch a career spanning nearly thirty years in the NAACP.

The newspaper report related the story of one Steve Greene, an illiterate black tenant farmer of Crittenden County, Arkansas, who, in self-defense, had slain his former white landlord. Although Greene escaped to Chicago, he was soon betrayed to the authorities, who employed inhumane methods to force from him a confession of murder. When the Crittenden County sheriff arrived to take the prisoner back to Arkansas, he boasted that a mob was waiting to burn Greene. Reflecting upon the Greene episode many years later, Spingarn explained that a man could never quite know "by what strange current of emotion he is moved . . . why one injustice appeals to him more than another, but I know that at that moment I said, 'I don't care what happens, Steve Green [sic] will never be extradited to Arkansas.'" Spingarn learned that the NAACP and the Negro Fellowship League, a Chicago organization established by blacks and principally designed to aid black Southern migrants, were seeking to block Greene's extradition and provide funds for his defense. He promptly contributed $100 to Greene's defense fund and requested additional information about the case from Edward Wright, Greene's attorney and Chicago's most influential black politician.[10]

There is no indication that Spingarn intended to become an active member of the NAACP, despite the intense interest which he had manifested in the Greene case. But this decision was virtually made for him when, in October 1910, Villard, who had become a member of the NAACP Executive Committee, seized the opportunity to add another prestigious name to the organization's membership roll by inviting Spingarn to join the Association. Apparently Spingarn's response was prompt and positive, for the following month, in November 1910, the Executive Committee adopted Villard's motion that Spingarn be elected to membership on the Committee. The motion had been befittingly seconded by W. E. B. Du Bois, the new friend whom Spingarn had contacted the previous spring regarding the operation of the Heart of Hope Club, and the Editor of the NAACP's official organ, the *Crisis*.[11]

While still a professor at Columbia, Spingarn brought to his new role in the NAACP all the idealism, intensity of interest, and enthusiasm which had characterized his efforts as a scholar, politician, and progressive reformer. By January 1911 he was liberally indulging his desire for practical struggle as an officer and activist in the NAACP's New York Vigilance Committee. As forerunners of what were later to become branches of the Association, the vigilance committees, as the name suggests, were designed to keep a close watch on race relations in a given locality, combating discrimination and segregation whenever possible, while at the same time serving as the local eyes and ears of the New York-based parent organization. The New York Committee confined its efforts to securing the civil and social rights of the city's blacks, deliberately avoiding work in the economic sphere in an effort not to conflict with the activities of the National Urban League. The Committee also confined its propaganda and appeals to blacks in order to avoid competition with the NAACP national office for the financial support of wealthy white New Yorkers.[12]

Spingarn chose to personally participate in the Vigilance Committee's sundry campaigns. When a group of black men whom he accompanied to a theater were refused seats, the Committee won a suit against the theater's management, thanks largely to Spingarn's testimony in court. Upon learning that a black man, Eugene Washington, had been accused of raping a white woman, Spingarn immediately asked his brother Arthur to serve as Washington's attorney, although the Spingarns and the Vigilance Committee later withdrew from the case when Spingarn learned that the defendant was "a most disreputable person." Meanwhile, Spingarn had been using his personal influence to prevent the son of Dr. Owen M. Waller, a black member of the NAACP Board of Directors, from being excluded because of race from New York's Central Preparatory School.[13]

Thus, when Spingarn's dismissal from Columbia in March 1911 brought his teaching career to an abrupt halt, he already had established substantial ties with the organization and the cause to which he was to devote the remainder of his life. There, Héloïse could be reunited with her Abelard. Some indication of the degree to which Spingarn's new calling had permeated his being was manifested in a list of last requests which he drafted in 1916, when he anticipated the possibility of death as a soldier in World War I. Enumerating those things which apparently were dearest to him, he asked his wife to take care of his mother, to remember his brother, to publish his poetry, and to carry on his work for the Negro.[14]

And, indeed, Spingarn's penchant for activism was sorely needed by the NAACP, especially during the formative years. The Association proposed to reverse the seemingly endless maze of inequities which confronted blacks through a simultaneous, two-pronged attack. Whenever possible, legal redress was to be employed in those cases in which a successful conclusion would enhance the status of the entire race. When legal redress could not be employed, the Association relied upon peaceful agitation and protest involving organized agitation by blacks acting through local branches of the NAACP, together with appeals to the public conscience by means of the written and spoken word. All in all, the program revealed its architects' deep and abiding faith in the inherent justness of the American people. An eight-year test of the effectiveness of the program was to prove that not only was it difficult to implement but also that much of that faith in the American people was unwarranted.

Although the success of the Association's program depended heavily on the widespread dissemination of information about the plight of black Americans, as late as 1913 an irate May Childs Nerney, the Secretary, complained that hardly a newspaper or magazine in New York would print NAACP material.[15] This problem was compounded by the fact that not until 1916 would finances permit hiring a full-time field secretary and national organizer. Thus the tasks of publicizing the Association's program and establishing local branches devolved upon Du Bois, Spingarn, Nerney, Villard, and other national officers and members, who were obliged to travel from city to city, orally spreading the organization's program and leaving branches in their wake whenever possible. Spingarn's forthcoming "New Abolition" tours, which were to take him to more than twenty cities over a three-year period, were as much a result of necessity as of his personal desire for active participation.

Initially, the Association concentrated on establishing branches in major cities above the Mason-Dixon Line, specifically in the Northeast and the Midwest; a concerted attempt at the organization of Southern branches was launched only after the first full-time field secretary and national organizer, James Weldon Johnson, was employed in 1916. In some instances, like Boston, a biracial group of citizens interested in the Negro problem formed the nucleus of what was later to become the city's NAACP branch. In other instances, as in the District of Columbia and Baltimore, specific cases of injustice—residential segregation ordinances or discrimination against black civil service workers—aroused the black community sufficiently to foster the rise of potent local branches. On the other hand, as late as 1914 major Midwestern cities, including Chicago, Detroit, Indianapolis, and St. Louis, either lacked NAACP branches or possessed units which were extremely weak, if not altogether ineffective.[16]

These failures appear to have been due to several factors. First, the Association's potential constituency consisted primarily of urban blacks, the majority of whom undoubtedly were wage-earners and members of the lower class. As a general rule, members of the lower class tend not to be avid joiners of voluntary agencies other than those involving livelihood and the family;[17] more important, perhaps, members of the lower class, as was noted in Chapter 1, are more likely to embrace a program of economic liberalism rather than one of noneconomic liberalism like that of the NAACP. Indeed, it is not an exaggeration to say that the NAACP, throughout the first thirty years of its history, sought to appeal to, and worked on behalf of, the masses of blacks but with a program which was more likely to attract middle- and upper-class blacks. This may, for example, help to account for the fact that in St. Louis the strong showing of the economically oriented local Urban League's unit prevented the NAACP branch from gaining a stable footing.

Nor should the seemingly omnipresent influence of Booker T. Washington be underestimated, for although by 1913 the ever-mounting discrimination against blacks had resulted in considerable slippage in his influence, his hold on the minds of countless thousands of black Americans was far from slight until his death in 1915. In that year the NAACP Secretary reported that many Northern Negroes found gradualism expedient, for militancy might jeopardize the limited gains which they had attained. Similarly, Southern blacks who had become accustomed to second-class citizenship status but who had migrated to the North, undoubtedly found it difficult to reorient their thinking toward a more militant philosophy. Washington supporters gained leadership positions in the infant Orange (New Jersey) and Indianapolis NAACP branches. Influential black newspapers, including the New York *Age* (which once had been subsidized by Booker T. Washington), the Washington *Bee*, and the Chicago *Broad-Ax*, defended the Tuskegeean against the NAACP's attacks.[18]

Conversely, the relatively radical program of the NAACP not only failed to attract some segments of the black community but also sometimes alienated wealthy white potential donors who found Washington's accommodationism more appealing than the Association's demands for immediate and total racial equality. For example, Nerney reported that Julius Rosenwald, Chicago philanthropist and contributor to Tuskegee, had been "quite disgruntled with us" ever since the NAACP's vigorous prosecution of those responsible for burning a Negro alive in Coatesville, Pennsylvania, in 1911. As Spingarn soon was to discover firsthand, influential white groups like the city clubs of St. Louis and Chicago attempted to ban adverse references to the Tuskegeean by guest speakers. In still another vein, Z. W. Mitchell, a black "professor" and founder of the Loyal Legion Cooperative Educational System, effectively distracted the Quincy (Illinois) branch's white supporters by insisting that his race was only fit for menial service and that he intended to train them for it.[19]

Finally, branch organization frequently was hindered by dissension within the local agencies. Sometimes men could not work with women, sometimes the members did not like the leader. Although the branches received their charters from the national office and were subject to the authority of the national Board of Directors, the absence of a full-time branch supervisor often made the Board's control of local affairs more apparent than real, especially during the formative years. Washington supporters' control of the Orange and Indianapolis branches already has been noted. In 1913 the viable District of Columbia branch was completely disrupted when the membership accused the President, J. Milton Waldron, of using the prestige of his office to secure a political appointment from the Democrats.[20]

In short, by 1914 the Association had barely begun to cope with the problems which confronted it. Mary White Ovington recalled that it was just one among the many "insignificant" reform groups housed in New York.[21]

It was in the midst of this, the darkest period in the Association's history, that Spingarn reached back in time to resurrect the spirit of nineteenth-century Abolitionism, the only major movement in American history which approximated the NAACP's ideal of equal rights and fair treatment for black Americans. The timing of his first mention of a "New Abolition" in December 1912 suggests that he had abandoned any hope of furthering the Negro's cause through Progressivism. A few months previously the Progressive Party's platform committee had flatly rejected a civil rights plank which Du Bois had drafted and which Spingarn had personally presented to the committee. In addition, the convention refused to seat black delegates and, as a crowning blow, Roosevelt himself advised Spingarn to beware of that "dangerous" Du Bois. On November 2, 1912, a disillusioned Spingarn resigned his membership in the Republican Club of New York, later observing that "reformers and prophets are always ahead of politicians." [22]

Beginning with the first New Abolition campaign in 1913,[23] Spingarn embraced the courage and determination of the nineteenth-century Abolitionists with a fervor which rivaled that of Garrison and Phillips. When the *Ohio State Journal* erroneously referred to him as a "Boston man," he angrily denounced the implication that only Boston men could take an interest in the Negro question, depicting himself and the small band of like-minded white liberals as the outnumbered and beleaguered forces of righteousness who, like their nineteenth-century counterparts, would withstand society's opposition. When a misunderstanding temporarily resulted in the barring of an NAACP conference at Johns Hopkins University in 1914, Spingarn refused to accept the university's apology, charging that the nineteenth-century Abolitionists had had church and press and university against them, too. As late as 1932 he denounced those descendants of Abolitionists who excused their lack of interest in the contemporary civil rights struggle by beginning with "But . . . ," derisively terming them "Abolitionist buts." [24]

The social uplift forces which epitomized Progressivism were singled out for special condemnation. "Politicians and puny statesmen" were not nearly as powerful a social force as reformers. Even Abraham Lincoln "did not have within his heart the courage of the least Abolitionist," for his "com-promise" Emancipation Proclamation had left those slaves owned by Northerners in bondage. Spingarn especially de-nounced the "social workers," "settlement workers," and "directors of recreation centres," charging that their failure to demand and practice racial equality made them the "mod-ern equivalents" of the social forces which the nineteenth-century Abolitionists had "lashed with fiery scorn." When a charitable organization's convention which convened in Mem-phis in 1914 refused to provide accommodations for black delegates, Spingarn and Du Bois traveled to Memphis and placed in the local papers a full-page advertisement of a pro-test meeting. The caption read: "All Those Who Love the Truth and Dare to Hear It Are Cordially Invited." Not only did the protest meeting succeed in breaking up the conven-tion's session but Spingarn's heated denunciation of the social uplift forces caused the New York *Evening Post* to comment that nothing like it had ever been witnessed in the South.[25] Clearly, Spingarn did not conceive of the New Abolition as an adjunct to the larger Progressive movement; rather, it was a manifestation of a white liberal's utter disillusionment with a Progressivism which was severely circumscribed by con-siderations of race.

Convinced that white America had little interest in up-lifting the Negro, Spingarn focused the New Abolition cam-paigns on attempts to arouse black awareness and aspirations. The modern movement—which he declared to be as sig-nificant as its nineteenth-century counterpart—would seek to organize blacks and their "friends" that they might actively, though peacefully, demand the black man's rights. The New Abolition's tactics and goals were synonymous with those of the NAACP: local and national organization of blacks (corresponding to the NAACP and its branches) to combat discrimination and injustice wherever it might occur; an organized publicity campaign to broadcast the good that blacks accomplished, as well as the bad deeds perpetrated against them; organized mass protest meetings to agitate against injustice; uncompromising insistence on the black man's total and immediate integration into every facet of American life. Spingarn especially urged bloc voting by blacks, insisting that the balance of power vote they held in seven critical states could be utilized both to elect sympathetic white candidates and to place blacks in important political offices. However, unlike Du Bois, who eventually embraced the concept of a Negro third party, Spingarn never wavered in his insistence that blacks should participate in both the major parties.[26] Thus, like the NAACP's program, Spingarn's New Abolition, which proffered no economic means of black uplift, was a classic exposition of non-economic liberalism.

Finally, the New Abolition sought to foster cultural nationalism among blacks as an intangible cement which would stabilize the more apparent manifestations of black unity. In March 1913 Spingarn offered a gold medal valued at $100, to be awarded annually to the man or woman of African descent who had attained the highest achievement in any field of elevated or honorable endeavor during the preceding year. The Negro was especially endowed in the arts, Spingarn maintained, and therefore had a great cultural and spiritual gift to offer America. In the arts, the Negro should think of himself as "rich, rich by inheritance and by temperament, but willing to share your great gifts with your poor, cold, uninspired brothers of white blood." The medalists and their achievements would serve as a reminder that America was not solely a country of, by, and for Anglo-Saxons.[27]

In the broadest sense, the Spingarn Medal betokened its donor's adherence to the concept of cultural pluralism, the belief that a given race or ethnic group should preserve its unique cultural heritage, while, at the same time, seeking full integration into all other facets of the larger society. Preservation of the black cultural heritage remained one of Spingarn's concerns throughout his life. In 1923 he sought to interest the firm Harcourt, Brace in publishing an English translation of Leo Frobenius' *Atlantis*, which Spingarn described as a "ten or fifteen volume treasure-house of African myth and folklore."[28] As young black leaders cast about during the 1930's for a new ideology and a new direction, Spingarn was to insist that a greater emphasis upon black cultural nationalism must be a vital aspect of any new direction taken by the Negro.

Yet, the New Abolition speeches, when delivered extemporaneously from the podium, often assumed a militancy which betrayed Spingarn's impatience with peaceful protest and, perhaps, belied his faith in the efficacy of the Association's program. In 1913 he incurred Villard's wrath by counseling Baltimore Negroes not to confine the means of securing their rights to peaceful methods. New Jersey Negroes heard Spingarn refer to the black man standing at his cabin door with shotgun in hand as a means of protecting what was rightfully his—a statement that one New Jersey Negro leader found appalling. Depicting Spingarn in one of his more militant moods, the Quincy (Illinois) *Herald*, observed that "he wishes to seize the U.S. Arsenal and be a John Brown the second." He delighted in recounting how his white audiences often would melt away long before the completion of his speeches, leaving only the waiters standing against the back walls; every newspaper reporter awaited him with a "handshake or a hammer." [29]

Yet Spingarn's words were to be more provocative than his actions throughout his career in the NAACP. Unwittingly, perhaps, he shared that dilemma of the progressives which Louis Hartz has described: "The Progressive mind is like the mind of a child in adolescence, torn between old taboos and new reality, forever on the verge of exploding into fantasy." [30] Spingarn was to witness the repeated failure of appeals to the public conscience and peaceful agitation and protest, but not until the 1930's would he attempt to embrace a new tactical approach to the race problem, an ever-so-slight but unmistakable modification of the noneconomic liberalism which held him so firmly in its grip.

Spingarn's disillusionment with the white social uplift forces was rivaled only by his utter disdain for the accommodationist philosophy of Booker T. Washington, for he believed more strongly perhaps than any of his colleagues except Du Bois that Washington posed the greatest single threat

to both the Negro's advancement and the success of the
NAACP's program. Unlike Villard, who took issue with
Washington privately but carefully refrained from publicly
attacking him, Spingarn's public attacks upon the Tuskegeean
assumed the proportions of a virtual passion—"I let myself go
about Washington tonight . . . ," he wrote after one speech.
He candidly asked his black audiences to abandon Washington's gradualism for the more militant program of the
NAACP and to switch their allegiance to Du Bois as the
symbol of blacks' ideals and ambitions. "It is possible that
Dr. Washington is in a delicate position and cannot fight
against Jim Crowism, segregation laws, and insulting intermarriage laws," Spingarn told a Memphis audience in 1914,
"but the friends of Dr. Washington certainly can, and should,
join hands with those who stand with Du Bois in the battle
against the erection of a monstrous caste system in this country." Spingarn likened those Negroes who would overlook
the ill treatment they received in exchange for the opportunity of acquiring wealth to a fictional black man sitting in his
countinghouse poring over the wealth of his race, and who,
upon learning that his house was in flames and his family perish-
ing, would reply: "I am carrying out my industrial obligation
to my race, I will put the fire out when I get through." Compromise with some forms of injustice in exchange for advan-
tages in other areas had retarded blacks' advancement,
Spingarn charged; compromise had increased, rather than
diminished, prejudice and had limited opportunity.[31]

These anti-Washington remarks did not go unchallenged.
Villard disapprovingly termed Spingarn a "firebrand" who
had started out with a "violent attack on B. T. W." The New
York *Age* countercharged that whites dominated the
NAACP. Later, in 1917, when expediency led Spingarn to
drop his staunch anti-segregation stance temporarily in order
to advocate a segregated Negro officers' training camp, the
Age took pleasure in reminding him of his earlier New Abolition attacks upon the then-deceased Washington. The Washington *Bee* also was highly critical of what it termed Spingarn's attempts to divide, rather than unite, the forces working

for Negro uplift. The *Broad-Ax*, Chicago's leading black weekly, completely omitted any mention of Spingarn or the New Abolition when Spingarn spoke in the city but, for several weeks after the New Abolitionist had departed, featured on its cover page a huge picture of Washington and extensive articles about his accomplishments. Although the Cleveland *Gazette* did not take sides, it extensively reported the New Abolition speeches, and its tone was decidedly friendly.[32]

Nor was Washington lacking in influential white supporters. When Spingarn personally called upon William Graves, secretary of the philanthropist Julius Rosenwald, in an attempt to woo Rosenwald from the ranks of Washington's supporters, Spingarn could report only that Graves had "seemed sympathetic." The City Club of Chicago, a prestigious white civic organization, threatened to withdraw its invitation to Spingarn to address the group if he did not give assurances that the speech would contain no adverse references to Washington. During one of his most vehement denunciations of Washington, at a mass meeting held at Chicago's Lincoln Center, Spingarn was publicly taken to task by Roger Baldwin, a wealthy white official of the St. Louis Urban League. Baldwin was "so much disturbed" by the Lincoln Center speech that he threatened to prevent Spingarn from addressing the St. Louis City Club (the next scheduled stop in the campaign) if the New Abolitionist did not promise "silence" where Washington was concerned. Although Baldwin rushed ahead to St. Louis to warn the City Club, Spingarn stood his ground and forced the group to accept his address (which, when delivered, was more temperate toward Washington than usual) without any prior reservations as to its contents.[33]

But even as Spingarn relentlessly denounced Washington's gradualism, he sought to effect a *modus vivendi* with the Washington camp. In May 1914, he sent his annual contribution for Tuskegee to Washington, professing to be appalled by the press's suggestion that he lacked appreciation for the Negro leader's accomplishments, and inviting Washington to confer with him during the Tuskegeean's next visit to the

North. (There is no indication that the two men ever met face to face.) Similarly, in addressing the NAACP Annual Conference that same month, Spingarn urged that "Bourbons and Progressives . . . white and black . . . those who follow Washington, those who follow Du Bois, . . . band together and fight for the rights of their race." [34] Nevertheless, in his concluding remarks Spingarn made it clear that unity must be effected under the banner of the NAACP, if at all. No one could then foresee Washington's death within a year.

While the attacks on Washington lent a tinge of excitement to the New Abolition tours, they were but the opening wedge of a much broader purpose. At some point during the day or evening, either before or after delivering his address in a given city, Spingarn would confer with the branch leaders or sponsoring committee, aiding them in formulating plans for increasing membership, helping to forge a stronger program for the coming year, or, if the city had no branch, providing guidelines for launching a local agency. Although the tours were designed primarily to arouse blacks to a more militant stand for their rights, Spingarn also attempted to interest influential whites in the Association's work. During the 1914 tour, for example, he addressed directors of the Board of Managers of the Columbus, Ohio, Chamber of Commerce, members of the Minneapolis Luncheon Club (reputed to be composed of the "best" white men in the city), and the congregation of the most "aristocratic" church in St. Paul. In Omaha arrangements were made for him to deliver his address in the council chamber of city hall. In an attempt to appeal to white college students, engagements were scheduled at Ohio State University, Wittenberg College (Ohio), the University of Pittsburgh, and the University of Cincinnati. When the entire student bodies could not be addressed, Miss Nerney, who arranged the tours, capitalized upon Spingarn's national reputation as a literary critic, asking the heads of English and literature departments to permit him to address their classes. In other instances, wealthy whites, like Mrs. Crosby P. Noyes of St. Paul, sponsored parlor meetings in their homes at which Spingarn expounded the cause of the New Abolition.[35]

The New Abolitionist's messages to white audiences were simply phrased but uncompromising. He assured an Omaha group that the Negro problem would persist as long as segregation and discrimination were substituted for justice. "All we ask," he concluded, "is absolutely fair treatment among men regardless of color." In Detroit he reminded his white listeners that slavery had brought the Negro to America and that "we must now pay the price of slavery." Pressing his favorite theme of linking the cause of the Negro with the well-being of the entire nation, Spingarn observed that the Negro must be guaranteed his rights "for our own sake, as well as for his —perhaps even more for our sake than for his." [36]

This facet of the tours bore tangible fruit. The Quincy, Illinois, branch reported that following Spingarn's visit many blacks and several whites, including a state legislator, had joined and that a new spirit toward Negroes had been manifested by many of the city's white citizens. The Detroit branch reported that, in the wake of Spingarn's lecture, about twenty-five prominent whites had expressed an interest in the branch's work and that the black community was still talking about his speech two weeks after his departure. Members of the Chicago branch, after conferring with Spingarn, voted to model their activities after those of the New York Vigilance Committee. As a sidelight to the first New Abolition tour, he visited the District of Columbia and launched the first NAACP college chapter at predominantly black Howard University.[37] All in all, the New Abolition message was heard by an estimated 70,000 people during the three tours, although it is difficult to precisely measure Spingarn's success since his goal was such an intangible one, the alteration of attitudes and the winning of men's minds.

Still another facet of the New Abolition tours reflected Spingarn's attempt to supplement the Association's campaigns against residential segregation ordinances, Jim-Crow transportation statutes, segregation of civil service workers, and lynching. He argued that residential segregation was a luxury which blacks could not afford, "for the segregated race is cheated out of its share of the complex organization it helped to build." When Negroes were forced to live in certain sections of cities, he charged, the white officials would exert no effort to improve the Negro district; rather, Negroes' taxes would be used to improve the white neighborhoods. He readily admitted that black neighborhoods were proverbial for their vice and disease. "Is it the Negroes' fault?" he asked. "No; it is the fault of the white man who have [sic] it in their power to remedy them." He told a Wilmington, Delaware, audience that "crime is a question of poverty and ignorance and not of race and if the intelligent white people of this city have done nothing to assist their less fortunate brothers they must bear the burden and share the blame for the black crime." In January 1914 Spingarn helped to thwart an attempt by several white real estate firms to oust Harlem residents from their homes by using his personal influence to prevent one of the largest firms from participating in the action.[38]

Spingarn, Du Bois, and William Pickens (the dean of Morgan State College and an active black member of the Baltimore branch) traveled to Louisville, Kentucky, in the summer of 1914, to personally lead the city's blacks in their struggle against a recently enacted residential segregation ordinance. The Louisville statute was especially significant, for the NAACP's Legal Committee saw in the structure and wording of the law the ideal opportunity for a test case, which, if successful, would result in the banning of all such ordinances. Spingarn's Louisville address, delivered at a Negro church before a predominantly black audience of more than 800, was one of his most eloquent pronouncements on the question of segregation. In the name of "all right thinking people, I come here to protest the wrong being done . . . to let you know that there are men who do not approve of such injustice," he began. The black man had helped build Louisville just as had the white man. The result of blocking off a minority group from the larger society "can be only one to develop a permanently inferior civilization in our midst," he insisted, "which must serve forever as a corrupting force in the movement of the larger civilization of which it must continue to remain a part." He reminded Louisville whites that "there is no such thing as a 'Negro problem': it is an American problem, for, while injustice exists, the whole country is in danger . . ." To blacks Spingarn held out a special admonition: "Rather die now than live 100 years in a ghetto." [39]

The Legal Committee's protracted struggle against enforced residential segregation culminated in 1917 when the United States Supreme Court ruled the Louisville ordinance unconstitutional. Earlier, in 1915, the Legal Committee had won an equally momentous decision against disfranchisement when it secured from the High Court a ruling against the use of "grandfather clauses" in state constitutions.[40] These early legal victories foreshadowed a trend which was to be evident throughout the first thirty years of the NAACP's history— that tactically legal redress would bring more frequent and more positive results than agitation and protest: first, because the Association was fortunate in securing highly competent attorneys; second, and more important, because the inherent nature of legal redress required only minimal dependence upon organized mass black protest or the public conscience. Indeed, Spingarn and the Association soon discovered that when sole reliance was placed upon appeals to the public conscience for the redress of grievances, usually the result was dismal failure.

The tactics of agitation and protest received the first major test in late 1913 when the NAACP launched a full-scale campaign against the segregation of black civil service workers in the federal government departments. The practice of segregating employees did not originate during the Wilson administration, for the Bureau of Printing and Engraving had "always" provided separate dressing and locker-room facilities for its black and white employees and had imposed certain limitations on the assignment of blacks to certain divisions. But shortly after Wilson's inauguration, the Bureau of Printing and Engraving broadened its segregation policy, while the Treasury and Post Office departments issued official orders requiring segregated restrooms, lockers, and eating facilities for their workers. President Wilson and other government officials defended segregation on the general grounds that blacks would be more secure in their positions and less likely to experience discrimination if assigned to wholly Negro sections and bureaus. However, the gravity of the situation became manifest in September 1913, when the Democratic caucus passed a resolution calling for the replacement of all Negro civil service workers by whites in the Capitol, Senate, and House offices. By November 1913, segregation of postal workers had spread from Washington to Atlanta and thence to Philadelphia, often resulting in the dismissal of blacks and their replacement by whites. By the summer of 1914, the Civil Service Commission had instituted the unprecedented requirement that all prospective federal employees must submit photographs with their application blanks, a practice which the Association feared was designed to circumscribe the hiring and promotion of blacks.[41]

While Miss Nerney, Villard, and the branches sought unsuccessfully to appeal to President Wilson and the heads of government departments, Spingarn attempted to bring the government segregation issue before the public as part of the 1914 New Abolition campaign. He blamed the upsurge of discrimination on Negroes' apathy in general and Washington's accommodationism in particular. He admitted that anti-Negro sentiment was widespread but argued that the government segregation issue must not be confused with "social convenience"; if a man did not want to invite a Negro to his home, he was not obliged to do so, but the government could not afford the luxury of distinguishing between its citizens merely on the basis of color. In March 1915, Spingarn wrote President Wilson, charging that since the directive requiring civil service photographs had become operative in the Philippines, not one black had been appointed to the federal service there. In a letter to the editor of the Chicago Post, he lamented that a President and his cabinet had deemed it necessary to segregate workers who possessed the same qualifications merely because their ancestors had "a drop of Negro blood . . ."[42]

The efforts of Spingarn and the Association proved futile. Wilson forwarded the protests to the Civil Service Commission, which ruled that photographs were necessary in order to prevent fraud and impersonation and, therefore, that there were no grounds for rescinding their use. In the fall of 1915 a defeated and embittered Spingarn admitted that even if an ulterior motive of the Civil Service Commission were proved, it would not "affect any Bourbon anyway." Subsequent events revealed the truth of his words. Segregation of federal employees persisted throughout the Wilson administration, discrimination through the use of photographs became commonplace, and as late as 1928 the NAACP was still battling segregation and discrimination in the government service as if the events of 1913–15 had never transpired.[43]

Ironically, perhaps the most important result of the government segregation campaign came about almost accidentally, when William Monroe Trotter, editor of the Boston *Guardian*, president of the National (Negro) Independent Political League, and a long-time foe of Booker T. Washington, was dismissed by President Wilson during an interview regarding government segregation, because of his allegedly rude and discourteous words. Although Trotter had never been affiliated with the NAACP, the Association publicly supported him in the dispute with Wilson. Spingarn openly conceded that the Trotter incident, which received nationwide press coverage, had succeeded in garnering the national publicity for the race problem and, incidentally, the Association's program, which the NAACP had unsuccessfully attempted for several years.[44]

Like some latter-day Don Quixote, Spingarn continued to tilt at the seemingly endless maze of segregation and discrimination, his personal triumphs and failures mirroring those of the Association. Outraged by the refusal of Smith College (Massachusetts) to provide dormitory accommodations for Carrie Lee, a black student, because Southern white students might be offended, Spingarn personally called upon the president of the college, threatening to see that the NAACP "unleashed the dogs of war" if the girl were not given equal treatment. Shortly afterward, Carrie Lee was assigned living facilities in one of the campus dormitories.[45]

But the glimmer of success emanating from the Carrie Lee

episode was dissipated by the crushing defeat that the New Abolition suffered in attempting to censor D. W. Griffith's motion picture *The Birth of a Nation*. First having appeared in 1905 as a novel entitled *The Clansman*, the story, which had as its setting the Reconstruction Era, was transposed into a brilliantly produced film in 1915. Nevertheless, the movie presented the Negro in the worst possible light. The magazine *Moving Picture World* summarized it this way:

> The Negroes are shown as horrible brutes, given over to beastly excesses, defiant and criminal in their attitude toward the whites and lusting after white women. Some of the details are plainly morbid and repulsive.[46]

The film's potential for inflaming public opinion was evidenced by the unprovoked slaying of a Negro boy in Indiana by a white man who had just viewed the picture, as well as by the alleged admission of the producers that riots would result if the film were shown in the South.[47]

The Birth of a Nation received Spingarn's and the Association's immediate attention, for by depicting the black man as more bestial and lustful than his white counterpart, it undermined the very basis of the argument for racial equality. The film "virtually assassinated" the character of ten million Americans, Spingarn charged, and was a complete "misreading" of the facts of Reconstruction. He admitted that any form of censorship was dangerous to the free expression of art, and that censorship could be directed against *Uncle Tom's Cabin* as well as *The Birth of a Nation*. But he rationalized that since the motion-picture industry subsidized a censoring agency (National Board of Censorship), it was left to the Association to see that that body performed its duty.[48]

But success proved an elusive mistress. Spingarn appeared before the National Board of Censorship on March 1 only to be cut short in his remarks. And, although members of the Board of Censorship, upon viewing the picture, summarily rejected the entire second part, they later, under pressure from the film's producers, reversed their decision and approved the movie in its entirety. Protests to the New York

City authorities signed by Spingarn, Villard, and other members of the NAACP were all but ignored on the grounds that no official action could be taken unless the film occasioned disorders. Next, Spingarn made an unsuccessful attempt to secure another hearing before the National Board of Censorship, including among his demands proper Negro representation on the Board. In addition, he headed a large biracial delegation to the mayor's office, securing from Mayor John Purroy Mitchel a promise (which was not kept) that the most objectionable scenes in the film would be cut. At the same time, Spingarn was making tentative arrangements with playwright Elaine Sterne for the preparation of a scenario in rebuttal to *The Birth of a Nation*, but this plan had to be abandoned in 1916 when the Association proved unable to raise $50,000 to finance Miss Sterne's film. Meanwhile, an attempt by the NAACP Legal Committee to block the showing of *The Birth of a Nation* through a court injunction had failed.[49]

By May 1915 both Miss Nerney and Spingarn had all but given up in disgust. In what amounted to a sad commentary on the agitation and protest phase of the New Abolition, Nerney observed that "if I seem disinterested kindly remember that we have put six weeks of constant effort on this thing and have gotten nowhere." She charged that "several" members of the NAACP Board of Directors doubted that the film was harmful and that the majority of New York Negroes had manifested "utter indifference." Similarly, Spingarn conceded the failure of appeals to the public conscience and expressed "no faith" in a second attempt at legal action to block the film. Shrouded in defeat he retreated to Troutbeck for his summer vacation.[50]

Even before the struggles against government segregation and *The Birth of a Nation* had reached their ill-starred conclusions, the Association had begun to turn its attention to the issue of Jim-Crow accommodations on interstate carriers. As early as January 1914, Spingarn's New Abolition speeches had included references to the "filthy Jim-Crow car" as one of the most blatant symbols of the Negro's degradation, but it was not until early 1915, following an unsuccessful test case of an Oklahoma Jim-Crow law (*McCabe et al. v. Atchison, Topeka, and Santa Fe Railroad Company*), by blacks acting independently of the NAACP, that the Association made the abolition of Jim-Crow transportation a primary goal. Both the NAACP's attorneys and the justice who delivered the majority opinion agreed that the Oklahoma case had been lost primarily because it had been poorly constructed and presented by the Negro attorney who had prepared it.[51]

In December 1914 Spingarn proposed that he would personally obtain the evidence necessary for a repeal of the Oklahoma law if the NAACP Legal Committee would but furnish advice and prepare the case after the evidence had been acquired. Accompanied by W. Scott Brown, a black member of the NAACP's Muskogee, Oklahoma, branch, and armed with a small camera, Spingarn launched his scheme to tour the state by train for the purpose of demonstrating that a white man could obtain sleeping and dining accommodations on a public carrier but that a black man could not. During the trip Spingarn made the mistake of explaining his liberal racial views to a group of fellow travelers, who made it quite clear that Oklahoma was no place for the "likes" of him.[52]

But success again proved elusive. After having spent three successive days and nights on Oklahoma trains Brown "unfortunately" had experienced no discrimination. Thus, the two men arrived at the Oklahoma City branch, where Spingarn addressed an enthusiastic audience but without the anticipated evidence. "I did not know whether to laugh or cry (metaphysically)," he confided to his wife, "it seemed such a fiasco, and yet we certainly had gained a point . . ." He was convinced that the mere challenge of the Oklahoma law had so thoroughly frightened the railroads that they would give equal accommodations to any Negro who had the nerve to request them and, more important, that his trip to Oklahoma had given blacks the courage to defy discriminatory statutes. Nevertheless, shortly before the venture ended, Brown was twice discriminated against on Oklahoma trains, affording the Legal Committee evidence for its test case. But the Association's case was abandoned in 1917 when Arthur Spingarn, the Chairman of the Legal Committee, took a leave of absence for active army duty.[53]

Although the major thrust of the New Abolition was concentrated above the Mason-Dixon line, the South was by no means excluded. Spingarn's private and public pronouncements indicate that throughout his life he viewed the Southern people with mixed emotions. During his youth he had spent a brief period in Kentucky, where he witnessed a genuine shooting "feud" between two families of the hill country, the Hargouses and the Cockrells. His scrapbooks contain numerous pages of clippings relating to that and similar Southern feuds which occurred between 1900 and 1910, together with personal notations which indicate dismay and, perhaps, horror of these phenomena. As late as 1938, he cited the Hargous-Cockrell feud as an example of the lawlessness and wanton disregard for life which so often characterized Southern history. During a visit to South Carolina in 1923, Spingarn lamented that he felt as if he were "exiled in a land of Climate without Civilization." On the other hand, he never wavered in his conviction that the overwhelming majority of Southerners were "right thinking" Americans who, because of apathy, had permitted a small, racist minority to speak on behalf of the entire section; that the "best thought" of the South could be aroused if the facts of the race problem were but brought to the attention of its people. The invasion of the region by a few "fanatics" like the nineteenth-century Abolitionists, he once suggested, might free its people of the darkness which engulfed them.[54]

In terms of historical development, the South, in Spingarn's opinion, had suffered the fate of all civilizations—including those of the Hebrews, Romans, and Germans—which had dared to proffer themselves as a "chosen people" or as otherwise superior to those in their midst. He observed that the South had attained a pinnacle of power and glory during the eras of Washington, Jefferson, Madison, and Monroe, before the cult of white supremacy and Negro inferiority had taken deep roots. He saw the beginning of the South's decline during the decades immediately preceding the Civil War, when "a madness came over the Southern people in the discussion of slavery and they developed the theory that the Negro was born to be forever inferior and the Southern white forever superior." A great war of the South's "own making" had ensued, and the section had been left helpless and hopeless for more than a generation.[55]

Nor did Spingarn find much reason for hope in the so-called New South that had emerged after 1880. Northerners had instituted the Thirteenth, Fourteenth, and Fifteenth Amendments to punish the South rather than to deal fairly with the Negro problem, he charged, and the ardor for enforcing the amendments had decreased proportionately as sectional hatred had cooled. As a result, the "noblest result of the Great Civil War" (the Fourteenth Amendment) had been frustrated; the South had succeeded in reinstituting every wrong assumed to have been dissipated by the war. Nor was the issue merely racial, he maintained, for the ever-increasing national political power of the South threatened to thwart the will of every other section of the country. Every black man must have the ballot not only for the sake of justice but "if only for the selfish interest of white men everywhere; he must have it in order that a few southern white men cannot control America in total disregard of the 14th and 15th Amendments." [56]

But even as Spingarn denounced the darkest aspects of Southern life, he seized every opportunity to visit the area and to court the attention of its silent, indifferent majority, both black and white. In December 1912, immediately prior to the first Midwestern New Abolition tour, he addressed the students of several Southern black institutions, including Fisk University (Nashville, Tennessee), Atlanta Baptist College (now Morehouse College), and Atlanta University. At the same time, his national reputation as a master of literary criticism provided entrée to Southern white universities. In 1916 he delivered guest lectures on literary criticism at the universities of North and South Carolina. While in the Carolinas he addressed a Negro educational conference at Durham,

North Carolina, and the students of Benedict College, a black institution in Columbia, South Carolina. He contributed to Southern organizations whose avowed aim was the betterment of race relations. For example, in 1912 he made a $50 contribution to the Nashville Urban League, and in 1917 he attended the Southern Sociological Congress, later donating $200 toward the Congress' work in fostering amicable race relations in the South.[57]

Perhaps Spingarn's faith in the efficacy of appeals to the Southern conscience was best illustrated by his virtual passion for sending pro-Negro literature, especially the *Crisis*, to influential white Southerners. In 1912, "as an experiment," he sent a paid *Crisis* subscription to Mary N. Moorer, president of Athens College in Georgia and a friend of some of his relatives. Mrs. Moorer's reaction exemplified the resistance the New Abolition was to encounter in the South. The social equality of the races which the *Crisis* advocated was a subject that could not be discussed in the South with safety to its exponent, wrote Mrs. Moorer, and, therefore, as the president of an institution for the education of "Southern gentile-womanhood," she could not permit such a publication to come to her, no matter how friendly the sentiments of the sender. Not easily deterred, Spingarn offered to "foot the bill" for fifty copies of the *Crisis* containing the relatively liberal speech of Professor C. H. Brough of the University of Arkansas to the University Commission on the Southern Race Question. "Those fifty copies of the *Crisis* will be distributed in the white South to very good advantage, I fancy!" wrote Spingarn. Upon learning that Peabody College for Teachers, a white institution in Nashville, Tennessee, planned to purchase for its library books dealing with the Negro, Spingarn offered to donate those which the college had not already purchased.[58] Throughout his career in the NAACP, Spingarn's faith in appeals to the white conscience through the medium of the written word was unabated; he rarely missed an opportunity to forward pro-Negro literature not only to white Southerners but also to white Northerners and even to acquaintances abroad.

The greatest single thrust of the NAACP's program in the South during the first decade of the organization's existence was directed against lynching, a phenomenon which Spingarn described as a "stain on our civilization." This cause was to occupy his efforts until his death in 1939. Historically, lynching was neither a distinctly Southern practice nor solely confined to black victims, and the total number of lynchings in the United States declined from an average of 187.5 per year during the decade 1889–99 to 92.5 per year during the following decade. But this improvement was marred by an equally perceptible and more sinister trend: Southern lynchings increased 10 percent during the decade 1899–1909, while, at the same time, the number of white victims decreased from 32.2 percent during the decade 1889–99 to 11.4 percent during the following decade.[59] In short, at the time of the launching of the NAACP in 1909 lynching had emerged as a distinctly Southern and racial custom.

The most hideous of crimes, lynching was nevertheless the most difficult to attack. Legal action usually proved futile, for local prosecuting attorneys and officials often deliberately thwarted attempts to bring guilty persons to justice. When Spingarn urged Governor Albert Gilchrist of Florida to punish those responsible for the lynching of five blacks at Lake City in 1911, the governor replied that he was hindered by insufficient funds and the legislature's failure to take action. The Association had begun investigating the possibility of the passage of a federal anti-lynching bill as early as the Taft administration, but Taft considered lynching a state crime, and his successor, Woodrow Wilson, displayed little inclination to place the prestige of his office behind a federal bill. America's entry into World War I seemingly provided an ideal opportunity for securing federal legislation, for the prevalence of the idealistic concept of a "war for democracy," coupled with the fact that thousands of black soldiers were defending their country yet lynch victims sometimes were potential draftees or soldiers in uniform, appeared to provide both moral and constitutional grounds for the enactment of federal anti-lynching legislation. Two federal bills, one sponsored by Representative Leonidas C. Dyer of Missouri and a second by Representative Merrill Mores of Indiana, were introduced in Congress in 1918, but both failed to pass largely because of the opposition of the powerful Southern bloc.

Meanwhile, in the summer of 1918, Spingarn, who had been commissioned an army major and assigned to the Intelligence Bureau in Washington, had one of his associates, Captain George Hornblower, draft a federal anti-lynching bill providing for federal jurisdiction in lynch cases where the victim was of draft age, the dependent relative of a draftee, or a member of the armed forces. However, before any progress could be made toward enacting the measure, World War I ended. Thus, the day-to-day tactics of the Association's anti-lynching campaign were of necessity limited to investigation, education of the public through the widest possible publicity, attempts to enlist the aid of influential Southerners, and the bestowing of accolades upon the few Southern officials who dared oppose the lynch mob.[60]

Although several members of the NAACP Board of Directors warned that appeals to the Southern conscience would never eradicate lynching, Spingarn adamantly insisted that the "best thought" of the South was opposed to the evil and could be mobilized against it if the facts were but made available. In 1919 he reiterated a suggestion he had first advanced in 1911: that the Association compile and publicize comparative statistical studies of rapes committed by both white and black men in order to prove "that rape [the alleged crime for which the majority of blacks were lynched] does not exist to a greater extent among Negroes than among whites of the same economic classes"; this would "make it easier to persuade America that the black race should not be judged by its criminal minority." He personally fostered investigations of lynchings and mob violence in West Virginia (1912) and Cherokee County, Georgia (1916), the former culminating in a magazine article which he prompted the investigator to prepare. Following a wave of Louisiana lynchings in 1914, Spingarn urged that the NAACP's letter of protest to the governor contain liberal quotations of Southern leaders and journals, and that the letter be written in such a manner as to indicate that "Northerners are not 'butting in' to a Southern problem." [61]

But contrary to Spingarn's prediction, the "best thought" of the South did not come to the fore; rather, the Association's Southern strategy became bogged down in an impossible dilemma. In February 1916, Philip G. Peabody, Boston attorney and philanthropist, offered to donate $10,000 to the NAACP if it could devise an effective means of eradicating lynching. But Spingarn's plan to expend the funds through an organization manned by Southerners had to be abandoned when William O. Scroggs, a liberal white professor in the University of Louisiana, warned that any Southern organization which did not disavow the NAACP's racial policies "would be eagerly seized upon by politicians of the Negro-baiting type and made a source of much embarrassment to the men of the South who are helping to wage war against lynching." Similarly, an Association-sponsored anti-lynching conference of Southern leaders planned for 1919 had to be converted into a national conference composed largely of Northerners because so few Southerners consented to participate. Moreover, the revival and rise of the Ku Klux Klan to full potency by 1919, coupled with a wave of riots and lynchings which characterized the so-called "Red Summer" of the same year, threatened to dissipate the limited gains which the Association's anti-lynching crusade already had accumulated. [62]

Meanwhile, in the midst of the Association's triumphs and defeats, Booker T. Washington had died in 1915. His philosophy of gradualism, fully as much as any other single factor, had been responsible for calling both the NAACP and the New Abolition into being. The black leader had been dead less than a year when Spingarn and Du Bois seized the opportunity to fulfill Spingarn's dream of drawing the Washington followers closer to the banner of the NAACP. Under the guise of seeking to avoid competing with a memorial meeting to be held for Washington in January 1916, Du Bois suggested that the NAACP's annual meeting, scheduled for the same month, be postponed in favor of a later gathering of leaders of the black race. From this suggestion grew the first

Amenia Conference, hosted by Spingarn at his country estate, Troutbeck, in August 1916.[63]

One of the first obstacles to overcome was that of inducing the Washington men to attend the meeting, a problem enhanced by Spingarn's earlier New Abolition attacks upon the deceased leader. This obstacle was surmounted by permitting Washington's followers to have a significant voice in the selection if Conference participants. After Du Bois had formulated a well-balanced list including both his own supporters and Washington men, Spingarn submitted the names to Robert Russa Moton, Washington's successor as principal of Tuskegee Institute, for his approval and suggestions. Spingarn immediately agreed to Moton's suggestion that the list be expanded to include others who had been sympathetic to Washington's program—among whom were Dr. Robert E. Jones, editor of the *Southwestern Christian Advocate;* Dr. Hollis B. Frissell, principal of Hampton Institute in Virginia; and philanthropist George Foster Peabody—and invitations were issued. Moreover, the names of potential conferees were solicited from other Washington adherents, including Fred Moore, editor of the New York *Age,* and Emmett J. Scott, Tuskegee's secretary. Moton initially expressed the intention of personally attending the Conference and of inducing Emmett Scott to be present. However, several days before the opening of the meeting, Moton telegrammed regrets to Spingarn, although expressing his best wishes for a successful gathering.[64]

The fifty conferees who met at Troutbeck ranged in philosophy and ideology from the conservative Scott to the "radical" William Monroe Trotter. Unlike the second Amenia Conference, which would be convened at Troutbeck some seventeen years later and from which whites would be explicitly excluded, the 1916 gathering welcomed the participation of whites who had displayed an interest in the Negro question. The meeting was opened by Governor Charles Whitman of New York, and among the whites who participated were Villard and Inez Milholland, daughter of John E. Milholland, one of the white liberals who had been active in the NAACP during the formative years. In order to preserve an atmosphere of conciliation, Du Bois, a long-time Washington opponent, remained in the background of the deliberations.[65]

The Conference findings indicated that significant concessions had been made by both of the contending groups. NAACP supporters could applaud the conferees' decision that all forms of education were necessary, and not merely the industrial education which Washington had emphasized. Again, NAACP adherents could rally to the call for the Negro's complete political freedom and the necessity for organization (like that which the NAACP could provide) as a means to such freedom. On the other hand, the Washington men could applaud the conferees' recognition of the "peculiar difficulties" that Southern black leaders (like Washington) faced, together with their pledge to respect the faith, methods, and ideals of leaders in all sections of the country who were working for blacks' uplift. Finally, the conferees called for the abolition of the old suspicions and factional alignments which had divided the race, and suggested the desirability of annual conferences of black leaders.[66]

Washington's death and the consensus emanating from the first Amenia Conference left the NAACP as the strongest voice speaking for blacks. But for those who observed closely, there were signs that all was not well with the organization. By 1919 an eight-year test of the agitation and protest phase of the Association's program, with its strong reliance upon the sympathetic response of the public conscience, had proved largely ineffective. It was a bad omen for the future. Conversely, the impressive showing of the legal department was but a prelude to the 1920's, when successive legal victories would catapult the New Abolition to unprecedented success.[67]

IN QUEST OF A MORE PERFECT UNION

The structure that the founders of the National Association for the Advancement of Colored People chose for their organization closely paralleled the corporate arrangement which is common to both the business community and many nonprofit voluntary associations. The NAACP's diverse and widely scattered membership is analogous to a business corporation's thousands of common stockholders who, largely because of their distant location from the national headquarters in New York City, delegate basic policy-making powers to a nonsalaried, elected Board of Directors. But as is usually the case in the relationship of the business corporation's stockholders to their elected executives, technically ultimate control of the NAACP has always rested in the hands of the dues-paying membership. Although the Board of Directors is the policy-making body, each successive constitution of the Association, dating from the first of 1911, has vested in the rank-and-file membership, acting through a January annual business meeting, the ultimate authority to elect or reject Board members. In addition, the membership, acting through the annual business meeting, possesses the power to amend the constitution.[68]

Yet, from the inception of the NAACP, a host of factors foreshadowed an oligarchic, rather than a democratic, administrative system. First, of the two major processes through which organizations are created—from the top down, whereby the founders of the polity organize other individuals or branches into a larger body, or where a federation or group of autonomous units unite to form a larger entity—the NAACP originated from the former process. Its founders and incorporators established a national headquarters in New York and drafted a constitution outlining the framework of the central bureaucracy before branches were called into existence. Although such development from the top down does not inevitably presage the undemocratic administration of a given polity, it does diminish the likelihood of such safeguards against oligarchic central administration as competition for leadership from members of autonomous component units or the opposition to the central bureaucracy's policies which is likely to emanate from viable subsidiaries.[69]

More important, the NAACP's rank-and-file membership, acting through the annual business meeting, failed to attain its full potential as a strong counterbalancing force to the Board's vast authority. Although every member who had paid his annual dues was entitled to attend and vote at annual meetings, an examination of actual attendance during the period 1912 to 1936 reveals that only an infinitesimal percentage of the membership exercised this important prerogative.[70] Even during the 1920's, when the total NAACP membership numbered over 30,000, attendance at annual business meetings ranged from thirty to sixty persons, some of whom were Board members, national officers, and their spouses. During the critical five-year period of 1930 to 1934, when the ravages of the Depression placed the organization's very survival at stake, the maximum attendance at an annual meeting was thirty members (in 1934), eleven of whom were Board members and national officers.[71] Fifteen members (increased to twenty-five in 1936) constituted a quorum at annual business meetings, although this body was charged with the responsibility of electing members of the Board of Directors.[72]

This wholesale default of the membership was due to several factors. Generally, the Association probably was experiencing one of the major problems commonly associated with the corporate arrangement: the inability or unwillingness of the average rank-and-file member to spend the time and money necessary to personally participate in meetings convened an appreciable distance from his own locality. It is significant that the overwhelming majority of those in attendance at annual meetings were residents of New York, the state in which the meetings were held.[73] On the other hand, the membership's laxity of participation in large-scale organizations sometimes reflects their satisfaction with the polity's administration and program. Indeed, during the 1930's, when the Association seemed unable to fully cope with problems arising from the Depression, the once relatively reticent membership would assume an unprecedented interest in both its administrative structure and its program, resulting in a new constitution of 1936, which technically

(though not actually) altered the historic administrative structure.[74] Finally, the degree of membership participation in
organizations bears a direct relationship to the precision with
which goals are defined. The more narrowly goals are defined,
the less likely is a member to feel the desire or need for
firsthand participation; conversely, the more diverse and im-
precise the goals, the greater the likelihood that a member
will find grounds for disagreement and, hence, experience a
desire to personally participate.[75] The revolutionary goals of
the Association during the formative years—especially in
comparison to Washington's accommodationism—coupled
with the hierarchy's general accord on an essentially noneconomic program, enabled the organization to boast both progressive and well-defined goals, especially during the first two
decades of its history. It is noteworthy that the greatest upsurge of membership participation during the period under
consideration occurred in the 1930's, and was centered in
the issue of the continuing adequacy of the organization's
historic program in the wake of the Depression.

The rank-and-file's influence upon the organization's administration was further weakened by its failure to exercise
the one prerogative—the independent selection of Board
candidates—which would have afforded the membership a
large measure of indirect control over the Board of Directors.
Although the Board of Directors maintained its own system
(eventually a standing committee) for the nomination of candidates for Board membership, the successive constitutions of
the NAACP also vested in the membership the right to
nominate Board members, with the final selections being made
by the entire membership assembled at the annual business
meeting. However, when the slate of Board candidates submitted by the Board's own nominating committee is compared
with the slate presented to, and usually accepted by, the
annual business meeting in almost any year during the period
1912 to 1936,[76] it becomes apparent that the membership
seldom exercised its prerogative to independently select
Board candidates. This arrangement was not altered until
1936, when a new constitution adopted in that year provided

for a standing nominating committee of which almost half of the members were to be chosen by the rank-and-file membership at the NAACP annual conferences.[77]

Thus, the NAACP became a closed corporation, largely through the default of its rank-and-file membership. The results were a tremendous narrowing of the broad base of authority suggested by the Association's constitutional structure, with a concomitant tendency toward a self-perpetuating Board of Directors.

Despite the shortcomings of the annual business meeting, a safeguard against the growth of oligarchic administration of the organization seemed, at first glance, inherent in the size and composition of the Board of Directors. Constitutionally designated at thirty members in 1911, the Board's membership was increased to forty in 1919 and to forty-eight in 1936.[78] Biographical sketches of each of the early Board members cannot be presented in a work of this scope [79]; instead, for the purposes of this study it is more fruitful to enumerate some of the basic characteristics of the collective Boards of Directors during the period 1912 to 1939.

First, the Board's members held sufficiently diverse ideologies and philosophies to ensure a wide spectrum of opinion on almost any given issue. Socialists and noneconomic liberals, Jews and gentiles, blacks and whites, pacifists and military preparedness enthusiasts, all found a common bond in some indefatigable desire to realize the basic citizenship rights of blacks. Second, throughout the first thirty years of the NAACP's history, Board membership generally was evenly divided among blacks and whites, although, for reasons which will be discussed below, the major top-level, nonsalaried executive positions—President, Chairman of the Board, Treasurer—were, without exception, occupied by whites until the mid-1930's. Although almost every major issue which confronted the Association occasioned sharp differences of opinion among Board members, the opposing sides were, without exception, biracial. Conversely, there was no instance in the NAACP's history to 1939 when the Board split strictly along racial lines on a major policy matter.

But what successive Board members had in common was more important to the long-range development of the organization than were their differences. The overwhelming majority, both blacks and whites, were educated, middle-class (or potentially middle-class) individuals. The professions most commonly represented by Board members during the period prior to 1939 were educator, physician, attorney, minister, professional social worker, and businessman. For example, William A. Sinclair, who established the best attendance record of any black Board member until his death in 1926— symbolically Sinclair suffered a fatal heart attack aboard a train while en route to a Board meeting—was an author and one of Philadelphia's most prominent physicians. Isadore Martin, Sinclair's successor on the Board and one of the most active black members throughout the second half of the 1920's and the 1930's, was the proprietor of a successful Philadelphia real estate agency. Louis T. Wright, elected to the Board in 1928 and the first black to be elected Board Chairman (1934), was a graduate of Harvard's medical school and was appointed New York's first black police surgeon. Conversely, one would search the Board's rosters in vain for a representative, either black or white, of the blue collar or unskilled categories. The homogeneity the Board enjoyed in terms of its members' socioeconomic status probably was the most important single factor accounting for both blacks' and whites' adherence to the tenets of noneconomic, rather than economic, liberalism in the search for a solution to the race problem.

It was the diversity of the Board's functions rather than of its composition, which became the greatest hindrance to its effectiveness. Partially through specific dictates of the Directors and partially through custom, the Board was structured to serve three basic functions: policy-making; representation of the NAACP membership and branches in every major geographical section; and enhancement of the organization's status in the larger community through the election of highly prestigious Directors.[80] But each of the three functions proved incompatible with the others.

An examination of Board attendance during the period 1911 to 1936 reveals that the individual member's attendance record bore a direct relationship to his residential proximity to New York, where meetings were held, with the attendance records of New York members consistently overshadowing those of nonresidents. By the 1920's, after the Association's branches had expanded into the far West and the South, and the Board encompassed members as far removed as Missouri and California, the problem of distance proved insurmountable. In resigning his Board membership in 1919, Charles Nagel, a St. Louis businessman, summarized the problem succinctly: "Experience has shown me that the result is always the same. These Board meetings are held in the East, and we men in the West . . . rarely ever find it possible to time our visits to suit the dates fixed for your meetings." The Directors persuaded Nagel to retain his membership, although he did not attend a single Board meeting during the succeeding six-year period (1919–24). Similarly, J. Max Barber, a black Philadelphian, resigned his Board membership in 1923 because, he wrote, "I find that I am unable to give a day a month from my work and the expenses of the trip as well . . ." By the late 1920's, only one of the approximately nine regular attenders of Board meetings—Isadore Martin of Philadelphia—was not a resident of New York.[81]

By the mid-1930's, an ever-mounting chorus of voices was demanding that the Board either consent to hold some of its meetings outside of New York or pay the travel expenses of its members,[82] neither of which had been done as late as 1939. The results were twofold: first, the potentially broad base of authority inherent in the Board's size was narrowed appreciably; second, administrative control of the organization passed to the Northeast, and particularly to New York.

The distance factor also had more subtle effects upon the organization's administration. Like most large-scale polities, the NAACP Board of Directors performed the bulk of its work through standing committees—Budget Committee, Nominating Committee, etc.—but Board members from as short a distance as the District of Columbia or Boston often were obliged to decline membership on major committees because of the time and expense entailed in weekly or bi-monthly attendance at such meetings. The incorporators of the NAACP made the Chairman of the Board, rather than the President, the single most powerful official in the adminis-trative hierarchy because the first President, Moorfield Storey (1911–28), resided in Boston, where he conducted a highly successful practice as one of America's foremost constitu-tional lawyers.[83]

The Association also discovered that prestige and regular Board attendance were highly incongruous attributes. Al-though the free legal services which Storey provided the As-sociation over the years proved invaluable, he displayed little interest in routine policy-making, attending less than six Board meetings during his eighteen years as President and Board member. Jane Addams, nationally renowned for her settlement-house work in Chicago, lent little more than the prestige of her name to the organization even during the formative years. Undoubtedly because of the distance factor and her interest in other causes, she did not attend a single Board meeting during the fourteen-year period 1918 to 1931, although she was faithfully renominated and re-elected at the expiration of each of her terms. Lillian Wald, noted for her work at New York's Henry Street Settlement house, was an active Board member until 1918. But in 1921, after three years of inactive membership, she resigned her position, in-sisting that "it is not right to permit my name to continue in the organization when I am doing nothing and can attend no meetings." Florence Kelley, secretary of the Consumers' League and an activist in the movement for the protection of women in industry, was the only one of the early pres-tigious Board members (aside from Spingarn and Villard) who remained active throughout the 1920's. Other distin-guished individuals who were elected to the Board during the 1920's and 1930's—Clarence Darrow, William Allen White, Governor Herbert Lehman of New York—usually provided invaluable services or monetary contributions but rarely, if ever, attended Board meetings or participated in routine policy-making.[84]

Finally, it should be noted that even if the entire Board had assembled at each monthly meeting, it is unlikely that all its members would have wielded significant influence over policy-making. On the contrary, some students of administration suggest that the larger the governing body of a polity, the more unwieldy decision-making becomes, creating a concomitant tendency toward the development of an inner circle of key policy-makers within the larger governing agency.[85]

But to a handful of white liberals—most notably the Spingarn Brothers, Mary White Ovington, and Oswald Garrison Villard [86]—the NAACP became virtually a full-time job and its cause their *cause célèbre*. Especially during the formative years, before an adequate salaried staff had been secured, no task was too mundane for them to perform if it brought the organization a step nearer to success. Villard gave of his personal funds to save the infant NAACP from seemingly imminent collapse. Spingarn traveled from city to city at his own expense, soliciting funds and memberships during the New Abolition tours, although it was not until 1919 that he began offering the organization sizable direct cash contributions. For a brief period (1911–12) Mary White Ovington assumed the duties of Secretary without remuneration.

The intensity of the white liberals' efforts was especially significant, for the pragmatic criterion of practical service appears to have been the major determinant in the selection of the first slate of top-level, nonsalaried NAACP executives. The perennially active Villard, who had served as Chairman of the first Program Committee and who had drafted the 1909 "Call," was elected the first Board Chairman, while all of the other major nonsalaried executive posts were awarded to whites who had been active in the organization before its incorporation.[87] In opposing the selection of a black Board Chairman in 1915, Mary White Ovington confided to Spingarn, "if we had a colored man in New York who had attended the Board regularly, had shown such an interest in the work as you or I have shown, I would hail him as Chairman, but we have no such person . . ."[88]

On the other hand, Miss Ovington's statement conveys

only half of the story. The white liberals' contributions—both financial and otherwise—probably were greater than those of their black counterparts, but this was because the former were more associated with what may be termed the aristocracy of wealth, with its attendant opportunities and leisure. There is a direct correlation between an individual's social status and his ability and willingness to participate in voluntary and non-voluntary associations other than those involving his livelihood and family. Wealthy individuals are more likely than the less affluent to be joiners and participants in such agencies, largely because they have more leisure time to devote to them. Although black Board members like William A. Sinclair and Isadore Martin were relatively successful in their professions, it is doubtful whether either was sufficiently independent financially to have undertaken a full-time, non-salaried post in the NAACP, or to have manifested their interest in the organization in the form of personally financed transcontinental tours or through sizable cash contributions. Even though W. E. B. Du Bois, one of the foremost black leaders of the day, received a full salary from the Association for his services, he frequently was obliged to solicit personal loans from Spingarn.

Members of the upper class also have a greater opportunity to develop skills vital to leadership roles. As will be discussed in a later section of this study, Spingarn's familiarity with New York's most reputable financial institutions and his expertise in the management of stocks and bonds enabled him to become one of the key formulators of the NAACP's financial policy. Indeed, the possession of skills which are vital to an organization's development is one of the major means by which individuals may attain and sustain themselves in leadership roles. The dearth of leadership skills among blacks as compared to whites during the NAACP's formative years was nowhere more evident than in the search for attorneys to conduct the Association's legal work. Arthur Spingarn recalled that there were few competent black lawyers, and there was none who could match the national prestige of Moorfield Storey, a former president of the American Bar Association and one of the country's foremost constitutional lawyers. Until 1940 the NAACP's Legal Committee was headed by Arthur Spingarn, who devoted much time to the organization without compensation.[89]

The tendency toward oligarchic administration of the NAACP national office was especially significant, for structurally the Association is a compound organization consisting of many component units (branches), which constitutionally are governed by and subordinate to the national office. The branches derived their charters from the parent organization, and the national Board of Directors possessed, and not infrequently exercised, the power to revoke a branch's charter.[90] More importantly, the national office, through both constitutional provisions and custom, exercised a large measure of indirect control over the subordinate units. For example, the constitutional provision that the national office was to receive up to 50 percent of the proceeds accruing to the branches from membership fees and donations not only regulated the number and kinds of programs in which the branches could engage but also reinforced the concept of their subordination to the parent body. In fact, complaints from the branches regarding the allocation of proceeds to the New York office remained a major point of tension between the central bureaucracy and its subordinate agencies throughout the period under consideration. As early as 1913 the national Board of Directors' Committee on Branches established a precedent for intervening in and adjudicating an internal dispute among the members of a branch (in the District of Columbia); and by the end of the 1920's, successive branch constitutions (which were formulated by the Board of Directors) had firmly established the national office's prerogative to determine the most minute details of branch operation, including, for example, the number of individuals who were to comprise a branch's local governing body, and the proper and acceptable procedure for conducting programs and garnering members.

In sum, the NAACP truly became a closed corporation, for not only did the central office's policy-making process come under the control of a handful of individuals but the central office's ostensibly tight control of the branches meant essentially that a few New York administrators determined NAACP policy on a nationwide scale.

On the other hand, extreme care should be taken in delineating theory and practice in the relationship between any large-scale, compound organization and its component parts. As the size of the polity increases and membership is more widely dispersed, it becomes virtually impossible for any one person or group, including the central bureaucracy, to have detailed knowledge of the entire structure.[91] The problem of strictly regulating the activities of branches was especially acute for the NAACP during the entire first thirty years of its history, for even after the branches numbered more than 300 (by 1921), scattered from coast to coast and in several foreign countries, the national office relied upon a salaried Director of Branches based in New York and his handful of assistants (approximately six Field Secretaries and Branch Organizers by the 1930's) to supervise branch activities and to keep the national Board of Directors informed thereof. Largely because of limited funds, the Board rejected the repeated suggestion that the branches be grouped into several major geographical divisions, with a full-time, salaried coordinator or secretary for each division. That the lack of close supervision resulted in an appreciable measure of branch autonomy (though often of a negative variety) is evidenced by the frequent complaints of national officers to the effect that large numbers of branches forwarded no funds to the national office and were delinquent in attracting new members—fully 55 percent were so classified in 1920. Some went undetected in these practices for nearly two years. Or, as Spingarn was to charge during the 1930's, many branches were "moribund" in the execution of those activities they did attempt.[92]

THE ART OF INTERPERSONAL LEADERSHIP

It was Spingarn's prowess as a great pacifier—the "interpersonal leader" among the Association's contending factions —which earned him the position of Chairman of the Board of Directors in 1914.[93] The interpersonal leader concentrates upon human interaction within the organization; he is primarily concerned with facilitating communication among the several personality types or potential groups which comprise the polity. He seeks to allay anxieties and, in the process, may even elicit personal devotion. He is more concerned with people than with policies; indeed, his expertise may lie outside the realm of content. Thus, the most important contribution of the interpersonal leader is a more harmoniously functioning organization. His role is appreciably different from that of the "institutional leader," whose primary concern is the promotion and protection of the polity's basic values.[94] Prior to 1914 the latter role appears to have been more decidedly Villard's.

Some indication of Spingarn's knack for interpersonal leadership was manifested in 1913 when the Board of Director's Committee on Branches (of which Spingarn was Chairman) undertook to adjudicate a serious conflict among members of the District of Columbia branch. The controversy reached explosive proportions when more than 100 members of the branch demanded the ouster of the black president, Dr. J. Milton Waldron, a Baptist minister and influential local Democratic politician, largely on the grounds that he was using the prestige of the branch presidency to secure a political appointment from the Democrats. Waldron, who enjoyed considerable support among some branch members, denied the charges and refused to resign. Both May Childs Nerney, who had been insulted by Waldron when she visited the branch, and Mary White Ovington strongly urged Spingarn to recommend to the Board of Directors that the anti-Waldron faction be designated as the official District of Columbia branch. Meanwhile, the conflict assumed even broader dimensions when William Monroe Trotter, a close associate of Waldron's and a long-standing critic of the NAACP, publicly charged that Villard personally had been opposed to Waldron for quite some time because of the latter's uncompromising demands for full Negro rights. Villard, concluded the *Guardian* editorial, was reverting increasingly to the accommodationism of Booker T. Washington.[95]

Spingarn, after having made a personal visit to the Washington branch, rejected the urgings of Nerney and Ovington, and recommended that the Board of Directors adopt a neutral position. He agreed with Nerney that Waldron's insults could not be ignored, but he insisted that "it seemed to me best to avoid a violent split, not only in Washington, but in the Board itself." Spingarn prevailed, and the Board refused to recognize either of the contending factions pending the outcome of a special election for a new slate of branch officers.[96]

More important, the early formation of interest groups within the national office made the services of an interpersonal leader indispensable. Interest groups, which are common to all large-scale organizations, represent energy. A group or an individual may develop a particular conception of the work to be done, the tactics to be employed, or the relationship of the group or individual to the other members of the organization. If the interest group thus formed directs its energies toward fulfilling the goals of the top-level leadership, its existence poses no threat to the organization. But if it harbors goals which are appreciably different from those established by the leadership, conflict will ensue and the unity and stability of the organization will be threatened. The leadership must act quickly to redirect the energies of the interest group, usually through concessions, toward fulfilling the polity's basic goals. The organization's unity is the leadership's foremost consideration.[97]

The most significant interest group to arise within the NAACP during the period 1911 to 1934 was centered in W. E. B. Du Bois, Editor of the Association's official organ, the *Crisis*, and Director of the Department of Publicity and Research. Du Bois' conception of his role in the NAACP has been documented elsewhere.[98] Endowed with an uncommon intellect, yet frustrated by the ever-present "color line," the Editor interpreted his role in the Association within a racial context. The only black executive officer (until 1916), he contended that it was absolutely necessary that he have a large measure of autonomy lest the Association, with its preponderance of white executives, should become a white-dominated organization with Negroes as mere helpers. It was virtually impossible for blacks and whites to work in the same office and at the same tasks without one group being in charge, insisted Du Bois. Yet if whites exercised authority, the Negroes would drop out; if Negroes headed the operation, the whites would gradually leave. In order to avoid this dilemma, Du Bois contended, "I've tried to see if we could not have two branches of the same work, one with a white head and one with a colored; working in harmony and sympathy for one end." [99] From an administrative standpoint, the Editor's demand for autonomy was a potential threat to the organization's basic unity.

Second, Du Bois demanded that he be afforded a large measure of freedom in editing the *Crisis*. He never considered the magazine a vehicle for promulgating only the official views of the Association; rather, he argued, the *Crisis* should encompass diverse and even controversial opinion, as partially shaped by the Editor and, most of all, reflecting the aspirations of black people. In 1929, looking back over his nineteen years of aspirations and failures with the magazine, Du Bois frankly admitted, "I have sought to retain as strong a hold over the *Crisis* as possible," partially in an attempt "to prove the possibilities of a Negro magazine." [100] Du Bois' dual aspirations—the autonomy of his department and in editing the *Crisis*—were to pose the greatest single test of Spingarn's prowess as an interpersonal leader.

Spingarn's initial contact with Du Bois was in the spring of 1910 regarding the operation of the Heart of Hope Club. Obviously Du Bois was aware of Spingarn's reputation as a progressive reformer, for although he cordially suggested a program which the Club's participants might find appealing, he also assured Spingarn, "from what I hear . . . you are probably in a position to give me more practical insight into the running of a club of this sort." [101] From this inauspicious beginning developed a unique, dual relationship between the two men, a relationship which often was to be strained to the breaking point by seemingly unbridgeable differences in personality and ideology.

First, the two men met upon a personal plane which largely was based upon the respect which each harbored for the intellectual faculties of the other. Both had attained the doctor of philosophy degree—Du Bois was the first black Harvard Ph.D.—and both had relegated the degree to what Spingarn termed "the proper perspective." Spingarn rarely, if ever, used the title Dr. before his name, and he observed that Du Bois too had freed himself of the "Ph.D. disease." Both men had experimented with the world of academe in the role of professors and writers; both had found it lacking in some measure. Each had made the descent from the cloistered study into a broader arena of practical struggle. Yet, although Spingarn was an avowed equalitarian, there are subtle indications that he assigned an elite status to the intelligentsia, placing them on a rung above the masses. Just as Du Bois once had been mesmerized by the concept of a "Talented Tenth" of Negroes who would lead the masses of their people, Spingarn also spoke of the "aristocracy" of talent and ability which every free society must eventually develop. Some men were thinkers and others were "doers," he once observed, but it was the thinker of Du Bois' stripe who deserved the plaudits of men, for it was the thinker who provided the doer with his task.[102]

Occasionally Spingarn and Du Bois cooperated in literary endeavors. The Editor's white friend invited him to write the story of the first Amenia Conference as one of the "Troutbeck Leaflets," a series of pamphlets dealing with diverse subjects commissioned by Spingarn and privately printed at his Troutbeck press. As late as 1933, the year preceding Du Bois' resignation from the NAACP, he wrote Spingarn asking for information to be used in a massive study of Reconstruction which Du Bois was then preparing. Similarly, when, in 1935, Du Bois was preparing to launch an encyclopedia of the Negro, Spingarn was one of the few whites invited to submit an article.[103]

Still another facet of the two men's relationship was exterior to their roles as co-workers in the NAACP. Du Bois

frequently experienced personal financial difficulties, and
Spingarn was always a source to which he could turn. For
example, in 1926 the Editor inquired whether he might be
able to borrow $5,000 from any financial institution with
which Spingarn had influence. Spingarn and his wife responded by each extending Du Bois a $1,000 personal loan,
and in addition Spingarn induced one of his wealthy white
friends, Mrs. Jacob H. Schiff, to increase the total to $3,000
by adding her personal loan of $1,000. Du Bois was permitted
to repay the loans at his convenience and without interest,
and Spingarn assured the Editor that he and his brother
would be willing to aid him in managing his personal funds.[104]

More important, it soon became apparent that Spingarn,
unlike Villard and most of the other members of the NAACP
administrative hierarchy, could talk *with* Du Bois; and, perhaps, Du Bois desperately needed, more than anything else,
someone with whom to talk. Possessed of a quarrelsome
temperament, which was abetted by Villard's domineering
manner, the Editor was convinced that of his white associates
only Spingarn and Mary White Ovington were free of race
prejudice. By 1914 few of his colleagues had escaped his
accusing finger: he had been "elbowed out" of the main
office work; May Childs Nerney harbored unconscious race
prejudice; Villard was even more prejudiced than she. Conversely, by 1913 Villard had given up Du Bois as impossible
to work with.[105]

But in his autobiography, published in 1940, Du Bois
referred to Spingarn as having had the greatest influence on
his life of any white man—a rare tribute from one to whom
considerations of the color line were ever present. Spingarn
developed a penchant for listening to Du Bois, sometimes
offering sharp criticism, but always assuring the Editor that
his criticism, though frank, was sincere "as the criticism of
friends should be." On the other hand, Du Bois recalled in his
autobiography that he was often peeved by Spingarn's
tendency to make snap judgments. But, as will be seen
shortly, Spingarn could understand and was sympathetic
toward Du Bois' desire for a measure of freedom in editing

the *Crisis*. By 1914 his unique relationship with the Editor was well known. "Because of the friendliness of our relations and my constant championship of you," wrote Spingarn to his friend, "I have been thrust forward by your friends and enemies as internmediary [sic] or arbiter in all cases of disagreement with you." Villard, seeing that he could not work with Du Bois, had begun as early as March 1913 to entertain the idea that Spingarn should succeed him as Board Chairman.[106]

Yet the two men's affinity for each other did not spring from mutual agreement on major policy matters. By 1913 Du Bois had begun suggesting in his *Crisis* editorials that the struggle for the Negro's civil rights must be buttressed by a strong program of black economic uplift, but Spingarn opposed the Association's adoption of an extensive economic program on the grounds that the NAACP's structure was not geared toward such a program and that the adoption of a major economic program would bring the Association into conflict with other organizations (undoubtedly a reference to the Urban League). In his autobiography Du Bois lamented that his white friend had been such a staunch noneconomic liberal: "He wanted for Negroes freedom to live and act," wrote the Editor, "but he did not believe that . . . revolution in industry was going to bring the millennium." [107] Similarly, Spingarn was sympathetic toward Du Bois' bid for a measure of freedom in editing the *Crisis* but not with any attempt to separate the Editor's department or the magazine from the Association. Indeed, Spingarn's twenty-five-year relationship with Du Bois was to be an anomalous one, in which he would be obliged to choose between his high personal regard for the Editor and his utter disdain for Du Bois' views regarding his own and the *Crisis'* relationship to the Association. Du Bois or the unity of the NAACP would be the fundamental choice continuously confronting Spingarn. He would always choose the unity of the Association, although making concessions to Du Bois whenever possible.

At the same time, Villard and Spingarn found even fewer grounds for mutual agreement. Villard considered Spingarn an excellent speaker, but he felt that the New Abolitionist's pronouncements sometimes were too radical. While jointly addressing a mass black audience in Baltimore in 1913, the two men had a public altercation after Spingarn arose with his usual unrelenting candor and "coolly" disputed Villard's advice that Negroes use only peaceful means to secure their rights. Spingarn, who by then fancied himself a reincarnated Abolitionist, contended that William Lloyd Garrison would not have employed such meek methods. Villard, the grandson of Garrison, interrupted Spingarn's speech and "set him right." However, the audience sided with Spingarn. Villard later confided to his uncle, Francis Jackson Garrison, that Spingarn had made a "very poor appearance." When Spingarn was invited to speak in Baltimore the following year, he declined, suggesting that Villard or other members of the Association probably would be able to do a better job.[108] With the exception of official NAACP Conferences and annual meetings, there is no indication that the two men ever appeared on the same platform together after the Baltimore episode. Thenceforth, when Spingarn was accompanied by a speaking partner, he usually chose Du Bois or a colleague other than Villard.

Villard also thought Spingarn too brash in his public attacks on Booker T. Washington during the New Abolition tours. Although Villard, a former Washington supporter, did not hesitate in privately chiding the Tuskegeean for his accommodationist philosophy, he was opposed to any deliberate public airing of differences between the NAACP and the rival Washington group. Indeed, as late as March 1913, Villard was earnestly cooperating with Washington in planning a conference of small Negro industrial schools. At almost the same time, however, beginning in January 1913, Spingarn launched one of the strongest attacks upon the Negro leader that the black community had ever witnessed. Villard confided to his uncle that Spingarn was a "firebrand"; Spingarn confided to Du Bois that he would not permit his freedom of speech to be curtailed in any way.[109]

Other differences in outlook also must have made it difficult for Villard and Spingarn to effect a close relationship. Even as Villard was concluding that Du Bois must get out of the Association, Spingarn was publicly hailing the Editor as the symbol of all that the organization stood for, "the Frederick Douglass" of the modern movement for Negro rights. In still another vein, the two men were at opposite ends of the political spectrum. Theodore Roosevelt had been Spingarn's political idol since 1899, and he had faithfully followed Roosevelt into the Bull Moose ranks in 1912. But Villard, who virtually despised Roosevelt, used every ounce of his prestige to ensure Roosevelt's defeat in 1912. What impact, if any, these differing political views had upon Villard and Spingarn's relationship is not clear. In the final analysis, Spingarn's disdain for Villard reached a point where, in commenting upon Villard's many threats to resign because of Du Bois, Spingarn noted that he was just up to his same old "capers." [110]

More important, Villard and Spingarn could not agree on the rights and duties Du Bois should have as Director of Publicity and Research and Editor of the *Crisis*. The issue reached explosive proportions in late 1913 when, after a heated altercation with Villard at a Board meeting, Du Bois wrote Villard, insisting that he must have "reasonable initiative and independence" in the performance of his duties, although the Editor conceded that Board members were entitled to criticize his work. Du Bois insisted that he was not Villard's subordinate—the Editor occupied the dual roles of Board member and employee of the Board—and, therefore, that his actions should not be considered disrespectful toward Villard's official position as Board Chairman. Rather than reply directly to Du Bois, Villard explained his position to Spingarn. However, Spingarn apparently took the position that Du Bois should have a measure of independence, for Villard later wrote Spingarn, insisting that "there is a fundamental difference in our positions, and that is that the Chairman of the Board . . . is the executive of the Association and must exercise certain authority over the paid employees . . . , whether they be editors or clerks." Villard maintained that he could not accept the responsibilities of a position without its attendant powers. A meeting between the Spingarn brothers, Mary White Ovington, and Du Bois failed to resolve the dispute.[111]

It was at this point, when an obvious impasse had been reached, that Spingarn departed from his position of neutrality to side openly with Du Bois against Villard. In recalling the event many years later, Spingarn maintained that he had espoused De Bois' cause in 1913 because he felt that there should be at least one publication in America in which a Negro could express his views without any interference from any white person whatsoever. He considered the basic issue to be that of freedom of expression, a privilege which he always had demanded for himself, and one that he felt Du Bois should enjoy as Editor of the *Crisis*. According to Spingarn his support of Du Bois had led directly to Villard's resignation as Chairman of the Board in late 1913.[112]

On the other hand, it is important to note that Spingarn confined his support of Du Bois to freedom of expression in the *Crisis;* he did not endorse any plan to separate Du Bois' department or the magazine from the Association, a move which would have destroyed the basic unity of the organization. In fact, attempts to resolve this latter problem eventually would all but destroy the two men's cordial relations.

It is not surprising that Spingarn supported Du Bois' bid for a measure of freedom in editing the *Crisis*, for throughout his career in the NAACP the New Abolitionist gave indications of being more sensitive, perhaps, than any of his white colleagues to the possible contradiction in the Association's call for black militancy and independence as opposed to the power which whites like himself wielded within the organization. In one of his first speeches on the race problem, delivered in November 1911, Spingarn offered this comment on whites' participation in the civil rights struggle: "I am tired, too, of the philanthropy of rich white men toward your race. I want to see you [Negroes] fight your own battles with your own leaders and your own money." [113] Financial records indicate that during the first eight years of

Spingarn's affiliation with the NAACP he donated approximately $500 in cash to the organization; his contribution was manifested largely through his time, his energy, and his interest. In 1914 he told a mass black audience that "we white men of whatever creed or faith cannot fight your battles for you. We will stand shoulder to shoulder with you only until you can fight as generals all by yourselves." [114] On two occasions, in 1915 and in 1933, he would resign his offices in the NAACP, partly because he equated the Board's failure to accept his view with the fact that he was white. Each time he would suggest that a Negro succeed him. Spingarn's discomfort over his somewhat precarious position would reach its apex in 1933 when he would frankly ask young black leaders gathered at the second Amenia Conference what role white liberals like himself were to have in the continuing struggle for black advancement.[115] Undoubtedly, Du Bois' ever-present emphasis upon the color factor further heightened Spingarn's awareness and sensitivity.

Yet Spingarn's failure to relinquish the power he wielded in the NAACP comprised one of the greatest paradoxes of his career. Those who occupy high-level positions within organizations usually are reluctant to relinquish them, especially when, as in Spingarn's case, only subordinate positions would be available. Thus, as if attracted by some irresistible lodestone, Spingarn would cling to the Association throughout the years, fulfilling his own prophecy that he would never desert the organization's cause, "not until I am dead." With the exception of the 1920's, when illness plunged him into an administrative semi-eclipse, the New Abolitionist's considerable influence within the NAACP administrative hierarchy was unabated. Indeed, after his election to the presidency (and simultaneously the Board Chairmanship) during the 1930's, one can detect a deliberate attempt on his part to recoup much of the administrative influence he had wielded during the formative years.[116]

Upon Villard's resignation in January 1914, Spingarn was elected Chairman of the Board, which placed him in the uneasy dual role of Du Bois' superior and friend. Although

Spingarn would staunchly oppose the Editor on a variety of matters, he upheld Du Bois' right to freedom of expression in the *Crisis*. One of the most important tests of the freedom of expression doctrine came in late 1914 when W. S. Scarborough, the president of Wilberforce University, complained to Spingarn about a *Crisis* editorial which was critical of Negro higher education in general and of Wilberforce in particular. Not only did Scarborough make Spingarn "suffer" by inundating him with letters, newspaper articles, and copies of letters addressed to Scarborough in regard to the *Crisis* editorial, but the educator also published a heated reply to Du Bois in the New York *Age*.[117]

Spingarn made no attempt to have Du Bois retract what he had written. Rather, he somewhat coolly asked Scarborough specifically what he found unfair or untrue in the article. At the same time, Spingarn told Du Bois that if Scarborough had any complaints he should address them to the *Crisis* Editor for publication in the magazine. Nevertheless, he suggested to the Editor, "I assume of course that you would welcome such a letter in the interest of fairness and good feeling." Du Bois initially treated Scarborough's complaints as a "joke," even publishing a satirical skit on the affair in the next issue of the *Crisis*. However, when Spingarn persisted in taking the matter seriously, Du Bois agreed to consider the publication of any rebuttal Scarborough might submit, although he informed Spingarn that he was not inclined to yield much to the educator's insults, especially since the article had not been offensive.[118]

Throughout 1914, as Du Bois proceeded to antagonize the Negro clergy, the Negro press, and other groups with his critical editorials, Spingarn generally refrained from violating the Editor's right to freedom of expression. Indeed, the new Chairman of the Board gave freedom of expression a new dimension by defending the Editor's right to freedom of speech in his public addresses. In December 1914 a Boston member of the Association complained to Spingarn that Du Bois, in a speech delivered to a suffragist meeting, had used a recent reorganization of the NAACP Board as an illustration of the dangers of usurpation of power. Spingarn promptly wrote the Editor, maintaining that he could not believe that Du Bois would "reveal our family secrets to outsiders" or make use of "family quarrels to illustrate a point on an unrelated matter." Spingarn assured the Editor that he was writing "not in any official capacity but as a friend" in order to end the story once and for all. Probably it would be better "for me to ignore stories of this sort," he wrote, "and yet I am always tempted to take up the cudgels for my friends." On Du Bois' assurances that his speech had not in any way betrayed the Association's internal affairs, Spingarn informed the complaining Bostonian that he had been mistaken. For Du Bois to have been guilty of the Bostonian's charges "would have been a breach of good manners on his part of which I simply cannot conceive him to be guilty at any time," wrote Spingarn, "but even if he were, I do not for a moment consider him responsible to the Association for his manners, any more than for his logic . . ." [119]

On the other hand, Spingarn had no sympathy with any plan to accord the Editor so much autonomy that the *Crisis* or the Department of Publicity and Research would be separated from the Association. In March 1914, less than three months after having assumed the Board Chairmanship, Spingarn reminded Du Bois that "more than ever now, I feel that we must present a united front, with courage and common sense, against defection and opposition." At the same time, Spingarn proceeded to use his authority as Board Chairman to exercise a general supervision over Du Bois' management of his department. In September 1914, when the NAACP was experiencing tremendous financial difficulties, Spingarn and the Editor could not agree on the question of economizing. Du Bois contended that additional space was needed for the *Crisis* office, and he was opposed to any attempt to effect the bulk of the economy cuts at the expense of his department. Spingarn replied that he had "always felt that the *Crisis* was rather extravagant" in terms of rent. He had always held what was, perhaps, the fictional idea that "any attic or garret was good enough for a newspaper office," although he conceded that Villard, the owner of the office which currently housed the Department of Publicity and Research, "would not be averse to our going." Spingarn warned Du Bois that the financial situation would grow worse daily, and suggested that the question of new *Crisis* offices be discussed more fully.[120]

In the final analysis, Du Bois prevailed and was permitted to move to new offices. However, when Spingarn received the first financial statement of the new facility, he was appalled by the increased expense. He complained that not only was Du Bois' statement of expenses much higher than those tallied by the Treasurer—for example, the printer had submitted the Treasurer a bill for $1094.48, while Du Bois had listed the same bill as $1968.22—but also that the new *Crisis* rent was double that of the old: fifty-nine dollars per month as compared to $118 per month in Spingarn's estimation. Obviously displeased, the Chairman of the Board informed the Editor that "I do not compare the convenience of the old and the new offices, but if these figures are correct, it would seem as if it were a serious error of judgment to have purchased so much 'convenience' before the *Crisis* was wholly self-supporting." Du Bois retorted that in the case of the printer's bill, his office recorded the bill as being due when it was incurred, thereby causing the apparent indebtedness to be doubled. Secondly, even if the old *Crisis* office had been retained, explained the Editor, additional space would have been required, thereby entailing a similar increase in rent.[121]

This unaccustomed bickering with his one close friend obviously disturbed Du Bois, for on the same day he wrote a second letter to Spingarn, requesting a candid explanation of the suspicion which his white friend appeared to have manifested toward him. He could not quite put his finger on the exact difficulty, yet he felt that Spingarn doubted his honesty. One indication of this, noted the Editor, was his friend's tendency to approach him cautiously, rather than openly, when discussing a matter. Du Bois had become so uneasy that a mere letter from Spingarn was received with great consternation. The Editor assured Spingarn that he desired the cooperation of all his co-workers, and urged his friend to openly express any inward doubts he might harbor.[122]

Spingarn's extensive reply exemplified the dilemma which would always surround his relationship with Du Bois: his deep personal understanding and regard for the Editor but also his annoyance with what he considered to be Du Bois' personal and professional shortcomings. His words might be so frank that they would wound a friend's feelings, began Spingarn, but at this critical time he could not waive a friend's right to the frankest criticism. He did not doubt Du Bois' absolute honesty or sincerity, but he did feel that, like Theodore Roosevelt and other men he admired, Du Bois simply could not admit an honest mistake. For example, the Editor had proceeded to move into new offices which he insisted would not be of additional cost to the Association; yet when a sizable cost resulted, Du Bois had contended that it was merely an illusion rather than admit he had been wrong. But this was only a "trifle" in comparison to the larger issue, continued Spingarn. The antagonism that surrounded Du Bois in the office was not confined to the Board or to Villard but existed in the entire colored world as well. Much of this was due to the Editor's devotion to principle and the sacrifice such principle must entail; it was also a result of Du Bois' boast that he could not accept even the appearance of inferiority or subservience without betraying the race ideals for which he was fighting, "although in this matter it may be weakness rather than manliness to protest too much," [123] insisted Spingarn.

No matter how much Du Bois might blame others, much of the fault lay within himself, continued Spingarn. Even his friends had come to feel that the Editor often mistook obstinacy for strength of character, a very poor substitute for managing men. Du Bois' friends had begun to feel that he would demand his own way even when no matter of principle was involved; that he would prefer to wreck the larger cause rather than give up a preferred point. Perhaps the Editor may have imagined that in many instances his victory derived from successful argument or strength of character, "but often it seemed as if these men yielded to you for the reason that parents yield to spoilt children in company, for fear of creating a scene," declared Spingarn. Nor was this based on hearsay, for Spingarn too had experienced these shortcomings in his friend. Du Bois had to be approached with diplomacy and "wheedling" rather than with openness; if the issue involved a personality whom the Editor did not like, nothing could be done for the cause until that personality had been eliminated or disguised. Thus, it was a distrust of Du Bois' temperament and not his character that was involved.[124]

Finally, Spingarn served notice that Du Bois' bid for autonomy and his seeming unwillingness to submit his will to the collective interests of the Association would not be tolerated. "There can be no *Crisis*, no non-*Crisis*," insisted the Chairman of the Board, "this way of dividing our work has failed; both must be one." If the Editor and everyone else were not willing to work for the common good, the Association would be doomed; and there were many who would welcome its downfall, warned Spingarn (perhaps referring to Villard), "now that they can no longer completely control its destinies." Spingarn suggested that Du Bois meet with him to discuss the matter further.[125]

Du Bois made an equally lengthy reply to Spingarn's charges. Spingarn had a way of changing his attitude and approach on a given matter, he retorted, the issue of the *Crisis* office rent being a case in point. The Editor admitted that his temperament might be trying, but this was due to his peculiar education and experiences. He was not obstinate; he merely wanted a chance to do a big piece of work without being hindered by those who did not yet see the larger ideal. Nor was he the cause of the friction in the office. In fact, he had been "elbowed out" of any real connection with the general work of the Association without complaining, although in his own "realm" he had insisted that equal respect be accorded his judgment as would be the case if he were white. Spingarn's continued urging of cooperation and understanding showed how little he understood the existence of the "color line" within the NAACP. Miss Nerney, the Secre-

tary, harbored unconscious race prejudice, while Villard was
even more prejudiced than she. Finally, Du Bois insisted that
some degree of autonomy for himself and his department was
an absolute necessity as a means of maintaining balance between white and Negro authority within the organization.[126]

After this exchange of views, the relationship between the
two men steadily deteriorated as each adamantly held to his
respective position. The following week, during the November Board meeting, Spingarn charged that the unrest within
the Association was due to the childish bickering of one
individual. A few days later Du Bois replied with a reorganization plan which called for the abolition of his department in
lieu of his taking "charge of the *Crisis* assuming all liabilities."
A Crisis Committee was to retain a veto power over the
magazine's contents.[127] In short, the Editor was willing to
relinquish the precious right to freedom of editorial expression in return for autonomy in the larger sense.

This proposal met a stone wall of opposition. The
NAACP Executive Committee (a subcommittee of the
Board), which had been preparing a proposal for administrative reorganization, completely ignored Du Bois' suggestion
in its report. Instead, the Committee recommended that "the
Director of Publications and Research with the advice of the
Crisis Committee shall be responsible for the administering of
the Crisis Fund and the formulation of the policy of the
Crisis, ranking as a head of Department." As a final blow
the Committee recommended that all department heads be
subject to the authority of the Board Chairman and make
monthly reports to the Board and the Chairman. Still determined not to be relegated to the position of a mere department head, Du Bois strenuously opposed the report, offering
instead a minority report in which the phrase "head of department" was deleted and his title stated merely as Director of
Publications and Research. Similarly, the Editor's minority report specified that he was to report to the entire Board, with
no mention being made of the Board Chairman.[128] Hence, Du
Bois jealously guarded his autonomy even against the encroachment of his friend Spingarn.

But Spingarn was equally determined that the *Crisis* and the Association would remain one. After Du Bois had presented his minority report to the Board, Spingarn, upon the urging of Villard, left the chair in order to argue the view of the majority report of the Executive Committee. When a final vote was taken, the majority report presented by Spingarn and the Committee was adopted, but with five Board members, including Du Bois, Ovington, and Paul Kennaday, opposing. A motion to make the vote unanimous in favor of the majority report was not acted upon.[129]

Thus, the interpersonal relationships within the Association had assumed the appearance of a strange game of musical chairs: Spingarn and Du Bois had opposed Villard in 1913; now, less than a year later, Spingarn and Villard were opposing Du Bois and Ovington. Nor was this to be the final arrangement. Upon becoming Board Chairman in 1919, Ovington's exercise of authority would be challenged by Du Bois, transforming her into one of his most severe critics. After years of wrangling with the Editor, Villard would drop out of active participation in the NAACP in 1919. Du Bois and Spingarn soon would recoup their affinity for each other and pit their united strength against the Board of Directors when the issue of Du Bois' acceptance of an army commission would arise in 1918.[130]

Meanwhile the lines of battle remained taut. In November 1915 Du Bois published a statement of his position in the *Crisis*, contending (erroneously) that he alone had sustained the magazine since its inception, that the NAACP had not expended one dime for its upkeep, and that he therefore was entitled to the *Crisis* by moral right. At the same time, the Editor's critics on the Board of Directors had begun to question the propriety of the considerable time he devoted to personal lecturing and writing ventures, as opposed to giving full time to his work with the Association.[131]

Spingarn opposed Du Bois on both counts. In December 1915 a three-member committee (including Spingarn) on delimiting the work of executive officers recommended that Du Bois' activities be confined to management of the *Crisis*, although he was to be permitted as much freedom as would be consistent with the Association's needs. However, the Board voted that it would be "inexpedient" to accept the report.[132] This pro-Du Bois vote probably reflected the impact of his November 1915 *Crisis* editorial regarding his contribution to the magazine's development and, perhaps, some Board members' belief that his personal achievements indirectly enhanced the NAACP's status. The vote should not be interpreted as reflecting Du Bois' influence over the Board, for the Directors had ruled against him repeatedly in the past and would continue to do so in the future. Nor should the vote be considered as representing a split along racial lines among Board members, for both Moorfield Storey and Mary White Ovington, two key white liberals, disagreed with Spingarn's views regarding the relationship of the *Crisis* to the Association. Ovington frankly told Spingarn, "As to the *Crisis* I am afraid there we can't agree." The magazine could not be both a house organ and a popular, successful periodical, she warned, and she suggested that it might be better to allow the *Crisis* to become an independent magazine. Moorfield Storey also felt that if Du Bois could make the *Crisis* self-supporting, then he should be permitted to sever all connections between the magazine and the NAACP.[133]

What was more important, the Board's pro-Du Bois vote indirectly gave rise to the issue of whether whites should continue to occupy the organization's top-level executive positions. Thoroughly taken aback by the Board's adverse decision, Spingarn displayed his major weakness as an administrator—the inability to gracefully accept the majority opinion when it was opposed to a view he strongly advocated. Ovington recorded a candid description of him as he withdrew to one corner of the Board room and turned away from the other members after the pro-Du Bois vote had been rendered. Shortly afterward, Spingarn confided to Ovington that he felt that he should resign his position as Board Chairman and support a black successor—the first of several occasions on which he would urge that a Negro succeed him when he felt that he no longer enjoyed the Board's support on a major policy matter. Villard too announced his intention of resigning shortly after the Board had rendered its vote, informing his uncle, Francis Jackson Garrison, that probably there would be a clean sweep of all of the white executives.[134]

A confluence of forces militated against Spingarn's plan to relinquish the Chairmanship to a Negro. First, Mary White Ovington was squarely opposed to the idea. No Negro who resided in New York had attended Board meetings as regularly or otherwise displayed the interest in the organization that "you [Spingarn] or I have shown," she wrote. "When the colored man appears to whom the chairmanship would go as naturally as it went to you or Mr. Villard," Ovington told Spingarn, "then surely he should have it." However, Ovington maintained that since "you [Spingarn] feel that you must make a fight at this particular moment for colored leadership," the Association perhaps could divide its central bureaucracy along regional lines, with a white Chairman in New York and a black Chairman in Washington. She frankly admitted that she would like to serve as the white Chairman, for she had formulated many plans for the Association and could make them operative only if she were Board Chairman. "I would like to have it [the Chairmanship] for a short time," [135] she confided.

But as was the case with the other potential front runners for the Chairmanship—most notably Villard and Du Bois—Ovington's succession undoubtedly would have split the Board. Joseph Prince Loud, the white President of the viable Boston NAACP branch, was adamantly opposed to her ascendancy and was doubly opposed to Du Bois or any black Chairman over whom he might wield influence. Villard was not a logical choice, for the organization's unity depended upon the Chairman's ability to work with Du Bois, and Villard already had tried and failed at this all-important task. On the other hand, whatever Spingarn's shortcomings, his prowess as an interpersonal leader had not gone unnoticed by either his white or his black colleagues. William A. Sinclair of Philadelphia, one of the most active black Board members, insisted that Spingarn possessed "the talent, tact, temperament, character, enthusiasm, earnestness and a happy combination of conservatism and radicalism . . . representing the qualities so necessary in a great leader in a great propaganda." Equally flattering pleas for Spingarn to reconsider his resignation were received from a number of other Directors and NAACP members, both black and white. Thus, when the Board convened in January 1916 for the election of officers, it re-elected Spingarn and Villard to their posts of Chairman and Treasurer, respectively.[136]

But the issue of according blacks a larger measure of participation in the Association's administration was not to be so easily dismissed. Joseph Prince Loud, upon learning that Spingarn planned to resign the Chairmanship, candidly informed him that in his opinion the NAACP should have a black Board Chairman. Similarly, May Childs Nerney, who resigned as Secretary in 1916, urged the Board to select a Negro as her successor. As a result of protracted field observation, she had become convinced that the Association was not attracting the support of the black masses, apparently attributing at least part of the difficulty to the preponderance of white executive leadership. She pointed out to Spingarn that the NAACP should pattern its administration after that of the Urban League, in which the bulk of the salaried officials were black (although the top-level leadership was white).[137]

Unwittingly perhaps, Nerney had provided a compromise solution for at least partially resolving the dilemma of balancing white and black administrative influence within the central bureaucracy. Obviously influenced by her suggestion, Spingarn seized the initiative in the fall of 1916 in urging that a Negro be selected to fill the newly created salaried post of Field Secretary and National Organizer. Although the responsibility for the nomination of individuals to fill the position was given to a three-member committee appointed by the Board, Spingarn proceeded unofficially to contact John Hope, the president of Morehouse College in Atlanta, and, upon Hope's refusal, James Weldon Johnson, former

United States consul at Puerto Cabello, Venezuela, and currently on the staff of the New York *Age*. Spingarn informed
Johnson that there was no guarantee that the nominating committee would approve him, but he expressed a willingness
to "urge them to select you." [138]

Johnson's selection marked the first time in the
NAACP's history that a Negro (other than Du Bois) was
accorded a full-time, salaried executive position of any conse-
quence within the national office. Whether by accident or
design, the practice of relinquishing the salaried line-of-
ficer positions to blacks, while retaining whites in the nonsalaried, top-level posts, was to persist until 1934 when,
after the Association's traditional leadership and program had
come under attack from dissident Directors and members,
Spingarn would resign the Board Chairmanship, to be succeeded by Louis T. Wright, the first black Chairman. [139]

Meanwhile, Spingarn and Du Bois moved toward a *modus
vivendi*, although each retained his respective stand. At the
January 1916 annual business meeting, Spingarn lauded the
Editor's contributions to Negro advancement and, in tones
reminiscent of Ovington's words, complimented Du Bois for
having made the *Crisis* a successful magazine. Reaffirming
his belief in Du Bois' right to editorial freedom of expression, Spingarn reminded the Board that the *Crisis* editorials
must necessarily reflect the personality which had formulated them; all the Board could expect was that the Editor
would interpret the NAACP's cause nobly and never sink to
the level of pettiness and ignominy. But Spingarn also reminded Du Bois and the Board that the *Crisis* and the Association were one. [140] Spingarn departed for active army duty in
1917, leaving Mary White Ovington, who succeeded him as
Chairman, to wrangle with Du Bois during the 1920's.

3

FIRST IN WAR: THE
STRUGGLE FOR THE
NEGRO OFFICERS'
TRAINING CAMP

As war engulfed Europe in 1914, Spingarn was among the first Americans to denounce Germany as the aggressor and to urge American preparedness as a first step toward what he believed would be his country's inevitable entry into the conflict. Fearing that blacks would be relegated to the lowest military ranks, yet unable to secure training for the Negro officers in white camps, Spingarn undertook virtually alone and amid widespread opposition within both the NAACP administrative hierarchy and the black community to secure a segregated facility for the training of black officers. At the same time, Spingarn was commissioned a major (later promoted to colonel) in the army, serving on active duty in France and emerging from the war with an impressive personal military record.

THE MEANING OF PATRIOTISM

Spingarn interpreted the causes of the conflict which engulfed Europe in 1914 partially within a racial context and partially within an economic context. The real roots of the conflict, he insisted, were the stronger powers' contempt for weaker peoples, which found expression in a desire to acquire and colonize their land. He drew a parallel between the American Negro's seeming unwillingness to demand his full rights and the plight of the weaker nations of Europe. The weak would always fall prey to their stronger neighbors.[1]

In reflecting upon the causes of the war many years after it had ended, Spingarn blamed the conflict on the theory of Nordic superiority. Tracing the spread of the theory of the superiority of the Germanic race from its first enunciation by the Frenchman Gobineau to its espousal by German and Teutonized writers from H. S. Chamberlain to Bernhardi, Spingarn observed that the theory had spread like "wildfire" throughout Germany by the eve of the war. He interpreted Germany's crushing defeat as just another manifestation of the doom which inevitably awaited those peoples who attempted to exert supremacy over others.[2]

Slight of build and possessing the sensitive temperament of the poet, Spingarn seemed at first glance the ideal candidate for the pacifist ranks. But it was this very sensitivity which complemented and fortified his determination to combat what he believed to be Germany's attempt to crush freedom. Militaristic and poetic sentiment were merged as one when, in 1917, Spingarn set forth in verse his feelings on the challenge presented by the war. He wrote:

I have loved freedom more than anything else,
And freedom fades . . . I see her everywhere dying;
Her troops are scattered and her army melts;
On every hilltop the enemy's flag is flying.
But still she does not die. Insoluble man,
Haunting her shrine, hungry and hollow-eyed,

Vainly without her seeks for vision or plan . . .
We must be dead to think that she has died.[3]

Convinced that nothing less than the cause of freedom itself
was at stake, Spingarn ignored the opposition of those of his
friends who were pacifists or opposed to preparedness. "I
know that you gave me up as hopeless many months ago," he
wrote to Mary White Ovington, "and I bore the doubts of
my friends with a light heart, because I was absolutely certain
that circumstances would bring them around to the position
which I myself adopted at the outset of the European war." [4]

Spingarn's faith in the justness of the cause at hand was
fortified by his staunch belief in the patriotic obligation of
each man to serve his country, especially after America's entry into the war. "He [Spingarn] was fired with patriotism,
feared Germany and believed in America," wrote Du Bois.
In replying to a young Negro who expressed doubt as to
whether he should enter the military, Spingarn insisted, "I
believe that there is only one duty imposed on all Americans
now, and that is the duty to *serve*." [5] In one of his best-
known essays, "Politics and the Poet" (1931), Spingarn set
forth his interpretation of the sense of patriotism that must
have guided his personal decision to participate in World
War I. Not to love one's country meant not to love everything else, "because profoundly a real and noble love of
country symbolizes all human activity. . . . For virtue is
never solitary: it takes part in the conflicts of the world."
Yet there could be no virtue unless a man played some part,
if only in his imagination, within a larger world. To lack
love of country was "to be without real moral enthusiasm
and therefore decadent." Spingarn hastened to add that his
brand of patriotism did not mean that narrow and empirical
concept of nationalism which culminated in separateness and
eventual hatred for every rival aspiration; rather, it meant a
sense of belonging to the whole and that relationship to the
civitas which formed the "warp and woof of politics." [6]

Bringing to bear that intensity of zeal which usually characterized his endeavors, Spingarn by March 1917 had com-

pleted training in three of the nation's first military training camps, including that at Plattsburgh, New York, where
he served as an instructor with the rank of second lieutenant. Indeed, as early as 1915 Spingarn had begun purchasing
and eagerly reading every book on military tactics which he
could locate. By mid-March he had assumed a leadership
role in the preparedness campaign of Dutchess County, New
York, having been appointed by Governor Charles Whitman as one of the seven original members of the so-called
Home Defense Committee. The group, which consisted of
men from Poughkeepsie and neighboring areas, undertook
to cooperate with and coordinate the preparedness plans of
counties in the vicinity. Also in March 1917 Spingarn induced
Franklin D. Roosevelt, Assistant Secretary of the Navy and
a neighbor by virtue of the proximity of the Hyde Park
and Troutbeck estates, and Theodore Roosevelt to write
letters of recommendation for Spingarn's entry into a fourth
reserve officers' training camp at Madison Barracks, New
York.[7] While word from Madison Barracks was pending,
Spingarn avidly studied military tactics and agonized over
whether his extremely poor eyesight would cause him to be
rejected by the military. But he devoted the bulk of his
thought and energies toward securing a training facility for
black officers.

AGAINST THE TIDE

While the Association directed its attention toward ensuring that blacks would be accorded admission into the army,
Spingarn moved far afield with his bold plan for the training
of black officers. He eagerly accepted the offer of General
Leonard P. Wood, commander of the eastern division of the
army, to open a separate camp for training black officers if
200 applicants could be secured immediately.[8] Ostensibly
Wood's offer provided a solution to a potentially difficult
problem; in reality it posed one of the major dilemmas of
Spingarn's long career in behalf of the advancement of American Negroes.

By 1917 the name of Spingarn had become synonymous in the minds of countless blacks with the uncompromising stand against inequality and segregation which had formed the key-stone of the fiery New Abolitionism of a day not long past. The New Abolition truly had been uncompromising on the issue of segregation, for there is no recorded instance in which Spingarn had hinted that the Negro should bow to expediency even when temporary segregation promised the only avenue to advancement of the race. On the contrary, he had admonished blacks to "die now rather than live 100 years in a ghetto"; he had mercilessly flayed Booker T. Washington's gradualism with little apparent regard for the hostile Southern social milieu in which Washington was obliged to function. Spingarn had experienced no small share of dis-illusionment and setbacks—in the government segregation skirmish, in the *Birth of a Nation* struggle, in the anti-lynching campaign—but none of these struggles had necessi-tated public admission of defeat. But the issue of training Ne-gro officers presented a unique dilemma. There could be no temporary retreat in preparation for a return bout, for a sec-ond chance was as remote as a second world war. More important, as if by some cruel stroke of fate, the subtle ac-ceptance of a segregated camp would not suffice; rather, the uncompromising champion of racial equality must undertake still another public campaign, but this time he must persuade his listeners of the merits of segregation.

Beginning in February 1917, Spingarn launched a public campaign on behalf of the segregated camp that rivaled the forceful anti-segregation argument of the New Abolition. In a public letter addressed to the "Educated Colored Men of the United States," he insisted that "I do not believe that colored men should be separated from other Americans in any field of life," but that the crisis was too near to debate principles and opinions. "It seems to me that there is only one thing for you to do at this juncture," he wrote, "and that is to get the training that will fit you to be officers, however and wherever and whenever this training may be obtained." [9] There was the strong prospect that universal military train-ing soon would be instituted, Spingarn warned, thereby presenting the black man with the choice of serving or rebelling. The latter alternative was unthinkable, for "the colored people of the United States are the pride of the American people, because in their ranks there has never been found a rebel, or a traitor." He reminded Negro Americans that all of the black military heroes of the past had been private soldiers or, as in the case of a few, noncommissioned officers. "Is it not time that we should have colored heroes who are lieutenants, captains, colonels, and generals?" [10] he asked.

The segregated camp, argued Spingarn, was but the first step toward a more open racial policy in the armed forces. Too often in the past the military authorities had excused the absence of Negro leadership by asserting that not enough qualified black men could be found to lead black troops, but "with two or three hundred properly trained officers" a fight could be made for "a wide-open army" and "against segregation itself . . ." [11] In a strategic move, Spingarn sought to shift from a defensive to an offensive stance on the segregated camp issue by insisting that "enemies" of the Negro—forces he usually did not name—would be delighted to see the race fail to take advantage of the opportunity for trained black officers. "Mark their words, consider their motives," he admonished, "and then from that angle look at the plan of the proposed training camp." Instead of apologizing, Spingarn boasted of his pride in having obtained an opportunity for the preparation of black officers "against the unanimous desire of the whole American Government." [12]

Similarly, Spingarn continuously (and perhaps unfairly) equated Negroes' willingness or unwillingness to accept the segregated camp with the measure of loyalty or disloyalty which the race offered the war effort. He argued that "enemies" of the race (again unnamed) had accused the American Negro of disloyalty, and that a favorable response to the camp was a means of dispelling such accusations. He urged one black Baltimore citizen who was interested in supporting the camp to do everything in his power to "show that the colored people of the country are loyal to the flag, and to disprove the damnable charges of disloyalty that are being made by the enemies of the race." [13]

The personal dilemma that the advocacy of a segregated facility wrought upon Spingarn was rivaled only by the potential embarrassment which the proposal harbored for the NAACP. With the Association's historic *raison d'être* resting firmly on an unequivocal demand for full citizenship rights for the Negro—including total and immediate integration into every facet of American life—any about-face shift to open advocacy of segregation, for whatever reason, was a potential strategic *faux pas*. There was always the possibility that those "enemies" of the race which Spingarn so thoroughly excoriated would rise at some future date to demand segregated facilities for blacks, citing as a precedent the espousal of a segregated officers' training camp by the nation's foremost Negro advancement association. Ironically, it was to be Du Bois who, in 1934, would cite the segregated camp in partial support of his bid for a program of black chauvinism.[14] Fortunately, Spingarn spared the Association the unenviable task of officially endorsing or rejecting the camp before the reaction of the black community could be ascertained. Throughout February, March, and early April (1917), he seized every opportunity to give both private and public assurances that the segregated camp was solely his idea and that the NAACP should share neither praise nor blame for the venture.[15] Indeed, one may perceive in the general tone of his statements some subtle desire to claim sole credit for launching the plan.

Nor would Spingarn concede that there was any incompatibility in his serving as Chairman of the NAACP Board of Directors while attempting to disassociate his actions from the organization he headed. "I could hardly afford to remain a member of the Association if I could carry on no private work without its approval," he insisted. When an apprehensive Archibald Grimké, president of the influential District of Columbia branch, reminded Spingarn that it would be difficult, if not impossible, to disassociate his actions from the NAACP, Spingarn retorted, "I do not intend to allow my official position to interfere with my outside activities," and added that if necessary he would relinquish the Board Chairmanship and support any successor.[16] It was not until May 1917, more than a month after the United States declared war on Germany, and only after Spingarn had virtually ensured the establishment of the camp, that the NAACP Board of Directors voted its official endorsement of a segregated facility.

The segregated camp proposal divided the black community as few issues had succeeded in doing. As if conjuring up some strange replay of the topsy-turvy world of Alice in Wonderland where left became right and up became down, many of Spingarn's staunchest friends during the New Abolition now labeled him a traitor, while others who had championed Booker T. Washington's accommodationism suddenly became arch foes of anything that remotely smacked of segregation. The Cleveland *Gazette*, a black weekly which had virtually thrived on every fiery word of the New Abolition, responded to Spingarn's proposal thus: "No, thank you Doctor! there is enough governmental segregation already." On March 24, in a front-page editorial, the *Gazette* insisted that "we fail to enthuse over his suggestion that we fight SEGREGATION with a segregated volunteer officer-school or 'military training camp,' at this time or any other."[17] As Spingarn stepped up his efforts for the camp throughout March and April, the *Gazette* grew even more caustic, culminating in what was probably the most forceful editorial emanating from the hostile wing of the Negro press. The editorial read in part as follows:

> . . . It certainly begins to look to us as if the National Association for the Advancement of Colored People was promoted and has been maintained by New York City white men of wealth and prominence for the express purpose of controlling in as large a measure as possible our people of this country. . . . Villard and Spingarn are two of the three most active white officers of the organization and the latter was decidedly the most popular up to the time of his "bad break," a few weeks ago. . . .

This wholesale asking of our people just at this time to continue making sacrifice of rights and privileges in the face of "old and new insults and wrongs," and by the white officers of an organization supposed to be for "the advancement of colored people," forces one to do a lot of thinking that is not at all favorable to the NAACP.[18]

Thus, as Grimké had predicted, the name of Spingarn had become too closely associated with the NAACP for the connection to be severed merely by words of disavowal.

The struggle against the camp that the Cleveland *Gazette* waged in the West was mirrored in the East by the Boston *Guardian*, the Baltimore *Afro-American*,[19] and, most of all, by the New York *Age*. The *Age*, which previously had been subsidized by Booker T. Washington and which had been the Tuskegeean's staunchest defender against the New Abolition attacks, charged that there was a basic incongruity in Spingarn's earlier opposition to segregation of federal civil service workers and his current advocacy of a segregated military facility. In a volley apparently in behalf of the deceased Washington, the *Age* insisted that if a prominent Negro had advocated a segregated camp, he would have been branded a traitor to his race, but that "a well meaning white friend can hold a meeting and advocate segregation without provoking adverse comment." The entire episode was proof that the Negro's psyche had not undergone much change in fifty years, maintained the *Age*, "when it comes to accepting as 'gospel' all that we are told by some who think they understand and know, but regarding with suspicion and misgivings what is told us by those in a position to know." [20] The Washington *Bee* initially adopted a neutral position on the segregated camp proposal, frankly admitting to its readers that "beyond the preliminary considerations the *Bee* is not now prepared to go." [21]

Aside from opposition to segregation as a matter of principle, the hostile wing of the black press advanced what it considered more practical reasons for disavowing the segregated camp. The *Age* insisted that there was no guarantee that Negro officers would not be trained in white camps, and that until the War Department definitely refused integrated training, Negroes should not voluntarily segregate themselves. Spingarn had stated that if universal military conscription were enacted, there would not be a sufficient number of trained leaders in the four existing black regiments to fill the demand for black officers. A good education, high moral character, and intellectual training were more vital attributes for a good officer than mere skill in the use of fire-arms, he insisted. The Cleveland *Gazette* was offended by this statement, accusing Spingarn of believing that black soldiers in existing military units "are deficient when it comes to doing what he terms the 'paper work' regular army officers are required to do." Similarly, the *Age* insisted that the sea-soned black military men who had distinguished themselves in the Spanish-American War and the regular army were more qualified to serve as officers than many graduates of West Point and the white officers' training camp at Platts-burgh.[22]

The segregated camp proposal also failed to win the ap-proval of many blacks of varying degrees of influence. Gil-christ Stewart, a New York attorney and Spingarn's former associate in the New York branch, warned his white friend that he, Spingarn, was being "widely misunderstood and criticized" in Kansas City, St. Louis, Chicago, Indianapolis, Pittsburgh, and other cities which Stewart had visited. Stewart intimated that Spingarn stood in danger of losing the "con-fidence and trust and friendship of the race at large."[23] J. Q. Adams, a local Negro leader in Minneapolis, urged Spingarn to cease his efforts for a segregated camp, insisting that "no right thinking, far seeing colored man would ask for it."[24] George W. Crawford, Howard University administrator, ex-pressed "considerable doubts about the wisdom of the scheme." It was sometimes better to endure disadvantages than to yield to a principle that might lead to even greater dis-advantages,[25] Crawford cautioned.

The widespread criticism which the camp proposal en-gendered did not deter Spingarn for one instant. He admitted having been "hurt" by "the recent suspicion of some of my friends," but adamantly insisted that "if one is certain of his ground, and sure as to his aims he can afford to lose friends." He professed to be proud of the vigorous opposition of some of the black newspapers to his plan: "I should like to think that the National Association . . . and the *Crisis* had something to do with the bold and manly way in which colored opinion is now beginning to express itself." But he insisted that "in the end" they would realize that he was right. "In any event," concluded Spingarn, "they may be sure that I shall never desert their cause until I am dead." [26]

Despite the criticism of opponents, the segregated camp proposal received enthusiastic backing from many quarters of the black community. In a letter to the editor of the Cleveland *Gazette*, Lieutenant Colonel Charles Young, the highest ranking Negro army officer, supported Spingarn's contention that there would not be enough qualified men in the existing four black regiments to serve as leaders if universal military conscription were enacted. Young endorsed the segregated camp as a "constructive plan," contending that "when the storm is past we can take up the idealism of the cause." [27] Major Charles R. Douglass, son of the black Abolitionist Frederick Douglass, endorsed the camp in a letter to the editor of the Washington *Bee*, maintaining that "it is the advantage to be gained that we are after." [28] Even before the United States' declaration of war against Germany on April 6, 1917, Spingarn had been deluged with applications from Negroes as far removed as the Carolinas who desired to join and help recruit men for the camp. [29]

Meanwhile, throughout March, Spingarn had been initiating concrete steps for actually launching the camp. Because he was especially anxious to secure "educated" participants, his personal recruitment efforts were centered upon attracting black college students. The response from Howard University in the District of Columbia was immediate and overwhelming. Spingarn's circular letter addressed to the educated colored men of the United States had been printed in the Howard University *Journal* and had attracted the attention of George E. Brice, the university's student-body president. Brice enthusiastically endorsed the camp proposal, assuring Spingarn that his personal appearance before the student body was all that was needed for the plan to materialize on Howard's campus. Indeed, Spingarn needed no introduction at Howard, for he had launched the first NAACP college chapter on Howard's campus in 1913 and had addressed the student body at least once during the New Abolition tours. George William Cook, the university's secretary, reinforcing Brice's invitation, assured Spingarn that his forthcoming appearance had elicited the hearty cooperation of the president, deans, and finance committee. As a direct result of Spingarn's speech, which was delivered on March 20, the university authorities pledged to give consideration to the question of Negro officers' training.[30]

From Howard's students Spingarn learned of some of the practical problems involved in recruiting college students. Brice explained that recruitment might proceed slowly because many students were obliged to work during the summer months. This problem persisted despite Spingarn's offer to pay for 100 uniforms (costing approximately $10 each) from his personal funds. Brice and R. McCants Andrews, former president of the Howard University chapter of the NAACP, suggested that the problem would be solved if the military authorities and university officials authorized a student ROTC unit on the campus, as was currently the case at Harvard University and other white schools. But Spingarn held this suggestion in abeyance on the grounds that the first and most important step was to secure the minimum number of qualified applicants required by General Wood.[31]

Spingarn's fear of insufficient enrollments of college students proved unwarranted. Seventy-three Howard students had applied for admission to the camp before the end of March. H. B. Frissell, the principal of Hampton Institute in Virginia, informed Spingarn that forty-six Hampton students had volunteered after hearing the circular letter to educated colored men read in chapel, and that others were "greatly interested" but could not relinquish summer earnings. The response of Howard and Hampton, coupled with that of volunteers from other parts of the country, enabled Spingarn to boast that a "great deal beyond" the requisite number of applicants had been secured by March 31.[32]

The United States' declaration of war against Germany on April 6, less than a week after Spingarn had secured the camp quota, placed a different light on the entire situation. General Wood's jurisdiction over officers' training was shifted to Major Johnston of the Adjutant General's office, thereby creating uncertainty regarding the new official's attitude toward Negro officers' training. On April 11 Spingarn reported that all plans for military training camps were vague, even in the mind of the Secretary of War, but that he, Spingarn, was "very sanguine about having a colored camp established." He urged George William Cook to have the Howard volunteers visit the Secretary of War in a body and "plead" for the chance to train as officers. In the meantime, Spingarn induced several sympathetic congressmen, including Senator Edmund Platt of New York, to exert whatever influence they could.[33] By April 20 a "representative" whom Spingarn had sent to Washington reported that Major Johnston had given assurances that the only question still pending was whether blacks would be trained in white camps or given a separate facility. Seizing what appeared to be an opportunity for integrated training, Spingarn headed a large, biracial delegation of prominent citizens to the War Department, but secured from Secretary of War Newton D. Baker only the vague promise that "as soon as it was decided that colored troops were to be called out an opportunity should and would be given colored men to train as officers." [34]

Meanwhile, the United States' entry into the war, with its inherent implication of universal conscription, had marked the turning point in garnering the black community's overwhelming support of Negro officers' training, even if it should entail a segregated facility. Howard University again assumed the forefront among black educational institutions. George William Cook assured Spingarn that a diploma probably would be granted to any senior who interrupted his studies to attend the camp. An "executive committee" of thirty-two Howard students (later renamed the Central Committee of Negro College Men) set up 24-hour-a-day headquarters in the basement rooms of the university's chapel to dispense information regarding the camp and to deal with emergencies and other aspects of the work. The committee drafted an eight-point brief stating that since the War Department refused to train black officers in white camps, the Negro race desired a reserve officers' camp for blacks.[35] Kelly Miller, dean of arts and sciences, optimistically promised a list of 500 volunteers "by the first of the week," and ultimately 1,000. "We owe the idea, our own interest—in fact *everything* to you [Spingarn]," Miller wrote, "we are merely attempting to carry out your ideas and suggestions—to fulfill your wishes." [36]

Other institutions quickly joined what was now approaching the proportions of a small crusade. Frissell of Hampton Institute wrote ex-President Taft and other friends of Hampton, urging them to support training for black officers. John Hope, the president of Morehouse College and a friend of Spingarn's since the latter's visit to Atlanta in 1912, expressed the wish that "hundreds of our young men would enter [the camp]." Fisk University, Nashville, not only endorsed the camp but considered wholesale volunteering of all its students and faculty.[37] The only discordant note emanated from Tuskegee Institute, which had been headed by Robert Russa Moton since Booker T. Washington's death in 1915. Moton refused to distribute the camp application blanks which Spingarn sent, insisting that one of the school's trustees had applied to the War Department for permission to recruit a black cavalry regiment to be comprised and officered by Tuskegee men. Moton conceded that the men probably would receive better training in Spingarn's camp but added, "the whole matter hinges very largely on the reply from the War Department and the wish of this Trustee." Spingarn replied that Tuskegee and the trustee could do more for the country by furnishing leaders for all black troops rather than a single cavalry regiment.[38]

By May 2 four hundred and seventy had applied for admission to the camp, and additional applications were being received at the rate of fifteen or twenty per day. Although college students formed the bulk of the volunteers, older men were well represented. The applicants included approximately twenty physicians, ten lawyers, three editors, five dentists, two college presidents, ten ministers, about twenty-three college teachers, and twenty government clerks and officials. Spingarn boasted that two-thirds were college students or college graduates and that virtually all of the remainder possessed at least a high school education. He had always insisted that the men must possess maturity and high moral character, undoubtedly in keeping with his belief that an excellent showing by black officers would provide a future avenue for advancement of the race.[39] The Abolitionist could not then foresee that many of the victims of lynch mobs during the "Red Summer" of 1919 would be black soldiers in uniform.

By mid-April the outlook for the success of the camp was so promising that Spingarn diverted some of his attention to the private black soldier, whom he had almost totally neglected previously. While he had been working for the officers' training camp independently of the NAACP, the Association had been directing its attention toward securing equitable admission of blacks into the armed forces. Its most notable struggle in this connection was an extensive and sustained campaign of publicity and political lobbying against attempts by Southern states to eliminate blacks from the draft. This effort culminated in the passage of an amendment to the Selective Service Bill that instituted the quota system, thereby making any Southern state which rejected black draftees liable for inducting a full quota of whites. Once having ensured that Negroes would be included in the draft, the NAACP worked toward instituting black regiments in branches of the service other than the cavalry and infantry.[40] Spingarn expressed the hope that black units would be included in the medical corps, coast artillery, field artillery, and quartermaster corps, although he admitted that that might "be perhaps too much to hope for immediately." He urged Roy Nash, the NAACP Secretary, to press the government to make 5 percent of the total United Stages regiments black, since Negroes constituted about 10 percent of the population.[41]

But the exuberance of victory again paled into despair when, on May 2, 1917, Spingarn departed for the officers' training camp at Madison Barracks, New York, without any definite commitment from the War Department regarding a training facility for black officers. "I go with a heavy heart," he wrote, "because I cannot share the opportunity with the hundreds of colored men who are more competent than I to take advantage of it." For the first time, Spingarn suggested that the NAACP officially endorse the camp and take up the struggle in his absence. He urged the Association to commit itself to securing training for black officers, preferably in an integrated camp, "but with its eye on results other than anything else." At the same time, Spingarn gave the Board of Directors the option of selecting another Board Chairman or appointing a Vice-Chairman to serve during his absence. He assured the Board that nothing could alienate him from the cause for which the Association stood and that whatever its decision regarding the Chairmanship, he would like to remain a member of the Board. On May 14 the Board officially endorsed a separate officers' training camp for blacks if white camps were not made available. Two Board members, Joseph Prince Loud, the white President of the NAACP's Boston branch, and Dr. Owen M. Waller, a Negro, requested that the Board minutes record their negative votes. The Board also voted to retain Spingarn as Chairman during his absence on military duty, and appointed Mary White Ovington to serve as Vice-Chairman.[42]

Even as the Board was endorsing the camp, Howard University's administration was intensifying its efforts for black officers' training. George William Cook had secured the consent of the university's president and trustees to open Howard's facilities for the training of 1,000 Negro officers in the event that the War Department should contend that there was no available site for a Negro facility. "Before this matter should fail," Cook wrote to Spingarn, "I would turn even my private house into part of a camp."[43] After the NAACP Board of Directors endorsed the camp, James Weldon Johnson, Acting Secretary of the NAACP, and President Stephen M. Newman of Howard relentlessly pressured the federal authorities for a definite commitment regarding the camp. Finally, on May 25, Adjutant General Grenville Clarke informed Johnson that a camp for training black officers (a segregated facility) had been established at Fort Des Moines, Iowa, and was to receive the first enrollees on June 18, 1917.[44]

A HERO WITHOUT HONOR

Spingarn's personal army career was characterized by both triumph and tragedy. He was one of three men out of a total of 2,500 to graduate from his officers' training camp with the rank of major. He was then assigned the command of the 311th Infantry battalion, consisting of twenty-six officers and 1,000 men. Mrs. Spingarn recalled that her husband enthusiastically urged his men to sing while marching and meticulously looked after their welfare, even going so far as to poke his head inside the mess hall ovens during inspection tours in order to be certain of their spotlessness.[45]

But in the autumn of 1917 Spingarn's once promising army career was marred by tragedy. His battalion, upon completion of basic training, was scheduled to sail for France, a venture Spingarn greatly anticipated. However, after having intensively trained with his men for weeks, Spingarn became gravely ill with a severe case of ulcers while en route to Hoboken, New Jersey, the port of embarkation. His battalion sailed for France while he remained behind to undergo surgery and subsequent treatment, which confined him to a hospital for nearly two months. Shortly afterward, in December 1917, Troutbeck, his beautiful country estate, was almost totally destroyed by fire, with damage estimated at $150,000, including the loss of many priceless artifacts and documents.[46]

Despite Spingarn's pleas that he be permitted to join his battalion in France upon his release from the hospital, he was assigned a desk job in the intelligence division of the army's general staff in Washington, D.C., where he remained for two months and eight days. One can only imagine the anxiety and disappointment which a man possessing his bent for rugged physical activity must have experienced. But rather than merely marking time, Spingarn was determined to use his position in the Intelligence Bureau to advance the cause of the Negro. Although he never clarified the specifics of his plan,[47] he intended to have the Bureau adopt what he termed "constructive measures" in dealing with blacks, apparently meaning that the agency would concentrate on redressing the grievances which beset Negroes during the war and encouraging Negroes' loyalty and patriotism rather than merely attempting to censure and uncover disloyalty.[48] This "constructive programme," as Spingarn liked to call the venture, now became a burning passion and his most recent *cause célèbre*.

Old antagonisms between Spingarn and Du Bois over the relationship of the *Crisis* to the Association were forgotten as Spingarn turned to the Editor for aid in perfecting the Intelligence Bureau program. He was convinced that the plan would be assured of success if Du Bois would accept an official position in the Bureau, presumably in the expectation that the Editor's fiery pen would stir the black community's loyalty and cooperation during wartime just as the *Crisis* had wielded strong influence among blacks virtually since its inception. Through the cooperation of his superior, Colonel Churchill, Spingarn secured a tentative promise for a captaincy for Du Bois, with the understanding that the Editor was to serve as Spingarn's assistant in the Intelligence Bureau.[49]

No one foresaw the furor the Du Bois commission was destined to raise. Like Spingarn, the Editor believed that accepting the captaincy would afford an opportunity to enhance the welfare of the entire race, but he was unwilling to relinquish control of the *Crisis* during his tenure of military duty. Initially, Du Bois claimed that he did not wish to permit the magazine to be edited by James Weldon Johnson,[50] the Acting Secretary, but later he offered additional reasons. In 1918 Du Bois was fifty years old, and he was concerned lest a man of his age should be unable to find suitable employment after his army duty had been completed. Similarly, he was concerned as to whether a captain's salary could support his family, which included young children. He concluded that the ideal solution would be to retain the editorship of the *Crisis* while serving in the army and to supplement his military salary with the money the Association would continue to pay for his editorial services. Thus, Du Bois informed the NAACP Board of Directors that he would be willing to accept the commission only under three conditions: (1) that the NAACP view his work with the Intelligence Bureau as part of the cause for which the organization stood and in which it was engaged; (2) that he retain the directorship of the Department of Publications and Research, and editorship of the *Crisis;* (3) that his military earnings be supplemented by the Association in the amount of whatever part of his current salary would not be needed for editorial assistance during his absence.[51]

However, the Board voted against Du Bois' accepting the captaincy, ostensibly on the grounds that it would not be wise to deprive *Crisis* readers of a full-time Editor.[52] Du Bois informed Spingarn that the adverse vote was the result of small attendance at the Board meeting and the strong pacifist sentiment of some of those present, citing Villard, Archibald Grimké, Florence Kelley, and Joseph Prince Loud as the chief opponents. The major factor leading to the Board's decision, Du Bois insisted, was Grimké's belief that accepting the captaincy would disrupt the work of the Washington branch and spread suspicion and discouragement.[53] Those Board members favoring acceptance of the commission included Mary White Ovington, George William Cook, Col. Charles Young, Dr. Owen Waller, and Charles Nagel. Du Bois estimated that, with his own vote included, those in favor of his accepting the commission might have prevailed, but that the Board would have been sharply split as a result.[54]

The Board's adverse decision caused Du Bois to fluctuate between defiance and submission. He informed Spingarn that he would not hesitate to resign from the NAACP if he were younger, did not have a family to support, and could be assured of a job after the war ended. On the other hand, he speculated that if he and Spingarn were to resign from the Association, the NAACP's work would be seriously crippled. Then, too, he reminded Spingarn that there was widespread opposition within the black community[55] to his accepting the commission and that he, Du Bois, wondered to what degree it was his duty to flaunt the opposition. In the meantime, Du Bois had written John Hope explaining his desire to accept the commission as opposed to the widespread opposition among Negroes, and asking Hope's advice.[56] Probably this was Du Bois' subtle way of seeking to ascertain whether a job might be waiting for him in Atlanta after the war ended.

While Du Bois was engulfed in indecision, a letter arrived from Spingarn urging that the Editor not give up hopes of accepting the commission. He blamed the entire controversy on a "few bitter men," predicted that the furor would soon subside, and warned Du Bois that it would be "madness" not to seize the opportunity to accept the commission. The Association must grant Du Bois a leave of absence, Spingarn insisted, and pledge that he would be restored to his position when the war ended. But Du Bois' friend assured him that money with which to supplement his salary was not a major obstacle, "for that can be taken care of in other ways if need be." At the same time, Spingarn urged Du Bois to make the sacrifice of temporarily relinquishing control of the *Crisis*, for there would be others on guard to see that all went well. Spingarn reminded Du Bois that his whole "constructive programme" was on trial and was in danger of toppling if the Editor did not join forces with him.[57]

When the Board of Directors displayed no inclination to

alter its opposition to Du Bois' acceptance of the captaincy, and an impasse obviously had been reached, Spingarn submitted his resignation from the Board Chairmanship in late July 1918. He interpreted the Board's refusal to permit Du Bois to participate in his "constructive programme" as a manifestation of the Board's general lack of appreciation for military men. Despite the vehement denial of this assertion by John Shillady, the NAACP Secretary, Spingarn insisted upon being released from his duties as Chairman.[58] Thus, Spingarn had again fallen victim to one of his greatest administrative weaknesses: his inability to abide by a majority decision of the Board when it conflicted with a proposal he favored strongly.

In late summer of 1918, plans for Du Bois' captaincy and Spingarn's "constructive programme" were dealt a mortal blow from an unexpected sector. The Intelligence Bureau suddenly abandoned the project on the grounds that the contemplated work would exceed the jurisdiction of the military authorities. Du Bois, however, was convinced that the reversal of policy was due to the opposition of Southern whites, the criticism emanating from the black community, and, perhaps, adverse reaction to Spingarn's plan within the Intelligence Bureau. Additional suspicion of the Bureau's motives was aroused when Spingarn's long-awaited assignment to active overseas duty was announced shortly after the Bureau abandoned his program.[59]

Spingarn emerged from active duty in Europe with an impressive record. Initially, he was assigned to the Sixth Army Corps as commander of the corps troops. Shortly before the Allies' advance on the Toul sector, he was reassigned to the Sixth Corps headquarters to reconnoiter the front lines for the headquarters' staff. Later, during the Allies' advance on Metz, he served as liaison officer. Spingarn was the first American officer to enter Metz, Saarbrücken, and Zabern. In recognition of his services, he was offered the position of occupational commander in Coblenz, but refused in favor of accepting membership on a military commission headed by General Westervelt. Service on the commission brought him into personal contact with Gen. John J. Pershing, for whom he secured special intelligence information in several occupied areas in France and on the Italian front. These reports for General Pershing were completed before the opening of the peace conference, and Spingarn sailed for America in March 1919.[60]

Although hailed as a local hero upon his return to Dutchess County, Spingarn disclaimed any heroic qualities, but emphasized his pride in having been one of America's first preparedness advocates. He insisted that he would not have exchanged his wartime experiences for all the money of the Belmonts and Morgans.[61]

As a sidelight to his military activities in France, Spingarn had supported Du Bois' efforts to convene a Pan African Congress in 1919. The Congress, which met in Paris, hoped to persuade the members of the peace conference to internationalize Africa and to afford the darker races in Germany's colonies a measure of self-determination. While in Paris in February 1919, Spingarn talked with the historian George Louis Beer, who was serving as the peace commission's official adviser on Africa. He informed Du Bois of Beer's interest in the Pan African Congress and suggested that Du Bois send Beer a full report of the Congress' proceedings and perhaps arrange a conference with the historian. At Beer's suggestion Spingarn also urged Du Bois to write Colonel Edward M. House, President Wilson's confidant and a member of the commission. Later, Spingarn was among those who addressed the Pan African Congress, together with two other NAACP Board members, Charles Edward Russell and William English Walling.[62]

4

LAST IN PEACE: ECLIPSE

THE SPINGARN who returned from active army duty in 1919 was perceptibly different from the enthusiastic and energetic New Abolitionist of prewar days. Broken in health and disillusioned by the fruits of the "war for democracy," it was natural that his participation in the Association should be curtailed.

More significantly, during the 1920's the NAACP passed from organizational to institutional status, and its increasing maturity and growth wrought administrative changes that rendered obsolete Spingarn's brand of personal activism. For the first time since the organization's incorporation, the Abolitionist looked longingly toward a return to his former academic career, while, at the same time, seeking to assure his continuing stake in the NAACP through increased financial donations.

TRIUMPH OF THE NEW ABOLITION

Perhaps the most notable achievement of the NAACP during the decade of the 1920's was its evolution from organizational to institutional status. An organization is a technical instrument for marshaling human energies and directing them toward a given goal. It is rationally structured to do a given job. More important, it is an expendable instrument. But to institutionalize is to infuse with value beyond the task at hand. An organization is transformed into an institution when it becomes a product of social needs and pressures. The goals it seeks to fulfill and the functions it serves come to be viewed by the larger community as almost indispensable, even vital. The unique historic experiences of the institution —its responses and adaptation to earlier internal and external pressures—has afforded it a distinct "character," a self. At the same time, the acquisition of character entails taking on basic values—modes of behaving which are deemed right and proper for their own sake. When external and internal pressures arise, the major concern of the personnel is not mere survival but the maintenance of the uniqueness of the group, the preservation of the institution's values. In this sense, institutionalization can entail a hardening process in which change is resisted.[1]

Several underlying factors paved the way for the NAACP's institutionalization during the 1920's. Booker T. Washington's demise and the truce which had derived from the first Amenia Conference transformed Spingarn's dream of the NAACP's triumph over gradualism into reality. Undoubtedly, many could not believe what they read when in 1919 the once hostile New York *Age* praised the work of the Association and called for unity under its banner. Any lingering doubts regarding the triumph over gradualism were dissipated in 1929 when Robert Russa Moton, Washington's successor as principal of Tuskegee Institute, was awarded the Spingarn Medal for the militant stance on the Negro rights question which he had displayed in a recent book. By 1929 a group of Tuskegee matrons, headed by Moton's wife, were among the most regular financial supporters of the Association.[2]

Still another factor that promoted institutionalization was increasing militancy in the black community after 1920, a phenomenon for which the Association's earlier efforts were partially responsible. At the beginning of the decade, a group of black intellectuals centered in Harlem precipitated the "Harlem Renaissance" from which emanated a bevy of books, novels, and poetry glorifying blackness and the need for racial identity. The cult of blackness reached an apogee with the emergence of Marcus Garvey, a coal-black Jamaican whose preachments exalted all that was black and called upon American blacks to return to the African homeland. At the peak of his movement, Garvey probably gathered upward of two million followers. An equally militant tone was struck by Asa Philip Randolph and Chandler Owen, two black Socialists whose *Messenger* magazine denounced the NAACP's failure to place greater emphasis on the economic uplift of the black masses. Even the fiery Du Bois was attacked as a conservative Negro who was entirely too fond of whites.[3]

By 1921 Spingarn had perceived the changed outlook which permeated much of the black community. "But more wonderful still," he wrote, "a great change has come over the men and women of Negro descent throughout the country." After recalling his attempts to arouse blacks during the earlier New Abolition tours, he rejoiced that "now the danger is past; a new sense of their power and destiny is in the very soul of black men and women; . . . our country is at least safe from the danger of . . . having a large minority who are willing to admit their eternal inferiority and serfdom." The new militancy would not decrease race prejudice, Spingarn predicted; rather, it might temporarily increase friction between whites and blacks. But even the resulting friction would serve a useful purpose, he prophesied, for "in the end it will force both races to seek and find some form of compromise or adjustment by which they can leave [live] peacefully and with self-respect together."[4]

The signs of the Association's institutionalization often were subtle but unmistakable. By 1920, largely due to the effort and skill of James Weldon Johnson, the NAACP boasted more than 300 branches scattered from coast to coast and in several foreign countries. An examination of the list of financial contributors reveals that the Association had begun to attract $1 to $10 donations from groups of blacks ranging from the Mothers' Charity Club of Butte, Montana, to obscure branches of the YWCA.[5] The community had begun the vital process of infusing the organization with value.

The emergence of new sources of income was another manifestation of the Association's increasing respectability and power, even within the white world. During the formative years much time and care had been expended in wooing a handful of white philanthropists like Julius Rosenwald and Philip G. Peabody. By 1929, however, the Association's soliciting and publicity skills had become so sophisticated and its status sufficiently commanding that more than $20,000 in legacies and bequests established by wealthy whites during the 1920's accrued to the Association in a single year, 1932. Similarly, the handful of early large donors were joined during the 1920's by over a half-dozen others, including John D. Rockefeller, Jr., the future Governor Herbert Lehman of New York, and automobile manufacturer Edsel Ford. Still another manifestation of the NAACP's growing stature within the larger community was its ability to compete successfully with other organizations for sizable grants from philanthropic foundations like the American Fund for Public Service (Garland Fund). By 1928, on the eve of the Depression, the NAACP had amassed a sufficient surplus of funds to invest part of its income in an impressive array of stocks and bonds—a situation which contrasted sharply with the lean years prior to World War I.[6]

A new look and a newfound strength also permeated the Association's postwar program. Discriminatory employment practices, the exclusion of black workers from white unions, and other economic hardships confronting the masses of blacks who had migrated to Northern cities during the war, led the organization to devote more attention to the economic condition of blacks than ever before in its history, although tactically it continued to eschew job placement of individual blacks and the use of direct-action techniques like the strike and the boycott. Rather, the success of the new economic orientation was sought through the conventional methods of agitation and protest in the form of the written and spoken word, with emphasis on legal and political victories in the economic sphere that would benefit all black workers. Beginning during the war and continuing throughout the 1920's, the NAACP waged an unsuccessful struggle to have the American Federation of Labor, the Brotherhood of Locomotive Firemen and Enginemen, and other unions open their ranks to black workmen. It readily placed its propaganda and legal machinery behind efforts to prevent wage and hours discrimination, discriminatory hiring practices, and the passage of congressional legislation deemed inimical to the interests of black workers. By 1930 the organization could boast of having helped obtain a salary increase for black trainmen, of having furthered the organization of black steel workers in Pueblo, Colorado, and of having aided A. Philip Randolph's Brotherhood of Sleeping Car Porters in organizing Negro maids employed by the railroads.[7] On the other hand, despite sustained efforts, the Association failed to eradicate the exclusionist policy of the American Federation of Labor, and, therefore, the major goal of its postwar economic program—the opening of the major craft unions to black workers—was not realized.

Yet these forays into the economic sphere did not mean that the quest for full civil and political rights for blacks had ceased to be the NAACP's primary goal or that the organization had moved beyond the orientation in noneconomic liberalism which its founders had projected. Resolutions drafted by Du Bois for the Annual Conferences of the 1920's rarely failed to call upon the Association to delve more extensively and forcefully into the economic sphere; these resolutions were enthusiastically accepted, then filed and forgotten. As late as 1927 James Weldon Johnson explained to Moorfield Storey that it was out of the question for the NAACP to become too extensively involved in economic matters for fear of encroaching upon the activities of the National Urban League. The NAACP Annual Report of 1919 reaffirmed both the primacy of the organization's civil liberties program and the principle that "public opinion is the main force upon which the Association relies for a *victory of justice.*" [8]

In short, the NAACP was reaping the fruits of institutionalization—stability, prosperity, acceptance—but it was also falling victim to the hardening process which so often attends institutionalization. Its distinctive character, its goals, its response patterns to external stimuli were becoming set.

Meanwhile, the Association's civil liberties program advanced apace during the 1920's with the Legal Department's victories continuing to dwarf all other efforts. The rulings which the Legal Department had secured from the United States Supreme Court against "grandfather clauses" in state constitutions (1915) and residential segregation ordinances (1917) were followed by two equally momentous decisions during the 1920's: a 1923 ruling (*Moore* v. *Dempsey*) against mob dominance in the courtroom and, conversely, defendants' right to a fair trial; and a 1927 ruling (*Nixon* v. *Herndon*) against the exclusion of blacks from participation in the Democratic primaries.[9] Less spectacular but no less meaningful victories often were won by the Association and its branches in lower courts.[10] On the other hand, the Southern filibuster in Congress, coupled with the general apathy of the Republican administrations of the 1920's, doomed the struggle for federal anti-lynching legislation to failure. Upon the suggestion of Mary White Ovington, the Board of Directors voted in 1923 to divert the time and resources devoted to the quest for a federal anti-lynching statute to the campaign to eradicate inequities in education. With Florence Kelley as the guiding light, the Association centered its strategy during the 1920's in attempts to secure equal apportionment of federal funds for education wherever law or custom dictated separate facilities, and especially in the South. This tactical approach would be continued during the 1930's and expanded to encompass demands that the states provide equal educational facilities and teachers' salaries for both races in the hope that the states would find separate facilities too expensive to maintain. Nevertheless, it was not until the 1950's that the NAACP scored its greatest triumph against educational inequities in the celebrated *Brown* v. *Board of Educa-*

tion of Topeka decision, which outlawed public school segregation on the grounds of the inherent inequality of so-called
separate but equal facilities.[11]

The administration of the NAACP also underwent changes
of major significance during the 1920's, the most important of
which was the diffusion of power and responsibility within
the administrative hierarchy. The organization and supervision of branches—functions that had partially necessitated
Spingarn's earlier New Abolition tours—had been given over
to a full-time salaried Field Secretary, James Weldon Johnson,
in 1916. In 1918 the Association found what may be termed
its first professional Secretary in John R. Shillady, a young
white social worker. To a greater degree than any of his
predecessors Shillady undertook the responsibility for raising
funds, coordinating the work of the branches, and mapping
out future plans for the execution of the Association's program. James Weldon Johnson, who succeeded Shillady as
Secretary in 1921, was even more industrious than his prede-
cessor (according to Mary White Ovington). A further division of labor was effected in 1919 when Herbert J. Seligmann
was appointed the first full-time Director of Publicity.[12] In
short, by 1920 there was no longer a pressing need for the
intensive personal activism which a handful of upper-echelon
officials like Spingarn had displayed during the organization's
formative period.

Concomitant with the tendency toward the diffusion of
power and responsibility was the disintegration of the once-
viable grouping of white liberals that had been so prominent
in the NAACP's administration during the formative years.
John E. Milholland, a wealthy manufacturer who had served
as the organization's first Treasurer, was not re-elected to the
post of Vice-President in 1919 because his service and attendance records had become so poor. After having wrangled
with Du Bois for eight years, Villard resigned his position as
Treasurer and dropped out of active participation in the
NAACP in 1919. By 1924 Mary White Ovington was complaining that William English Walling, the man who, more
than anyone else, had been responsible for launching the

Association, was so sporadic in terms of participation that his services amounted to no more than "a flash in the pan." Moorfield Storey, the aging President, continued to reside in Boston, where he conducted a full-time law practice. Although Storey's legal services to the NAACP were invaluable, he had never been closely associated with the organization's routine policy-making process. Spingarn, sick and war-weary, was also destined to undergo an administrative semi-eclipse during the 1920's. In sum: by the mid-1920's the coalition of white liberal leadership had been narrowed to Mary White Ovington and Arthur Spingarn, who held the posts of Board Chairman and Chairman of the Legal Committee, respectively.[13]

It is at this point that the internal workings of the NAACP's administration become extremely difficult to perceive with clarity. Despite the diffusion of power and responsibility, constitutionally the organization's basic administrative structure was unaltered. Technically the Board of Directors continued as the policy-making body, exercising full authority over the salaried executives. The Directors continued to hold their monthly meetings, although by the mid-1920's Board attendance had narrowed to approximately eight regular members, including Ovington, Arthur Spingarn, Du Bois, Florence Kelley, Paul Kennaday, and Isadore Martin.[14]

On the other hand, in 1923 the Board established a Conference of Executives, consisting of all of the major salaried national officials—Secretary, Director of Branches, Director of Publicity, and the like, many of them black—plus the Chairman of the Board (Ovington), the Chairman of the Legal Committee (Arthur Spingarn), and the Treasurer (J. E. Spingarn, who had succeeded Villard to the post in 1919). The Conference of Executives, which met bimonthly between Board sessions, often was given full power to act on matters which arose between Board meetings.[15]

At the same time, it is clear that the trend, begun by Shillady, of the Secretary assuming the responsibility for administering day-to-day operations of the organization was continued and intensified by James Weldon Johnson after his succession to the secretaryship. Indeed, Mary White Ovington later recalled that Johnson had taken charge of office affairs.[16] Thus, at least one author has suggested that the 1920's marked the changeover of control of the NAACP to blacks, citing as an indication the heavy representation of blacks on the Conference of Executives.[17] Johnson's strong showing also could be used to support this contention.

Although a definitive pronouncement on this question must await a far more intensive examination of the organization's structure during the 1920's than this study has warranted, it is clear that control of the NAACP by Johnson and the black salaried executives was far from total. For example, the ultimate control of the organization's finances rested firmly in the hands of the Board of Directors, with only the Treasurer and those Board members specifically authorized by the Board being permitted to sign checks or otherwise disburse monies. More important, the Association had had only white treasurers since its inception, and although the Board had always been biracial, a study of the Board members empowered to sign checks and disburse monies reveals that in the majority of instances they too were white.[18] Probably one of the main reasons for this phenomenon was the belief that the control of the organization's monies by wealthy whites would minimize the possibility of charges of mismanagement of funds.

In 1926 the Pittsburgh *Courier*, one of the nation's most influential black papers, accused the NAACP of mishandling its funds and charged Johnson with being "boss" of the organization. Upon Johnson's request, Spingarn, who was then Treasurer, issued a press release in which he assured the public that neither Johnson nor any other salaried executive had ever signed a single check. Spingarn pointed out that he personally had selected the current auditors of the NAACP's books and that the salaried executives had served well "under the supervision of a distinguished Board of Directors."[19] In 1925 Johnson complained to the Board of Directors about the inconvenience entailed in having to secure the permission of one of the persons empowered to sign checks, even for petty cash. Upon the motion of Arthur Spingarn, the Board voted to place a $250 petty cash fund at the Secretary's disposal.[20]

There are other surface indications that the Board of Directors (through which the white liberal leadership manifested itself) retained much of the critical decision-making power. Critical decisions are those which bear upon the long-range goals and values of the organization. They are the special concern of the true leadership of any group. Critical decision-making is to be distinguished from routine decision-making: the latter is concerned with the question of how available resources can be utilized to implement the critical decisions which already have been made.[21] For example, the decision (suggested by Ovington and voted by the Board) to shift the thrust of the organization's program from the quest for federal anti-lynching legislation to the eradication of educational inequities represented a critical decision, for it had long-range effects upon the Association's future program. That the Secretary may then have found ten different ways to implement the new education program marked him as an excellent manager, but not necessarily as a formulator of critical policy.

There are sufficient grounds to speculate that administratively the NAACP was undergoing during the 1920's a process that is normal for large-scale organizations during some phase of their life cycles. The sociologist Philip Selznick has described the phenomenon: ". . . leadership declines in importance as the formal structure approaches complete determination of behavior. Management engineering is then adequate to the task." [22]

REQUIEM FOR THE ABOLITIONIST

The unaccustomed rigors of army life had broken Spingarn's health, necessitating two major operations for ulcers during the 1920's. The fiery words of the New Abolition were heard no more, as Spingarn consistently declined all speaking engagements and even ceased attending the Annual Conferences of the Association. In 1926 Arthur Spingarn informed

Walter White, the Assistant Secretary, that it was "absolutely out of the question" to expect his brother to accept a speaking engagement at the Annual Conference. Trips into New York City from Troutbeck declined to a trickle; in 1922 Spingarn informed Ovington that he was in the city only about two days a week, and not every week. An active man by both temperament and habit, Spingarn lamented in 1924, "I must continue, I fear, to live more or less like a vegetable for the rest of the summer." His attendance at Board meetings slackened appreciably until by 1928 the incredulous Clerk of the Board, Richetta Randolph, could hardly believe the accuracy of her records, which showed that J. E. Spingarn had attended no meetings during that year.[23]

Undoubtedly Spingarn's physical disability was partially responsible for the alteration in his behavior, but there are indications that his general mental attitude also changed significantly. Some inkling of his disillusionment with the fruits of the "war for democracy" was evidenced in a speech before the NAACP Annual Conference of 1919, delivered immediately after his return from the battlefields of France. After denouncing the backwardness of Southerners who had been placed in charge of black troops, Spingarn suggested that perhaps force of arms might be necessary to win the black man's rights in America—a statement he retracted immediately. At home, too, Spingarn saw ample evidence of the failure of postwar democracy, as a series of violent race riots swept America during the "Red Summer" of 1919. During that summer, while visiting the poet Carl Sandburg, he witnessed a bloody race riot in Chicago, later reporting in detail the horrors of the event. Also in 1919, Spingarn wrote an impassioned appeal to the governor of Arkansas, pleading on behalf of eleven blacks who had been sentenced to death for alleged crimes committed during a race riot precipitated by their opposition to the peonage in which they had been held. He was greatly "disturbed" by rumors of still another race riot in the nation's capital in 1919. In refusing a speaking invitation as late as 1929, Spingarn observed that "somehow or other, I still feel that America is too full of speech-making."[24]

Nor did the general international outlook seem any more promising to Spingarn in the wake of the war. He told his friend and admirer Lewis Mumford that the liberals thought their postwar treaties would solve the problems confronting the world, but, he predicted, there would come a time when men would know a greater slavery than ever before. In writing the obituary of his former colleague in 1939, Villard recalled that Spingarn remained to the end one who was thoroughly disillusioned by the fruits of the "war for democracy." [25]

This disillusionment, coupled with ill health and the administrative changes that had transpired within the NAACP, undoubtedly accounted for the ambivalence Spingarn displayed toward resuming his career with the Association. On the one hand, upon his return from army duty, he insisted that "my interest in the Association is unabated." Prior to his first operation in December 1922, he accepted the chairmanship of the Crisis Committee (1919) and Budget Committee (1920), and he enthusiastically welcomed renomination to the Board of Directors.[26] Yet there was obviously much less need for Spingarn's brand of forceful, active administration. The Board chairmanship from which he had resigned upon entering the army was now held by Mary White Ovington. Branch organization and the Association's publicity work—tasks which partially necessitated the earlier New Abolition campaigns—had been given over to full-time, salaried officials.

Thus, the only nonsalaried executive position available to Spingarn upon his return from army duty was that of Treasurer, a post recently vacated by Villard. Upon Miss Ovington's prompting, Spingarn reluctantly accepted the treasurership, specifying that he was not to be held responsible for soliciting funds and that he would relinquish the position as soon as a suitable successor was secured. Only his high regard for the NAACP had induced him to permit the use of his name for the post.[27] (Spingarn continued as Treasurer until his election to the presidency in 1931, leaving in his wake an impressive record of professional financial administration.)

On the other hand, Spingarn displayed an inclination to devote a sizable portion of his time to interests outside the NAACP and the cause of the Negro—a factor which apparently was both a cause and a result of his decreasing activities within the NAACP. In 1919 he had helped to found Harcourt, Brace and Company and had become a major stockholder in the publishing firm. Rather than serve as an absentee owner, he accepted a responsible working position as literary editor. After Spingarn had devoted more than eight years of virtually full-time service to the NAACP, his colleagues now witnessed the strange sight of his communications appearing under the letterhead of another organization.

There were other unmistakable indications of Spingarn's renewed interest in scholarly pursuits throughout the 1920's. In 1922 he again actively entered the academic fray, issuing a "Manifesto to the Younger Generation," which called upon young poets, philosophers, and writers to effect a return to tradition and history. Very few listened; very few followed. In 1924 appeared Spingarn's second volume of poetry, a volume which the enforced solitude and inactivity occasioned by illness probably facilitated. Before leaving Harcourt and Brace at the end of the 1920's, Spingarn edited a twenty-five-volume *Home Library* of short stories and representative samples of the world's greatest literature.[28]

THE ROAD BACK

Yet, as if attracted by some irresistible lodestone, Spingarn clung to the NAACP during the 1920's—if, indeed, he had ever harbored serious thoughts to the contrary. But his stake in the organization now was manifested in a different form. In 1911, at the outset of his work with the organization, he had spoken with disdain of the "philanthropy of rich white men" toward the black race, presumably implying that their financial contributions had been a prime source of their influence.[29] Whether by accident or design, prior to 1919 Spingarn had pursued a different course. His primary contribution to the NAACP had been a dynamic continuum manifested through his time, his interest, and regardless of his shortcomings, his genuine concern. There is no evidence that he contributed more than $500 in cash to the NAACP during the entire period 1911–18.

However, beginning in 1919 and continuing throughout the 1920's, Spingarn and, for the first time, his wife, Amy, awarded modest but steady financial contributions to the NAACP.[30] Spingarn started out in 1919 with a $500 contribution to finance a thorough audit of the Association's books (with the proviso that he have a voice in the selection of the auditors), followed by an additional $200 contribution as a member of the Board of Directors. In 1922, as her husband prepared for an operation, Mrs. Spingarn sent the NAACP her personal contribution of $300, congratulating Johnson for the organization's achievements. The following year, in May, Mrs. Spingarn wrote Johnson, declaring that she and her husband felt the Association would be able to render more effective service if it possessed its own building (national headquarters), and offering $5,000 toward a building fund contingent upon the organization's raising an additional $10,000 by December 1923. Without awaiting the outcome of the building fund project, Mrs. Spingarn forwarded the Association a check for $500 in November 1923 and, at the same time, her husband enclosed his check for $100.[31] Thus, by the beginning of 1924, not only could Spingarn boast of strong financial contributions to the NAACP but Mrs. Spingarn had begun an active interest in the organization—a role she was to perpetuate and intensify into the 1930's.

As the 1920's progressed and the limelight of publicity centered upon Johnson and, to a lesser extent, Ovington, the contributions of Spingarn and his wife formed a steady flow into the Association's coffers. In January 1924, Mrs. Spingarn awarded the organization $1,000 toward meeting a contingent offer of Philip G. Peabody. Smaller though substantial contributions were forthcoming from the Spingarns in support of the several mammoth drives for funds undertaken by Johnson and his staff during the 1920's. They made a joint contribution of $500 to aid a $50,000 Legal Defense Fund drive undertaken in 1925. In 1929 Spingarn subscribed to a $500 life membership in the NAACP in support of the organization's efforts to amass a substantial cash reserve in the form of a Life Membership Reserve Fund.[32]

But the Spingarns' most ambitious financial effort came in 1929 in response to an impressive twentieth-anniversary drive (of the NAACP) with a projected goal of $200,000. The Association conceded that branch contributions, though expected to be substantial, would have to be supplemented with contributions from whites. Spingarn supplied a list of wealthy whites in the New York area who might be induced to contribute to the drive and, for one of the few times in his career, offered to write letters of solicitation. Proclaiming that the NAACP had "more than justified its right to ask the American people for $200,000 in order to continue its activities," Spingarn expressed his and Mrs. Spingarn's "faith" in the work which had been accomplished and which remained to be done by offering $1,000 toward the twentieth-anniversary campaign—$500 from Mrs. Spingarn when the first $50,000 had been raised and $500 from Spingarn when the first $75,000 had been obtained. The following September, Spingarn altered the terms of the original offer, summarily forwarding the Association a check for $2,000—$1,000 to fulfill the original pledge; $500 for a life membership in the NAACP for Mrs. Spingarn; and the same amount for a life membership for his brother Arthur. Spingarn requested that no publicity be given the donation: "Why should a mere money contribution receive publicity anyway?"[33] he asked rhetorically. Nevertheless, with or without publicity, his stake in the NAACP was assured by such substantial donations.

Although his attendance at Board meetings was practically nil during the 1920's, Spingarn proceeded to take his job as Treasurer seriously. He had been the director of two mills and a partner in the Harcourt and Brace publishing firm, yet he intensely disliked routine financial management.[34] Yet his tenure as Treasurer of the NAACP was to demonstrate not only his strong penchant for professional financial organization and administration but his enviable expertise in financial matters—especially the purchase and disposal of stocks and bonds. During the 1920's, as the NAACP amassed more funds than ever before in its history, it found in Spingarn one of its most astute and professionally minded financial advisers.

Spingarn's insistence upon careful, long-term investment of the NAACP's surplus funds was perhaps his greatest single contribution as Treasurer. Prior to the mid-1920's, the Association had separated its monies into special funds—anti-lynching, legal defense, and the like—but any surplus monies usually had been deposited in regular savings accounts at nominal rates of interest. This was largely due to the fact that the organization conducted a hand-to-mouth existence whereby any surpluses were so rapidly consumed to meet current financial obligations that long-term investments would not have been practicable. By 1926, however, the influx of bequests, philanthropic contributions, and grants ensured that the Association would have a sizable surplus for an extended period. For example, by January 1926 the NAACP had $50,000 on deposit in the National City Bank of New York, yet the bank's policy stipulated that only 2½ percent interest could be paid for deposits exceeding $10,000.[35]

In January 1926 Spingarn suggested to Johnson that a considerable portion of the Association's surplus monies be invested in first-class bonds. He urged that a five-member Investment Committee be established, to be charged with the responsibility of purchasing, exchanging, and selling such securities as the Board of Directors might set aside for that purpose, and that the written authorization of three of the members of the Committee should be necessary for withdrawal, sale, or exchange of the securities. At its initial meeting, held at Spingarn's home in February 1926, the Investment Committee launched an ambitious program, beginning with the investment of $30,000 of the Legal Defense Fund (then on deposit in the National City Bank) in bonds.[36]

Spingarn became the trusted and ever-knowledgeable source to which Johnson could turn for advice in selecting the proper securities and the most beneficial financial institutions.

Spingarn recommended the Guaranty Trust Company as the best institution at which to open a custody account for the Association, and, obviously as a result of his personal connections with the bank, provided Johnson with a letter of introduction to the bank officials. When Guaranty Trust seemed reluctant to open an account for the NAACP without the deposit of a sum against which the bonds could be charged, Johnson suggested to Spingarn, "I do not suppose this will be necessary if the order comes from you." Similarly, Spingarn carefully pointed out to the Investment Committee the differences in New York State requirements for investments in savings banks and those for trust funds. He displayed an amazing working knowledge of specific stocks and bonds, frequently quoting current and potential securities earnings and pointing out to Johnson the pitfalls awaiting the unwary investor.[37]

Spingarn's policies regarding the disposition of the NAACP life membership fees further illustrate his financial acumen. First inaugurated in 1927, tht NAACP Life Membership Drive represented an attempt to garner additional income by inducing interested individuals to subscribe to a $500 life membership rather than provide small annual contributions. By the end of 1928 only four life memberships had been paid in full, but many individuals had pledged or paid installments on their $500 fees. In December 1928, Spingarn apprised Johnson of the fact that almost all organizations similar in nature to the NAACP funded life membership fees rather than using them for current expenses. If the NAACP had not formulated such a funding program, he suggested, it should do so without delay. Johnson informed Spingarn that the Board had not established life memberships with the idea of having the proceeds funded; rather, it was intended that the income should provide the Association a steady revenue (for current expenses) extending over a period of years. The proceeds from the life memberships were being placed in the General Fund (from which salaries and other current expenses were paid).[38]

This arrangement proved totally unsatisfactory to Spingarn. He warned Johnson that it was "dangerous" to consider life membership fees as current contributions, insisting that the Association must consider an individual's life membership fee as the only annual contribution from that person as long as he lived. By funding the fee, the organization would receive a return of approximately $25 annually, not only during the person's lifetime but forever. The decision not to fund life memberships "seems to me an inadequate financial arrangement," concluded Spingarn. Nevertheless, no action was taken on his suggestion until February 1930, after the Association's auditors, W. C. Heaton and Company, had substantiated Spingarn's opinion. In keeping with the auditors' suggestion, Spingarn (and later the Board) endorsed a plan calling for a ten-year Life Membership Reserve Fund, whereby the interest and $50 of the principal of each life membership fee would be expended annually over a ten-year period. In the final analysis the NAACP was penalized heavily for its failure to fund the fees from the outset, for it became necessary to switch money from the Special Legal Defense Fund in order to launch the new Life Membership Reserve Fund with the total amount ($6,600) that had been contributed to the latter fund since 1927.[39]

As was suggested previously, part of the subtle reasoning behind having a white liberal as Treasurer of the NAACP probably was the belief—whether real or imagined—that the organization's enemies would be less likely to level charges of mismanagement of funds. This reasoning received its first major test when, in 1926, the Pittsburgh *Courier*, an influential black paper edited by Robert L. Vann, accused the Association of malfeasance and gross mishandling of funds. Specifically, the *Courier* labeled a $34,000 appropriation to the NAACP from the American Fund for Public Service a "slush fund," charging that the Association had given no public accounting for the expenditure of the money. The NAACP also was a "closed corporation" in regard to the selection of officers, the *Courier* charged, since it did not give the public any voice in the selection of its officials although it relied on public support. The newspaper accused Johnson of having been "boss" of the NAACP for years, and insisted that he was likely to continue "for the next so many years, so far as the public knows." The NAACP was determined to advance the Negro public "in spite of itself," concluded the *Courier*, "but the only thing the Negro public can have to do with the NAACP is contribute its money and accept the 'Advancement.' "[40] Johnson felt that a suit against the *Courier* for libel would be detrimental to the cause, but he urgently requested that Spingarn, in his official capacity as Treasurer, issue a public statement in answer to the *Courier*'s charges.[41]

Spingarn sought to counterattack partially by relying upon his personal reputation. Listing the offices he had held within the Association, he insisted that he was in a position to state frankly and precisely the organization's business methods. After recounting the elaborate system of checks and balances used in the signing of checks and the disbursement of monies, he assured the public that neither Johnson, Du Bois, White, nor any other salaried executive officers had ever signed a single check. The disbursement and handling of funds were confined to the purview of the Board of Directors, stated Spingarn, and only those members authorized by the Board were empowered to sign checks. He noted that he personally had selected the current auditors of the Association's books because of his faith in their competence and impartiality. He expressed strong resentment over any imputation which might be cast on the honesty and good faith of the salaried executives who, "under the supervision of a distinguished Board of Directors," had devoted their lives to race and country. The mere success of the NAACP invited attacks, warned Spingarn, and blacks must learn to recognize those who worked disinterestedly in their service.[42] Johnson also issued a statement to the press in which he quoted extensively from Spingarn's statement.

Spingarn's somewhat veiled attempt to project his personal standing as a means of refuting the *Courier*'s charges met with only partial success. In an article prepared for the Preston News Service (a syndicated service of the black press), Ernest Rice McKinney, a black reporter, all but summarized the reasoning which must have led the NAACP to select white treasurers throughout its history. The Treasurer of the NAACP was Joel Spingarn, a leading scholar, militant friend of blacks, and "fairly wealthy," wrote McKinney. Similarly, he referred to Mary White Ovington as "a white woman who certainly would not seek to elevate herself in the estimation of white America by close association with our group." These were the men and women whom the *Courier*, a black paper, had seen fit to denounce, concluded McKinney. A number of white and black papers, some of which used McKinney's argument, also sprang to the defense of the Association, including the Chicago *Bee*, the Philadelphia *Tribune*, the New York *News*, the Baltimore *Afro-American*, and the Richmond *Planet*.[43]

On the other hand, Spingarn and Johnson's statements failed to mollify a large segment of the black press. The Pennsylvania *Guard* not only denounced Johnson's statement as inadequate but proceeded to satirize Johnson's decision to quote from Spingarn's statement. When Johnson "read a statement from J. E. Spingarn, treasurer of the NAACP, the sky cleared—the long sought-for explanation of just why the *Courier* figures had so upset the executive camp of the Association was made known," quipped the *Guard*. Johnson had quoted Spingarn, "the man who gave Johnson a medal . . ." (Johnson was a recipient of the Spingarn Medal.) Meanwhile, throughout December, the *Courier* continued its attacks, being joined by the Cleveland *Gazette*, the Chicago *Whip*, the Arizona *Times*, and the Detroit *Owl*. Hostility between the Association and the *Courier* continued until 1929, at which time both issued public statements in which each vowed to "bury the hatchet" and cooperate in the common cause.[44]

Two events, both of which occurred in 1929, facilitated Spingarn's return to intensively active participation in the Association. Having secured a Julius Rosenwald Fund fellowship for a year of creative writing, Johnson applied for a leave of absence from his post as Executive Secretary in 1929. He had been overcome by sheer mental and physical fatigue after nearly a decade of piloting the Association through its most exciting decade. Seeing Johnson at the NAACP Annual

Conference of 1929, Spingarn was "disturbed by the fatigue and strain" the Secretary manifested. Spingarn wrote the Board of Directors, urging that Johnson's request for a leave be granted and pointing out that it was important that Johnson's health be preserved for future service. Spingarn arranged an appointment for Johnson with his personal physician, requesting that he offer any help or advice he could. Shortly afterward, in the fall of 1929, Moorfield Storey, who had served as President of the NAACP since its incorporation, died.[45]

The selection of Storey's successor proved a difficult task. Spingarn initially declined the post, probably because of the long spell of poor health which had plagued him during the 1920's and perhaps because his disillusionment with the general postwar American scene had not entirely dissipated. After considerable deliberation, the committee charged with nominating individuals to fill the post submitted the names of five candidates, none of whom was satisfactory to the Board "in all respects." After five additional months of deliberation, the committee reported that it still had not come to any decision regarding Storey's successor. Faced with this impasse, the Nominating Committee spoke briefly with Spingarn in November 1930 while the Board was in session, then secured from the assembled Directors the authorization to extend to him a second invitation to serve as President.[46] By that time thirteen months had elapsed since the death of Moorfield Storey.

Some dissension over Spingarn's election to the presidency erupted almost immediately, originating with the Amsterdam *News*, a Harlem paper edited by George Harris. The *News* raised the question of why a white man had been selected, and implied that Johnson's departure from the Association at virtually the same time as Spingarn's election reflected the Secretary's disagreement with the choice. Although Johnson denied the *News*'s charges, the story was perpetuated by the white press in New York. The New York *World* reported that "many Negroes" had favored Johnson as Storey's successor, and that Johnson had temporarily or permanently ceased to take an active part in the Association after Spingarn's election. The New York *Evening Journal* reported that black leaders in Harlem had prophesied "fireworks" at the NAACP annual business meeting of 1931 because they were convinced that a white man, no matter how well qualified, should not have been made President of the Association.[47] Nevertheless, the predicted fireworks did not materialize and the controversy appears to have been short-lived and confined almost solely to the New York press.

Spingarn enthusiastically accepted the NAACP presidency, although he insisted that there were others who were more qualified for the post and that he would serve only until a suitable successor could be found. In his letter of acceptance, he recounted the "predicament" that the selection of a President had occasioned and of his "clear duty" to serve under the circumstances. He reminded the Board of "what an extraordinary Association ours really is," with every shade of political, economic, social, and religious opinion represented among the Directors and the rank-and-file membership. He urged that this diversity, which he depicted as one of the main sources of the organization's strength, be continued and that the NAACP maintain its militant and disinterested help to the millions.[48]

5

THE ABOLITIONIST AS
ADMINISTRATOR

B y 1930 the NAACP had passed through two major stages
of administrative development. The period from 1911 to
roughly 1918 had been characterized by the virtually uncontested administrative leadership of a handful of individuals,
most of them white liberals who had served as both administrators and activists. The second developmental stage,
which encompassed the period from 1918 to 1930, had witnessed the extensive diffusion of authority and responsibility
among full-time salaried executives who, of necessity, were
accorded at least a modicum of decision-making power in their
respective realms. At the same time, the organization had
evolved from organizational to institutional status, complete
with the prosperity, security, and other benefits but also with
the hardening of goals, values, and response patterns almost
inherent in the process of institutionalization.

Spingarn's ascendancy to the presidency in 1930, followed
by his election to the Board Chairmanship in early 1932, marked

the beginning of the third stage in the institution's administrative development—the revival of viable white liberal leadership in the top-level policy-making process. Even the largely
honorary historic functions of the presidency underwent
significant changes during Spingarn's tenure. Unlike Moorfield Storey, who had resided in Boston and who had manifested little interest in routine administrative problems, Spingarn was only a phone call away from the national office,
attended Board and committee meetings regularly, and insisted
on being kept apprised of even routine administrative matters.
Indeed, Spingarn proceeded to exercise a close, though often
subtle, watch over the salaried executives, calling an abrupt
halt to policies which he deemed unsound.

This chapter especially focuses on the management of the
Association's funds, an area of administration with which the
white liberals had been closely associated since the organization's incorporation in 1911. The white liberal leadership
exercised virtually uncontested control of the NAACP's financial policy-making during the most crucial stages of the
Depression, from 1930 to 1933.

PRELUDE

The administrative history of the NAACP during the
1930's—and especially the period from 1930 to 1935—in large
measure revolves around the relationship between Spingarn
and Walter White. A mulatto with blond hair and blue eyes,
White had begun his duties as Assistant Secretary in 1918,
shortly after Spingarn's departure for active army duty. It
was not until after the war had ended that mutual literary
interests provided an initial basis for the two men's first
meaningful relationship. In 1922, after six years as Assistant
Secretary, White, having garnered a wealth of firsthand information about Southern race relations and mob violence, decided to attempt a novel. Never having written professionally,
he turned for advice to Spingarn, who was some fifteen years
older than he and an editor at Harcourt and Brace. The novel,

The Fire in the Flint, presented a strong anti-lynching theme within a compelling and passionate story of love, racial antagonism, and mob violence in the South. Spingarn found the story "overwhelming" and capable of inducing the reader to follow the career of the protagonist "breathlessly"; some of the scenes were "powerful." But the Master of Literary Criticism was much less pleased with the manner in which White presented his characters; they simply did not "live," thereby giving the work the appearance of a "melodrama," rather than drama. Spingarn told White that "until you have learned how to create characters you have not learned how to write a novel, however breathlessly you may persuade people to follow a story from incident to incident." With these words of encouragement and candid criticism, Spingarn returned the novel to White, assuring him that he would be willing to discuss the novel or any other matter "whenever you think my advice worth having." [1]

Thus, like Du Bois, White reached an accord with Spingarn on an intellectual plane which transcended the routine business affairs of the NAACP. But unlike Du Bois, White's initial relationship with the celebrated literary critic was to be characterized by the deference and, perhaps, subservience which not infrequently attends the contact between master scholar and aspiring young student. Du Bois had possessed a large measure of professional status at the time of his initial contact with Spingarn; although at times he too had sought his white friend's professional advice, the two men's relationship clearly had been that of professional equals. But the tone of White's letters to Spingarn during the 1920's suggest deference and adulation. White extolled his newfound mentor for having been "more than good to me . . ." "I need the guidance of an experienced hand," wrote the young author, "and, with no attempt at flattery, yours would mean more to me than any other." Using his extensive contacts with the nation's most illustrious literati, Spingarn helped to publicize *The Fire in the Flint*, having been instrumental in securing Sinclair Lewis to make favorable public comments about the novel.[2]

The success of *The Fire in the Flint* [3] prompted White to undertake the writing of two other major books during the 1920's, with Spingarn continuing to serve as a source of advice and encouragement. After the completion of his second book, *Flight* (1926), White seriously considered abandoning his work with the NAACP in order to pursue a full-time writing career. Spingarn was "much disturbed" by his young protégé's decision to "give up what I [Spingarn] had thought was to be your life-work." He urged that White discuss the matter with him, resulting in the Assistant Secretary's decision to request a year's leave of absence from the Association in lieu of severing his connections altogether. Spingarn also was instrumental in helping White secure a Guggenheim Foundation grant covering expenses for a year of creative writing in southern France. The result of White's efforts, *Rope and Faggot: A Biography of Judge Lynch* (1929), was a sociohistorical study of lynching and mob violence. Sociologically White had stated the case against lynching admirably, Spingarn wrote, for although the colorful tone of his young associate's earlier works was missing, the restraint of dramatic instincts had "increased the effectiveness of the argument for serious readers, most of whom may feel that emotion rather than reason has already too much governed in these matters." [4]

In essence, then, the 1920's served as an introductory period for White and Spingarn; a mutually congenial prelude to the turbulent 1930's, during which their relationship would shift from that of friendly literary associates to a more trying and official administrative basis. Ironically, however, it was not until 1932, after the two men had taken a train together to Boston, that, for the first time in their ten-year relationship, the two men began addressing each other on a first-name basis. Spingarn sent White $15 to cover the cost of his young friend's Boston train fare; White admitted that the trip had given him the opportunity to get to know Spingarn better than ever before in their long relationship. [5]

There is every reason to believe that Spingarn both liked White personally and was confident that he was capable of

filling the post of Executive Secretary after James Weldon
Johnson's resignation in 1930. While serving as one of the
three Associate Acting Secretaries during Johnson's leave of
absence, White had written Spingarn asking whether he
would consider urging the Board of Directors to "rule that
there shall be an Acting Secretary and abolish the positions of
Associate Acting Secretaries." White insisted that he preferred "not going into the reasons for this request," but that
it was difficult to be held responsible for affairs unless there
were some central person in charge of coordinating reports
and related policy matters.[6] In short, White was requesting the
same supervisory authority over the Association's salaried
employees which Johnson had enjoyed as Executive Secretary. In response to White's request, Spingarn told his brother
Arthur, "I think we ought to give W. W. ample opportunity
and responsibility to carry on effective work." Because he
was unable to attend the next Board meeting, J. E. Spingarn
asked his brother to propose the following resolution, or one
similar to it: "Resolved, That the [Executive] Secretary, and
in his absence, the Acting Secretary, shall be the Executive
officer of the Ass[ociatio]n and Associate Secretaries and all
other salaried officers of the Ass[ociatio]n shall be directly
subject to his authority." The resolution was passed by the
Board as offered. Similarly, when Johnson finalized his decision not to resume the post of Executive Secretary after
his leave of absence had expired, Spingarn proposed to the
Board of Directors that White succeed him.[7]

On the other hand, Spingarn formulated an elaborate network of checks and balances designed to insure that White
would be answerable to the top-level leadership of the organization. In the resolution proposing White's appointment as Executive Secretary, Spingarn also resolved that the Secretary be
subject to the authority of the Chairman of the Board under
the powers conferred upon the Chairman by the constitution.
The constitutional provision in question—the same one Villard
had attempted to invoke against Du Bois during the *Crisis* controversy of 1913—stipulated that all salaried employees of the
Association were subject to the authority of the Board

Chairman when the Board was not in session. Spingarn's
resolution also called for the creation of a Committee on Administration for the Secretary's "counsel and guidance." The
Committee was to consist of all the salaried executives of the
Association; the Chairman of the Board (Ovington); the
Chairman of the Legal Committee (Arthur Spingarn); and
three Board members to be appointed by the Chairman. The
Committee was to meet once each month, two weeks after
the regular monthly Board meeting, or whenever the Chairman of the Board deemed it necessary. This portion of Spingarn's resolution, like that naming White as Secretary, was
adopted by the Board as offered.[8] Spingarn and the Board had
taken an important step toward reaffirming and strengthening
the top-level leadership's functional as well as scalar status.

THE POWER OF THE PURSE

Spingarn assumed the office of President and White the
office of Secretary at the outset of the most trying period in
the NAACP's history, the age of the Great Depression.
Ideological and internal administrative conflicts—many of
which indirectly derived from the impact of the Depression
on American society—would plague the Association during
the first half of the 1930's, but the first and foremost task of
the executives was to forestall the organization's financial
collapse.

The effects of the Depression on the NAACP, as on
countless other organizations, were immediate and potentially
devastating. Given a choice between paying branch membership dues and using the money to purchase necessities of life,
the average black man apparently chose the latter. The amount
of funds forwarded to the national office from the branches
steadily declined each year during the period 1929 to 1933.
In 1929 only sixty-four branches had failed to contribute the
annual minimum of $50 to the national office; by 1932 the
total number of delinquent branches had increased to 109—
nearly one-third of the approximately 350 active branches. In

October 1931 the branches forwarded to the national office a total of $4,011.92; exactly one year later they sent only $1,365. Total returns from the branches to the national office in 1932 were $12,000 less than in the preceding year—a substantial blow to the Association's projected 1932 budget of $50,000.[9]

The impact of the Depression was also reflected in the marked decrease in contributions from individual philanthropists. Prior to 1929, a substantial portion of the organization's revenue had derived from donations (usually ranging from $1,000 to $500) from approximately twenty individuals. In many instances these sizable contributions had been contingent on the Association's securing specific amounts from other donors. During the 1920's, not only had the Association almost always succeeded in meeting contingent offers, but it appeared that a large contribution from one individual often served as a catalyst for prompting others to match the donation.[10] By 1933, however, the NAACP found it increasingly difficult to secure pledges or donations even from those philanthropists who had been regular contributors during the 1920's. Philip G. Peabody summarized the situation neatly when, in refusing to renew his annual contribution, he observed that "necessity knows no law." In May 1933, White informed the Board of Directors that "large contributions except in rare instances are most unlikely to be secured during the next few years," and he advised that the Association concentrate on securing $5 to $100 donations.[11]

Had it not been for legacies and grants from philanthropic foundations, the NAACP would, in all probability, have experienced a complete financial collapse by 1934. In June 1930 the American Fund for Public Service granted the Association $100,000, to be paid in installments,[12] to mount an extensive legal campaign against segregation and discrimination. Much smaller grants, ranging from $2,500 to $1,000, were received from certain agencies, including the Julius Rosenwald Fund and the New York Foundation. In addition, many bequests which had been made during the 1920's became payable to the NAACP during the early 1930's—approximately $20,000 in such legacies being received in the year 1932 alone.[13] Thus, while returns from branch memberships and individual contributions—the Association's traditional sources—declined, new financial avenues somewhat lightened the impact of the Depression, at least until the end of 1932.

Spingarn, with occasional assistance from Ovington and Arthur Spingarn, became the key formulator of the Association's financial policy during the most crucial phase of the Depression, from 1930 to 1933. Several general factors helped to pave the way. First, the skill in financial matters that Spingarn had displayed as Treasurer during the 1920's could hardly be ignored during the Association's most acute financial crisis. In fact, the dependence of an organization's members upon the special talents of experienced leaders often provides a basis for the self-perpetuation of leaders.[14] Second, the organization's extensive holdings in the form of stocks and bonds—a system inaugurated during the 1920's at Spingarn's behest—necessitated considerable expertise in the sale and transfer of securities, especially in light of the precarious position of the stock market. It quickly became apparent that Walter White lacked this expertise. He rarely ventured to suggest the sale, purchase, or transfer of any stocks or bonds before first inquiring of Spingarn whether the transaction should be made or what procedure should be employed.[15] This is not intended as a negative reflection upon White, for even Arthur Spingarn bowed to his brother's financial acumen, occasionally referring specific financial matters to J. E. Spingarn. Similarly, Spingarn either served on the Association's Budget Committee or was requested to sit in on its meetings each year during the period 1931–38.[16]

But it was a rift between Walter White and the other salaried executives over the management and allocation of funds that appears to have been the most important single factor in prompting the top-level leadership—especially the Spingarn brothers and Mary White Ovington—to intervene so forcefully in the organization's financial administration. In December of 1931 the Board of Directors received a memorandum signed by every major salaried official of the Association

—Du Bois; William Pickens, the Field Secretary; Herbert Seligmann, the Director of Publicity; Robert W. Bagnall, the Director of Branches; and even Roy Wilkins, the newly appointed Assistant Secretary—accusing White of giving the Budget Committee false information to the effect that his salaried co-workers were not doing their fair share of economizing within their respective departments as a means of aiding the organization through its most acute financial crisis. Apparently White had suggested, or was suspected of having suggested, retrenchment in the form of personnel and salary cuts, for the memorandum countercharged that more savings could be effected through "reasonable limitations of money wasted" than by decreasing salaries or dismissing officials. If White were not, among other things, "more conscientious in his expenditure of money," charged Du Bois and his colleagues, "the chief question before this organization is how long he can remain in his present position and keep the NAACP from utter disaster?" The memorandum also charged that the Chairman of the Board (Mary White Ovington), the Secretary (White), and the Budget Committee (which was biracial) had combined forces against the salaried officials. The signers left no doubt that they believed White's allegedly false information was the root of the evil. The memorandum called for a curb on the Board Chairman's power to appoint all committees—as Chairman of the Board, Ovington had appointed the members of the Budget Committee—and demanded that the President of the Association appoint a committee to study thoroughly the expenditure of funds.[17]

The memorandum had two immediate and highly significant results. First, it induced the top-level leadership to keep a closer scrutiny on routine office affairs in general and White's management of funds in particular. Second, the attack on Ovington led her to confirm a decision she had been contemplating before the memorandum was issued—to resign the Board Chairmanship. On December 15, 1931, six days before Du Bois and his colleagues penned their memorandum, she had confided to Spingarn that she felt useless as Board

Chairman because White never asked her opinion about office affairs and because she was never invited to attend committee meetings. Spingarn assured Miss Ovington that she would never outlive her usefulness, but suggested that the Chairman ship, which he agreed no longer entailed any significant exercise of power, be occupied by whoever was President (currently himself).[18] Thus, in January 1932 he succeeded Ovington as Board Chairman, while she became Treasurer of the Association, a post Spingarn had vacated upon his election to the presidency.

Shortly after the salaried executives had issued their broadside against White, Spingarn confided to his brother his lack of confidence in White's financial acumen. The NAACP's annual reports were too extravagantly printed, he complained, suggesting that the size should be cut in half, cheaper paper used, blank pages omitted, and less expensive printing employed. He asked Arthur Spingarn to take the matter up with White, because, said Spingarn, "I am afraid he does not know how to economize." "There are leaders for expansionist times," noted the new Chairman of the Board, "[and] leaders for deflationist times, and I wonder if he [White] will ever be able to adapt his psyche to the new state of the world." White complied with the bulk of the suggested economy cuts.[19]

But Spingarn's first major check on White's handling of monies derived from the issue of maintaining the integrity of the special funds.[20] The total separation of the special funds into separate bank accounts from that of the general fund had been effected in 1930, largely at the behest of Arthur Spingarn. When in 1930 the NAACP auditors had called Arthur Spingarn's attention to the fact that the Association's several funds had not been maintained in separate bank accounts, and that on occasion money from one fund had been drawn to supplement others, Arthur Spingarn expressed surprise. He requested that White, who was then Acting Secretary, bring the matter before the Committee on Administration. When White failed to do so, Arthur Spingarn instructed him to present the matter to the entire Board of Directors at its next meeting. At that time, the Board voted to establish a separate bank account for each of the several funds, with the understanding that the money in each fund was to be used only for the purpose specifically designated for the respective funds. However, by the end of 1931, as a result of decreasing revenues, the general fund from which salaries were paid was depleted and White had begun charging the salaries of office workers to the special funds.[21]

In February 1932, Spingarn joined with Mary White Ovington in calling an abrupt halt to this practice. They informed White that, having examined the last monthly balance sheet, "we are much disturbed by the amounts that have been borrowed from the Special Funds." Both Spingarn and Ovington included their official titles beneath their signatures, a technique which Spingarn frequently employed to ensure that an "opinion" would carry the weight of a pronouncement from a superior officer, and a practice that sharply contrasted with the absence of official titles which usually prevailed in interoffice communications. A conference that White requested with Spingarn and Ovington to discuss the matter apparently was to no avail, for shortly afterward White informed Pickens and Bagnall that "I have been instructed by the President and Treasurer to permit no further borrowing from special funds, even for the payment of salaries." At that time, on February 16, 1932, the general fund showed a deficit of $10,000.[22]

On the other hand, there are indications that it was not the maintenance of the integrity of the special funds *per se* which concerned Spingarn; rather, he wanted White to secure prior authorization before handling them, an authorization that happened to fall within the purview of the Spingarn brothers and Mary White Ovington. In August 1932 Spingarn informed White that he felt "strongly that no officer is authorized to sell bonds, especially those which belong to special funds, without explicit permission from the Board, and that matters should be so planned that Board action is taken at the right time." In October 1932 Roy Wilkins, the Assistant Secretary, informed Arthur Spingarn that bonds in the Legal Defense Fund needed to be sold in order to sustain the Association's current legal cases. Arthur Spingarn gave his approval and instructed Wilkins to "take up the matter with the President and Treasurer, to the end that they may determine what bonds should be sold and issue the necessary orders to that effect." [23]

Spingarn made it clear that in his opinion retrenchment was the desirable alternative to borrowing from the special funds. In a memorandum to the Budget Committee dated November 1932 and marked "confidential," he suggested that the two major questions confronting the Committee were: (1) Should severe cutbacks in the Association's monthly expenses be made? (2) How could the cutbacks best be effected? By June 1932, before the issuance of Spingarn's memorandum, the Board of Directors already had voted a reduction in the office staff and across-the-board cuts in the salaries of the remaining staff. The Budget Committee instituted additional staff and salary cutbacks throughout 1932 and 1933, with the most severe penalties being levied against Roy Wilkins, the Assistant Secretary, and Robert W. Bagnall. The Committee recommended that Wilkins be switched from full-time to part-time status and his salary cut in half. Bagnall, who had been Director of Branches since 1919, was dismissed (with three months' severance pay) and his office abolished.[24]

White vehemently protested to Spingarn the change in Wilkins' status, largely on the grounds that he, White, could not effectively sustain the duties of the secretaryship without the assistance Wilkins had rendered. Spingarn replied that if White could find another way of saving $1,153 (the projected savings from Wilkins' salary cut), he would be more than delighted to have the Assistant Secretary retained full-time. But, concluded Spingarn, "the Budget Committee in my opinion reduced expenses much too little." Nevertheless, White induced Spingarn to make a special trip from Troutbeck to New York City so that the matter could be discussed further. Adopting a more practical approach, the Secretary reminded the Board Chairman that switching Wilkins to part-time work would save the Association only $676.50 rather than $1,153 [25] for the year 1933 since only six months remained in the year. At the same time, White informed Spingarn of his recent contacts with William Rosenwald (son of Julius Rosenwald) and of the possibility of Rosenwald's making a small contribution to the Association before the end of 1933. White inquired whether Spingarn would be willing to "take the position with me that Mr. Wilkins be retained at full time" if the Rosenwald contribution were secured. Spingarn expressed the hope that White would be so successful with Rosenwald that the difficulties of the Budget Committee would be eased. In response to the Secretary's mention of the actual savings that would accrue from reducing Wilkins to part-time status, Spingarn curtly replied, "Of course a saving of $1500 'per annum' means a saving of $750 for six months. How could so simple a statement be otherwise understood?" [26]

Similarly, in response to a deluge of letters and telegrams from individual members and branches protesting Bagnall's dismissal after twelve years of service, Spingarn explained that the retrenchment measures were not personal but merely reflected the dire financial plight of the NAACP. Whether additional staff cuts would be necessary would depend on the financial response of the people of the country during the succeeding six months.[27]

Meanwhile, Spingarn had proceeded to block the practice of extending salary advances to office workers. Technically only the Treasurer and specifically authorized Board members were empowered to sign the Association's checks, but traditionally the authority to approve routine salary advances had been left to the overall jurisdiction of the Secretary, and usually his recommendation had elicited automatic acceptance from his superiors. However, the expert whom Spingarn had secured to investigate the Association's administration following the salaried executives' December 1931 broadside against White concluded that salary advances had become a constant practice in the office and recommended that the authority to advance salaries be removed from the jurisdiction of the (salaried) executives. The Board of Directors adopted this recommendation in April 1932, stipulating that thenceforth no salary advances were to be made to any executive or employee of the NAACP without the written consent of at least two of the following: the Chairman of the Board; the Treasurer, or one of the above officers and one Board member. The Board also adopted a new requisition form for the office that required White's approval of all requisitions before they were forwarded to persons authorized to sign checks. Shortly after the new form had been adopted, Arthur Spingarn noticed that they were not being used by the office workers. "May I suggest that you take this matter up with Mr. White . . . ," he wrote to Ovington, "as the Budget as adopted expressly provides that no future checks should be drawn without such requisition." [28]

In January 1933, White complained to Spingarn and Ovington about the inconvenience involved in securing so many signatures for salary advances, charging that it added to the already overwhelming office work, and cost money and time. The Secretary called the Chairman's and Treasurer's attention to the new requisition form which the Board recently had adopted and which required the Secretary's approval on all cash requisitions. In light of this new form, White requested that the rule requiring two additional signatures for salary advances be abolished. Spingarn replied that the investigator's report had shown that salary advances had become common practice and could be stopped by removing the authority to make such advances from the hands of the salaried executives. Even if the Board should rescind its April ruling and return the authority to advance salaries to the executives, he insisted, a written explanation from the person requesting the advance "should be read at the next Board meeting in each case, or presented to the Treasurer and Chairman of the Board and such advances should be reduced to an 'irreducible minimum.' " [29]

As White and Du Bois engaged in heated disputes over the *Crisis* funds during the period after 1930, Spingarn came to exercise the same supervision of the Association's appropriations to the *Crisis*. It was not until early 1935 that his intensive personal interest in the NAACP's financial policies began to abate, largely because of insurgent attacks upon the old-guard leadership, especially regarding the continuing adequacy of the organization's historic program. [30]

A HOUSE UPON THE SAND

It has been established that true leadership entails critical decision-making bearing on the long-range objectives and stability of the organization. But effective leadership also entails the more mundane task of adjucating immediate day-to-day conflict in the realization that the organization will have no future if these problems are not resolved quickly and satisfactorily. Ordinarily, as the chief salaried executive officer of the Association Walter White would have been the logical official to handle its internal disputes, but White himself was so often at the center of conflict that his potential role as mediator appears to have been seriously, if not irreparably, impaired. What became a perennial deadlock between the contending interest groups—White and Du Bois—often caused each to vie for the sympathy and support of a powerful third party, Spingarn. Thus, during the first half of the 1930's, Spingarn not only served as the NAACP's institutional leader by virtue of his voice in policy-making as Board Chairman and President, but his attempts to bring a modicum of peace between Du Bois and White caused him to play the role of interpersonal leader more intensively than he had since the early *Crisis* controversy of 1913–15. It was to be his task to chart a middle course between the contending interest groups, granting sufficient concessions to each in order to diminish conflict, yet doing so within the confines of what he believed to be the best long-range interests of the organization.

The onset of the Depression disrupted the financial stability which had attended the *Crisis* throughout most of the 1920's. In a January 1929 memorandum to the Crisis Committee, the once fiercely independent Du Bois candidly admitted that it was becoming increasingly difficult "to make ends meet." The burden of tiding the magazine over its immediate financial difficulties came to rest upon the already financially distraught Association. In 1929 the *Crisis* borrowed

$3,000 from the American Fund for Public Service, a debt that had to be repaid by the Association because of the magazine's depleted treasury. In April 1929, Du Bois informed the Board of Directors that the *Crisis* might require an annual subvention of about $5,000 "indefinitely," or else raise a capital and become a commercial venture. As a stop-gap measure, the Editor suggested that the NAACP relinquish the commission fee (about $1,500 annually) it traditionally received on *Crisis* subscriptions and permit the magazine to retain this money as an additional source of income. Spingarn, who was then Treasurer, joined with White and Ovington in opposing this sacrifice of the Association's much-needed income.[31]

In essence, then, by the summer of 1930 the Association was faced with one of the most critical long-range policy decisions in its history: whether the *Crisis* was to be continued and, if so, in what form. Spingarn was the first official to offer a solution to this critical policy question in the form of an extensive resolution presented to the NAACP Board of Directors in July 1930. "We consider the continuance of the *Crisis* in some form as of high importance to the Association and the American Negro," stated the resolution, but financial conditions necessitated a more integral correlation of the magazine with the executive organization of the NAACP. Therefore, Spingarn further resolved that the *Crisis* be managed thereafter by an Editorial Board consisting of four persons: the Secretary (Johnson); the Assistant Secretary (White); the Editor-in-Chief of the *Crisis* (Du Bois); and a fourth person to be selected by the Board of Directors. Spingarn reaffirmed that Du Bois was the Editor-in-Chief of the magazine but that under the new arrangement his salary was to be paid by the Association and he was to be under the direction of the Editorial Board. The Editorial Board, which was to be subject to the authority of the Board of Directors, was to have full charge of the editorial and business management of the *Crisis*, including the authority to revise and renovate the magazine's current business and editorial policy. Finally, Spingarn resolved that the NAACP assume the responsibility for appropriating such monies as would be necessary for the support of the *Crisis* upon the submission of a budget by the Editorial Board.[32] In short, despite the fanfare regarding Du Bois' retention of the position of Editor-in-Chief, Spingarn had chosen to save the *Crisis*, albeit at the expense of the Editor's last vestige of editorial autonomy.

Spingarn's resolution occasioned one of the first major overt signs of the impending, many-faceted struggle between White and Du Bois. One could detect some enmity between the two men beginning during the early 1920's, when White, who was then Assistant Secretary, occasionally took the liberty of pointing out to Ovington and Johnson what he believed to be the Editor's shortcomings in managing the magazine. Indeed, the general tone of White's letters throughout the 1920's and the early 1930's indicates that he believed that the *Crisis'* financial management and circulation could be improved by a change of Editor. How much of the enmity between the two men was the product of the seemingly endless personality clashes that attended Du Bois throughout his career in the NAACP can only be surmised. Nevertheless, in 1929 when the *Crisis* was on the verge of financial collapse, White suggested to Johnson that the Association retain all the magazine's commission fees until the Association was reimbursed for the $3,000 it had paid the American Fund for Public Service on the *Crisis* loan. In the spring of 1930, Du Bois had secured the pledge of the Rosenwald Fund that the *Crisis* was to have a share of the Fund's next appropriation to the Association. But when the appropriation turned out to be less than expected, White did not want to give the Editor a share. Arthur Spingarn had had to remind the Secretary that there was nothing to be gained by crippling the magazine and that in his "personal opinion" the money should be shared.[33]

Thus, Du Bois strongly objected to White's presence on the Editorial Board, which Spingarn had proposed. He insisted that Herbert J. Seligmann, the Director of Publicity, be substituted for White, and that Mrs. Lillian Alexander, one of the Board's most outspoken members and an acquaintance of Du Bois since the early 1920's, be named the fifth member of the Board. The Editor informed Spingarn that if White were not removed, he would resign from the *Crisis* editorship.[34]

As had been the case during the earlier *Crisis* controversy of 1913–15, Spingarn made every concession to Du Bois short of sacrificing what he believed to be the long-range interests of the organization. Since the Editor objected so strenuously to the composition of the Editorial Board, Spingarn offered an amendment to his July resolution that retained White on the Board, but added Seligmann, though not Mrs. Alexander. When an anonymous Board member complained to Spingarn of Du Bois' failure to give detailed financial reports of *Crisis* expenditures and suggested that the Editor could do more to economize, Spingarn initially maintained that he saw no reason why "all or nearly all of the suggestions in this letter cannot be carried out to the financial betterment of the Association." However, when Du Bois sent Spingarn a heated reply to the effect that he was doing everything possible to economize and that he would resign if the Board felt otherwise, little more was heard of forcing economy in the *Crisis* office.[35]

On the other hand, Spingarn was both annoyed and provoked by some of the Editor's actions. When, in the interest of the organization's public image and internal unity, all of the executives except Du Bois withdrew their signatures from the December 1931 broadside that had been directed against White and Ovington, Spingarn urged the Editor, too, to withdraw the charges against his fellow officers. Du Bois replied that he would not "retract or change a single word." Spingarn told the Editor that one Board member had commented that Du Bois was a badly brought-up child who needed a spanking. "It grieves me, as one of your friends," wrote Spingarn, "that you should subject yourself to such a characterization." When Du Bois demanded that all of the members of a newly created Crisis Press Conference be black, Spingarn, as Chairman of the Board, appointed a biracial committee, informing the Editor that the conference members represented a wide spectrum of opinion and that any questions arising between meetings could be referred to the Committee on Administration or the Board Chairman, "for the provision in our By-Laws giving the Chairman 'full authority over all officials and employees of the Association . . .' was intended to provide for just such emergency decisions." [36]

On the other hand, Spingarn made it clear that the *Crisis* was to be maintained in its current form as nearly as possible and that Du Bois was to be retained as Editor as long as he wished to be. When White suggested that the magazine might be converted into a semi-newspaper "with an attractive border" to distinguish it from other newspapers, Spingarn overruled this suggestion on the grounds that it would entail a radical transformation in the *Crisis'* tradition form. In the wake of widespread complaints from Board members to the effect that Du Bois was devoting too much time to personal writing and speaking ventures, Miss Ovington proposed to the Board that the Editor be relieved of full-time duties and be given a reduced salary and the option of performing for the Association whatever services his time and inclination would permit. Apparently Arthur Spingarn took Miss Ovington to task for this proposal, for she later felt the necessity of explaining to J. E. Spingarn that she did not know where his brother got the idea that she had suggested that Du Bois be relieved of the *Crisis'* management. Similarly, when Du Bois departed for a teaching position in Atlanta in 1933, with the magazine being left in the immediate charge of Roy Wilkins and a business manager, George Streator, the Editor wrote Spingarn, complaining that the Board was reneging on its promise that he be allowed to retain editorial authority over the magazine while in Atlanta. After Du Bois had had a five-hour talk with the Spingarn brothers, they induced the Board to reaffirm the Editor's authority.[37]

These early disputes were but the prelude to 1934 when the *Crisis* problem would shift to another and broader front, straining Spingarn's relationship with Du Bois nearly to the breaking point and culminating in Du Bois' resignation from the Association.[38]

6

THE ABOLITIONIST AS
TACTICIAN: TO ALL
THINGS A SEASON

ORGANIZATIONS, like individuals, are charged with the responsibility of performing a designated role. Here, we are generally defining "role" as a method of behavior associated with a given position in a social system. Nor should an organization's role be confused with its general purpose: purpose denotes *aim;* role implies the *means* that will be employed to realize the purpose or aim.[1] For example, both the NAACP and the National Urban League have the ultimate general purpose of advancing the American Negro, but each performs a different tactical role within the larger movement for Negro advancement. As was noted in Chapter 2, the NAACP deliberately relinquished the role of securing blacks' economic advancement to the Urban League, while itself assuming virtually the exclusive role of securing the civil and political rights of black Americans. Indeed, in instances where there are two or more organizations conducting a similar activity or seeking to fulfill the same purpose, each must carefully define its role in relationship to those of its rivals.

Although the Association's record in terms of the successful execution of its chosen role was far from impeccable at the onset of the Depression in 1929, its sweeping legal victories and its institutionalization alone were proof that it had acquired a significant degree of competence in enacting its chosen endeavor.

Yet, as an organization performs the same role over an extended period of time, it becomes extremely difficult to alter that role. Its personnel, its membership, and its resources are likely to have become geared to the performance of the traditional role, and all may have to be reoriented, if not completely changed, in order to accommodate a sudden shift in roles.[2] The leadership, the membership, and the larger community will have acquired a definite conception of what the polity is and should be, and the organization will have built up a definite pattern of response to pressures and problems which may arise—such is the process of institutionalization. Hence, any appreciable changes in the organization's historic purpose or role may necessitate sweeping changes in personnel, a completely new self-conception, and a new system of responses. Obviously, then, a sudden shift in roles is fraught with danger for the continuing stability of the organization. Indeed, some students of administration suggest that it may be easier and more plausible to disband the old organization and begin an entirely new one.[3]

Although the Association conducted an impressive program of agitation, protest, and legal redress against discrimination during the New Deal, serious questions were raised as to whether the organization, in the midst of the widespread economic deprivation which the Depression had wrought among the black masses, could afford not to expand its historic primary goal to place major emphasis upon black economic uplift. Abram Harris, a young black professor of economics at Howard University who was elected to the NAACP Board of Directors during the early 1930's, urged the organization to abandon as a primary goal the attainment of civil and political rights in favor of seeking to effect an alliance of white and black labor against the "exploitative" capitalist class. More important, a significant segment of opinion called upon the Association to alter its historic purpose. By 1934 Du Bois had completely strayed from the Association's avowed purpose of integration to its antithesis: espousal of black voluntary segregation. Similarly, the Communists offered a "way out" to the black masses which contrasted sharply with the NAACP's historic purpose of integrating the black American into the existing capitalist system. Each of these groups harbored differing ideologies, but all agreed that the Association's traditional program of integration through the attainment of full civil and political rights was no longer adequate.

The task of reappraising organizational purpose and role within the light of changing times is one of the most indispensable functions of effective leadership. The leader must carefully weigh the intensity of external and internal pressures for change in the realization that the organization cannot remain static in the wake of overwhelming demands for a new program or ideology. On the other hand, he must at all costs avoid becoming an opportunist who bows to immediate pressures merely because it is expedient in the short run to do so. Rather, he must carefully weigh the demands for change against the potential of the organization's existing personnel and structure to perform the projected new role competently. In the final analysis, the effective leader must strike a delicate balance between recasting the organization's general aims to a degree which will not corrupt its basic principles while, at the same time, responding to pressures for change sufficiently to ensure the organization's survival.[4] This task would be especially difficult for Spingarn for essentially he was a non-economic liberal; yet he would be obliged, in response to demands for change, to forge an economic program for the NAACP.

THE ABOLITIONIST AS NEW DEALER

World War I, the postwar prosperity of the 1920's, and the conservative, pro-business administrations of Harding,

Coolidge, and Hoover marked the death knell of the organized progressive movement. After the demise of the Progressive Party in 1916, Spingarn, like many old-line progressives, retired from active participation in politics. Indeed, to those like Spingarn who measured the worth of politics and politicians primarily in terms of their stance on civil rights, the political climate of the 1920's was especially discouraging, for neither of the three Republican administrations displayed any intention of taking a bold stand in favor of anti-lynching legislation, equal voting rights for black Americans, or other questions of vital importance to the Negro.[5]

Only once during the 1920's was Spingarn's political hiatus interrupted. In 1928 Al Smith, the Democratic presidential candidate, proffered a considerably more liberal program than his Republican opponent, even offering to issue a strong public statement on behalf of Negro rights. Spingarn enthusiastically voted for Smith, although he did not actively participate in the campaign. (Mrs. Spingarn recalled that she and her husband considered Smith a "breath of fresh air" in comparison to the administrations of the 1920's.) Spingarn's changeover to the Democratic ticket after his long-standing Republican loyalty foreshadowed a similar shift in 1936 on the part of black voters who, in overwhelming numbers, were to cast their votes for Roosevelt after having given allegiance to the party of the Emancipator since the Reconstruction Era.[6]

Herbert Hoover, despite his Quaker background, displayed little sympathy for black Americans. He had backed a "lily-white" delegation to the 1928 Republican convention in preference to an integrated one. Although fifty-seven blacks were lynched during his administration, the President offered no public protest. Du Bois complained that Hoover appointed fewer Negroes to first-class government posts than any President since Andrew Johnson. Black government workers were refused admission to federal cafeterias during his tenure. Vice-President Charles Curtis, who was of Indian lineage, refused to shake the hand of a black member of a biracial delegation that called on him. When the government sent the Gold Star Mothers to France to visit their sons' graves, black mothers were provided a separate ship with inferior accommodations. Hoover's staunch resistance to federally financed relief at the outset of the Depression was especially felt by black Americans, since they traditionally suffered the worst economic hardships. So suspect were the President's intentions that the NAACP Board of Directors engaged in extensive debate as to whether he should be asked to address the 1932 Annual Conference to be held in Washington, out of fear that his remarks might betray an anti-Negro bias. Spingarn urged that Hoover be invited to speak, insisting that he could be taken to task on the spot if he should make any utterance detrimental to blacks.[7]

Indeed, Spingarn had no qualms about publicly displaying his utter contempt for Hoover. In 1932 the President personally invited him to attend a conference on hoarding which was to be held at the White House. When Hoover asked the participants to raise their hands if they were willing to support his campaign against hoarding, Spingarn refused to raise his hand. As if to complete the insult, Spingarn gave his candid impression of both the conference and the Hoover administration to a group of reporters waiting on the White House lawn. For a Negroes' representative to have been invited to a conference on hoarding was analogous to inviting a starving man to a lecture on extravagance, he charged, since Negroes had nothing to hoard. The black man was facing the most serious crisis in his history, "and we have yet to find any indication that the national administration appreciates this fact or is doing anything to alleviate it." Betraying his personal conception of where some of the fault for the Depression lay, Spingarn expressed amazement at the conference's "superficial treatment" of the problem of hoarding, since "it was urged that a dollar hoarded if put into a bank would mean five or ten dollars credit, when the whole question depends on the profound suspicion of the American people as to how bankers have used this credit in the past and are likely to use it in the future." [8]

Since 1913 Spingarn had been cultivating the friendship of Franklin D. Roosevelt, the man who was destined to capture his imagination and political loyalty as no other politician since the Republican Roosevelt. The proximity of Spingarn's Troutbeck to Roosevelt's Hyde Park estate made the two men neighbors, a fact of which Spingarn liked to brag. Spingarn had secured Roosevelt's aid in blocking an anti-intermarriage bill which was introduced in the New York legislature in 1913 when Roosevelt was a young state senator, and the two men had occasionally cooperated in minor business ventures. In 1917 Roosevelt, who was then Assistant Secretary of the Navy, provided a personal recommendation for Spingarn's entry into officers' training camp. During the 1920's Spingarn sent Roosevelt copies of his poetry and contributed to the Georgia Warm Springs Foundation, with which Roosevelt was closely affiliated. Roosevelt's responses were always cordial and Spingarn was extended a personal invitation to visit Warm Springs.[9]

Nevertheless, both Spingarn and the NAACP approached the campaign of 1932 cautiously. Maintaining its historic nonpartisan policy, the Association decided to present resolutions on Negro rights to both major parties for incorporation into their respective platforms and to send to each presidential candidate a questionnaire designed to ascertain his stance on specific issues of importance to blacks. Spingarn urged that the resolutions be strong and uncompromising, for even if they were rejected by both parties, that would be preferable to "mild or vague" resolutions which might be acceptable to one or both of the parties.[10]

Spingarn's suggestions regarding the topics to be included in the questionnaire which was to be sent to each candidate, coupled with a policy statement on the Negro question which he drafted for Roosevelt in the fall of 1932, provided a broad outline of what was destined to be the Association's program under the New Deal. The candidates' views were solicited on the following seven points: (1) employment opportunities on national projects; (2) apportionment of federal funds for relief, education, etc.; (3) segregation of federal employees; (4) lynching and federal anti-lynching legislation; (5) voting privileges in national elections; (6) Jim-Crowism within any federal jurisdiction; (7) United States policy toward the predominantly black nations of Haiti and Liberia.[11]

Spingarn elaborated on these points in a policy statement on the Negro question which was designed for Roosevelt's issuance on the eve of the election. The statement pledged the future President to seek to ensure that the black American would have a chance to earn a living, develop to his highest potential, receive fair play in every walk of life, and have equal voting rights, an equal share of government appropriations for relief, education, and similar aspects of life. Roosevelt was asked to express his "abhorrence of the crime of lynching," and to promise to do everything in his power to "end this stain on our civilization." The statement emphasized American Negroes' concern about the plight of blacks in other nations, and pledged Roosevelt to view sympathetically the political aspirations of the people of Haiti and Liberia.[12]

Initially, however, the New Deal afforded blacks little more than hope. Black tenant farmers and sharecroppers were the first to lose their lands under the crop reduction program of the Agricultural Adjustment Administration. The National Recovery Administration codes initially worked to the Negro's detriment, since black workers often were forced to accept racial wage differentials or else risk displacement by white workers. Most of the jobs traditionally held by Negroes were exempted from the NRA codes and, even when the codes were applicable, their administration by local officials often made just complaint futile, especially in the South. The Tennessee Valley Authority readily accepted black unskilled labor but refused to admit Negroes to its training program. The Homestead Subsistence program proved equally discriminatory; blacks who applied for admission to the Arthurdale, West Virginia, colony were frankly told that it was reserved for native whites. Similarly, the Federal Housing Administration codes included restrictive covenants. Although organized labor made significant gains under the New Deal, black workers enjoyed few immediate benefits since the major unions restricted the admittance of Negroes.[13]

The minutes of the Committee on Administration and the

correspondence of the NAACP's principal officers, indicate that Walter White was afforded extensive leeway in working out the basic details and strategy of the organization's New Deal program. Constitutionally, the Board retained its supervisory powers over the Secretary, as did the Committee on Administration, which continued its regular, bimonthly meetings. But the Board and the Committee appear to have relied on the reports of the Secretary regarding the work which had been done and the tasks that lay ahead.[14]

Two major factors probably accounted for this diffusion of authority and responsibility. First, the Association's work in regard to New Deal programs became so varied and extensive that the salaried staff workers who were in direct and constant contact with day-to-day operations undoubtedly enjoyed a far better working knowledge of problems and procedures than the top-level, nonsalaried administrators. Indeed, it is an axiom of organizational development that diversification and extension of a polity's activities usually result in relinquishment of some decision-making to line officers, since it becomes increasingly difficult, if not impossible, for the top-level leadership to comprehend and administer firsthand the agency's sundry endeavors. Second, and more important, the basic tenets of the NAACP's New Deal program had received the approval of the top-level administrators as evidenced by the major points presented in Spingarn's questionnaire to political candidates and the statement he prepared for Roosevelt. Similarly, as was noted in the preceding chapter, ultimate control of the Association's monies, including the funds that financed the organization's New Deal program, remained firmly in the hands of the top-echelon leadership. Thus, there appears to be no basis for assuming that the top-level leadership relinquished critical decision-making to the Secretary during the Depression; rather, Walter White worked diligently to utilize available resources to fulfill such already agreed-upon goals; such is the function of effective management.[15]

The Association challenged discrimination under the New Deal with the basic response patterns it had utilized since its inception: agitation and protest, largely through the written and spoken word, together with legal redress whenever possible. Simply stated, the primary goal was the attainment of a proportionately equal share of the benefits accruing from the numerous federally sponsored programs for blacks. In pursuit of this goal, the NAACP launched the most impressive campaign of agitation and protest in its history. Even before Roosevelt was inaugurated, the Association had launched investigations of the Mississippi Flood Control project, the Hoover Dam project, and similar programs of the Hoover administration in an attempt to guard against discrimination in hiring, hours, and pay rates. By 1935 both the national office and the branches were hard at work lobbying against racial discrimination by the Public Works Administration, the Civilian Conservation Corps, the National Youth Administration, the National Recovery Administration, and the Social Security Administration. The branches were instructed to maintain a close watch on the local level for employment discrimination in both private and federally sponsored projects for construction and relief. Some of the branches, including those in Toledo and Baltimore, experimented successfully with "Don't Buy Where You Can't Work" campaigns, a bold, new direct-action tactic whereby businesses which refused to hire Negroes (but readily accepted them as customers) were boycotted.[16]

As notable as the Association's more overt agitation and protests was its sponsorship, in conjunction with other organizations, of in-depth, statistical studies of the condition of the Negro in virtually every sector of the New Deal program. This ambitious undertaking was initiated in the fall of 1933 by the Negro Industrial League, an organization based in Washington and headed by John P. Davis, a young black attorney who was later to be named executive secretary of the National Negro Congress, and by Dr. Robert C. Weaver, a young black Harvard graduate in economics. Weaver, the League's director of research, specialized in preparing briefs dealing with the effects of the various federal codes on black labor. Upon the young men's invitation, other organizations, including the NAACP, the Federal Council of Churches in Christ, the AME Zion Church, and some fifteen other groups, formed the Joint Committee on National Recovery in October 1933, with Davis as its executive secretary. Largely financed by the NAACP, the Joint Committee's investigations, together with the voluminous storehouse of statistical data it had amassed by 1935, provided an invaluable guide for the Association's scrutiny of New Deal legislation, and continues to serve as a major source for understanding the New Deal's impact on American blacks.[17]

At the same time, the Association devoted a considerable portion of its resources and energy toward efforts to secure federal anti-lynching legislation. It will be recalled that the NAACP, virtually from its inception, had adopted as a primary goal the eradication of lynching, initially having centered its strategy on attempts to induce municipal and state authorities to punish offenders, but around 1917 shifting the major thrust of its campaign toward the attainment of a federal anti-lynching statute. However, the defeat of the Dyer anti-lynching bill (1922) by a Southern filibuster in the Senate, coupled with the apathy, if not outright antipathy, of the Republican administrations of the 1920's, left the organization no alternative but to relegate the quest for a federal statute to an ancillary goal. The Association renewed the struggle for federal anti-lynching legislation after 1930 because of increased racial strife—some of which was directly attributable to the heightened job competition of the Depression—and because of the ascendancy of the potentially more friendly Roosevelt administration.[18]

Spingarn, who had taken a special interest in the anti-lynching campaign since the days of the New Abolition, devoted more personal attention to this aspect of the NAACP's New Deal program than to any other. He had not dispelled the belief that the conscience of the nation, including that of the majority of Southerners, could be aroused if the horror of lynching were but widely publicized, a view which was shared by Walter White. In 1933 the NAACP sponsored the Writers' League Against Lynching, composed of more than

fifty of the nation's most prominent authors—including
Spingarn, Sinclair Lewis, and Benjamin Stolberg—and designed to serve as a pressure group for mobilizing public
opinion. Amy Spingarn assumed the forefront in sponsoring
an anti-lynching art display, featuring works that depicted
vivid scenes from some of the nation's most brutal lynchings;
it was shown in major cities along the East Coast.[19]

But again Spingarn's faith proved unwarranted. When he
attempted to deliver a radio address on lynching in February
1934, the National Broadcasting Company censored all reference to the term lynching. "I knew the broadcasting com-
panies are pretty critical of speeches," an irate Spingarn
observed, "but I had no idea that any person nowadays would
want to strike out purely historical references to lynching,
which is a common enough American practice." Nor did the
Association's renewed quest for a federal anti-lynching statute
prove any more successful. In 1934 the organization sought to
mobilize public support for the Costigan-Wagner anti-
lynching bill, only to see the measure blocked in May 1935
by the filibuster of seven Southern senators. Greatly disillusioned, Spingarn wrote White, apologizing for his impatience and assuring the Secretary that "the people waiting
behind the lines are always more discouraged than those who
are in the thick of the fight." Next, the Association sought to
effect a slight shift in strategy by devising a bill that might be
less objectionable to Southern opponents. After consultation
with personal friends in the federal government, Spingarn
suggested that the desired legislation might be obtained in the
form of an amendment to the Lindbergh kidnaping law, or
that emphasis could perhaps be shifted to punishment of the
individual lyncher with no attempt to disparage the particular
county or state in which the crime had been committed.[20]
However, while this new strategy was still in the discussion
stage, the attention of the nation and the Association was
diverted to the Presidential election of 1936.

Although Franklin Roosevelt, during his first administration,
had done little more than his predecessors to secure a federal
anti-lynching statute, Spingarn was sufficiently satisfied with

the President's over-all performance to publicly endorse him as having done more for the Negro than any President since Abraham Lincoln. In casting about for a new coalition upon which to build political strength, Roosevelt became the first President in the twentieth century to view the black vote as a major component of a new political alignment. In addition, the President encompassed within his administration an unusually large number of officials who actively, often voluntarily, sought to end discrimination in the areas under their supervision. The most notable of these were Harold L. Ickes, Secretary of the Interior and former President of the NAACP's Chicago branch; Frances Perkins, Secretary of Labor; Harry Hopkins, relief administrator; and Clark Foreman, the administrator in charge of Negro affairs. At the same time, Eleanor Roosevelt openly championed fair play for American blacks, granting several interviews to Walter White and serving as an unofficial liaison between her husband and the NAACP.[21]

Unlike many old-line progressives who viewed with consternation, if not horror, the sweeping changes which the New Deal wrought in the American system, Spingarn chose to judge the Roosevelt administration almost solely in terms of its efforts on behalf of black uplift. In his public letter endorsing Roosevelt, Spingarn recalled his disillusionment with the Republican and Progressive parties, his subsequent decision that the Negro must make the fight for his rights independent of any party, and his twenty-year eclipse from active participation in politics following the demise of the Progressive party. Yet withdrawal from politics had entailed no real sacrifice, Spingarn insisted, "for the cause of the Negro and the NAACP was dearer to me than any office that I or anyone else might have held."[22]

But, the statement continued, the very reason that had led Spingarn not to endorse any candidate for twenty years now caused him to support Roosevelt. Because Roosevelt had no race prejudice of any kind, Spingarn said, he could be trusted to do what he could for the American Negro; it was part of his "deep humanity," which had led him to remember all "forgotten men" and to give the brightest ray of hope to America's poor and humble. He had caused the Democrats to do what the Republicans had not done since Reconstruction —attempt to give the American Negro a fair deal. He had appointed more Negroes to positions in government than all Republican administrations combined, "and not mere peanut politicians but the ablest leaders of the Negro race." Because of Roosevelt there were 4,000 more Negro farm owners than in Hoover's administration; thousands of black youths had been helped by the National Youth Administration; millions of black people had received relief benefits commensurate with those of whites; Howard University had received over $3 million. Roosevelt had spent more than $50 million for black housing, "much of it in the South where Republicans would never dare to do anything." All of this, Spingarn prophesied, was a mere inkling of what the President would do when given the additional prestige of serving a second term.[23]

Shattering the last vestiges of his long political silence, Spingarn made a number of speeches on Roosevelt's behalf on the eve of the election, in Philadelphia, Chicago, Detroit, Cleveland, Indianapolis, Toledo, and other major cities with sizable black populations.[24]

Spingarn viewed Roosevelt's overwhelming majority at the polls in 1936 as a double victory for the Negro. The black vote, of which the overwhelming proportion traditionally had swelled the totals of the Emancipator's party, had shifted decisively to the Democrats in 1936. Spingarn rejoiced because Roosevelt had succeeded in freeing the black man of his "traditional partisan shackles." In his telegram of congratulations, Spingarn subtly reminded the President that his victory had been due in part to the black vote and that he was expected to use the prestige accruing from his impressive showing to take a bold stand against lynching. He congratulated Roosevelt "most of all on the wonderful opportunity that awaits you to remove the darkest blot on American justice and democracy." [25]

In December 1937 Roosevelt repaid Spingarn's support by

granting him a personal interview for a discussion of Presidential support of anti-lynching legislation. Wily politician that he was, Roosevelt so thoroughly monopolized the interview with discussions of general subjects that Spingarn emerged from the meeting with no commitment on anti-lynching legislation, but thoroughly enamored by Roosevelt's dynamism. Earlier, Roosevelt had confided to his wife that he did not believe the Supreme Court would uphold a federal anti-lynching statute, but that state authorities must take the necessary actions to curtail lynching. Similarly, the President felt that the intervention of Northerners would merely antagonize the South.[26]

While in Washington to visit the President, Spingarn called on Senator Theodore Bilbo of Mississippi, one of the staunchest and most long-standing opponents of anti-lynching legislation. Bilbo told Spingarn that the unchecked lawlessness of Northern gangsters and racketeers provided the South's best argument against the anti-lynching bill. Whereupon Spingarn had White compile a statistical study of Southern violence and lawlessness, emphasizing the classic Southern feuds and the fact that Memphis, Tennessee, currently had the highest homicide rate of any city in the world. Although a summary of White's study was read into the Congressional Record, it brought no discernible results.[27]

In the final analysis, Congress' anxiety to consider pressing New Deal measures, the President's failure to enlist the full power of his office in the quest for anti-lynching legislation, and the omnipresent Southern filibuster resulted in the defeat of the Gavagan Anti-Lynching bill (1937) and the Wagner-Van Nuys bill (1938). Upon learning of the defeat of the latter, Spingarn conceded that it was futile to renew the struggle for federal anti-lynching legislation. Although discussion of a federal statute occurred at almost every NAACP Annual Conference well into the 1940's, the quest for a federal law, as a primary goal, ended in 1938.[28]

Yet the Association's campaign against lynching, with all of its setbacks, provides a significant commentary on large-scale pressure-group activities. Technically a thirty-year campaign had failed, for the organization did not secure a concrete ban against lynching. On the other hand, there was both a proportionate and a real decline in the number of lynchings each decade after the organization launched its agitation in 1911, until by the 1960's lynchings had become rare occurrences. Whether lynchings would have undergone a similar decrease without the NAACP's thirty-year campaign of propaganda, publicity, and agitation is a moot point; but it seems likely that the by-products of the organization's efforts were in the final analysis as momentous as its failures.

The NAACP's legal-redress activities, especially in regard to discrimination in education, rounded out its program during the 1930's. Aided by substantial financial grants from the American Fund for Public Service (Garland Fund), the Association broadened the attack on educational inequities which it had launched in the 1920's, centering the new strategy on attempts to make segregated education in the South so expensive that its adherents would be forced to capitulate. Through a series of lawsuits brought against the University of Maryland and other institutions, the NAACP Legal Committee sought to force Southern states to provide out-of-state scholarship aid for black students who were refused admission to state universities solely because of race. By the end of 1937 the Association's efforts had resulted in the passage of acts providing for out-of-state scholarship aid by five Southern states. At the same time, the organization lobbied successfully for an amendment to the Harrison-Black-Fletcher bill for federal aid to education, securing a clause specifically prohibiting the exclusion of black children in the South from equal benefits of federal grants to secondary education. In still another vein, a rash of lawsuits, which were largely handled by individual branches, resulted in several victories on the local level for equitable salaries for black teachers in the South who possessed the same experience and education as their more highly paid white counterparts.[29]

Displaying its usual expertise, the NAACP Legal Committee won three victories before the Supreme Court during the 1930's. Two, in 1935 and 1936, resulted in the freeing of blacks sentenced to death by Mississippi and Oklahoma courts on the grounds that they had not been granted a fair trial. In 1932, for a second time, the NAACP secured a ruling from the High Court prohibiting the exclusion of blacks from the Democratic primaries. However, the Association suffered a temporary setback in its struggle against the white primaries when, in 1935, in a case with which the NAACP was not affiliated, the Supreme Court reversed its earlier decisions and ruled that the primaries were private organizations and therefore entitled to select participants. But the Association succeeded in having this decision reversed in a case brought before the High Court in 1944, which marked the end of the white primaries.[30]

BUT TIME MAKES ANCIENT GOOD UNCOUTH

Even as the Association began its impressive program under the New Deal, an ever-mounting chorus of voices proclaimed that it was offering too little too late. Du Bois was one of the earliest and easily the most vociferous of the organization's critics. In a speech entitled "What Is Wrong with the NAACP?" delivered in May 1932 before the NAACP Annual Conference, Du Bois declared that "the success of our program has been a gradual success. We have gradually progressed in nearly all of the lines in which we have been working. . . . But at the same time there are difficulties that come from a gradual widening of these principles so that more and more we are faced with the necessity for a positive program." [31]

There was much truth in Du Bois' words. Despite the expenditure of substantial amounts of time and money, the Association had failed in its attempts to obtain federal anti-lynching legislation. The organization had expended considerable time and energy throughout the 1920's in an attempt to open the American Federation of Labor to black workers, but it had not succeeded in doing so by the onset of the Depression in 1929. By 1932 the NAACP had won signifi-

cant, and even monumental, victories in the realm of voting
rights, but by no stretch of the imagination could it claim
total success in the battle against black disfranchisement.
Similarly, the Association had scored notable victories against
discrimination in education, but here, too, its greatest triumph, the celebrated 1954 school desegregation ruling of the
Supreme Court, was more than two decades distant. In short,
the dilemma of which Du Bois spoke derived not from the invalidity of the objective of integration which the Association
espoused; rather, it derived from the limited progress which
the organization had made by 1930 toward realizing the objective.

It is important to note that Du Bois emphasized the necessity for a "positive program" and not merely an economic
program. As Spingarn was to proudly boast, the Association
had never lacked an economic program *per se*, although traditionally the organization's efforts on behalf of black economic
uplift had constituted an auxiliary goal in relationship to its
primary goal of attaining full civil and political rights of
black Americans. During the post-World War I era it had
sought to have black workers admitted to membership in the
AF of L, had helped to unionize black railroad workers, and,
under the New Deal, had begun attempts to prevent discrimination in hiring and wages. But at best this ancillary economic program was *defensive* in terms of tactical orientation
as, indeed, the NAACP's historic tactics always had been
largely defensive. The Association waited for a law to be
broken or for cases of apparent discrimination, then it moved
to uphold the law or to effect a judicial ruling against discrimination. In short, the NAACP *responded* to stimuli of external
origin. Du Bois' projection of a "positive program" called upon
the organization to create the stimuli rather than the response;
to map out a program of black advancement which could be
carried forward in an offensive stance, regardless of changes in
the larger society. Whether to accept Du Bois' view and, if so,
how to implement it were questions that would engage the
NAACP's attention for the succeeding three years.

Nor was Du Bois the only official within the administrative hierarchy to criticize the organization's historic program and tactics. As early as 1930 Robert W. Bagnall, the Director of Branches, had privately expressed the opinion that "the time has come for the Association not to stand aside because of the existence of some other organizations, limiting its program to the matter of civil rights." Disturbed by the mounting black unemployment fostered by the Depression, Bagnall urged the organization to undertake a national black employment campaign, justifying this unprecedented modification of the Association's role under the guise of seeking to combat employment discrimination. By the summer of 1932 the heresy had spread to the Board of Directors. Dr. Louis T. Wright, a member of the Board since 1928 and New York's first black police surgeon, warned his colleagues that the NAACP was losing ground with the masses because "the work lacks inspiration"; more specifically, that it was not attracting and holding the interest of young people. Wright charged that even the Association's impressive legal victories were not receiving adequate publicity, partially because of the ineptitude of the branches.[32]

In still another vein, Roy Wilkins, the Assistant Secretary, suggested that the Association could garner much more financial support from the black masses if it would expand its legal program to undertake the defense of any black man who needed legal assistance, rather than confining its cases to those that could provide an "abstract" victory for all blacks. In the final analysis, concluded Wilkins, the NAACP's legal work would be judged on the basis of "whether or not it actually can come down to their [Negroes'] town and do something to make the law there give them a fair deal." Meanwhile, at Howard University, Abram Harris, a young black professor of economics, was advocating the unity of white and black labor against the capitalist class as the quickest means to black advancement.[33] In 1932 Harris was still only peripherally involved with the NAACP, but he was soon to become one of its most vociferous Board members.

Thus by 1933 there was widespread sentiment within the NAACP that an attempt must be made to expand the organization's historic program, that it might more nearly encompass the black masses, and to upgrade the effectiveness of the program. No one, however, seemed quite sure how this could best be achieved. By April 1932 White and Bagnall were privately discussing the possibility of a program of black consumer cooperatives, an idea whose chief exponent was George Schuyler, a young black author and economist. Anxious not to give the appearance of competing with the Urban League and seeking to guard against the League's usurpation of the Association's plans, White warned Bagnall that the utmost secrecy must be maintained in discussing any program, "especially in view of the Urban League and other groups . . ." In fact, Edwin Embree, one of the whites who made substantial financial contributions to the League, suggested to White that a merger of the Association and the League would be desirable since it would eliminate competition for financial resources between the two organizations. Undoubtedly because of the prodding of whites who exerted considerable influence financially, the Urban League took a step toward uniting with the NAACP in 1933, extending an invitation to Spingarn to become a member of the League's national Advisory Board. Spingarn flatly refused the invitation, and there is no indication that the NAACP hierarchy seriously considered merging with the League. At the same time, White and Spingarn had been discussing plans for drawing more young people into the Association's work as a means of revitalizing the organization. Meanwhile, a disgruntled Du Bois refused to have anything to do with the 1933 Annual Conference on the grounds that his suggestions regarding the adoption of positive activities had been ignored by the NAACP for more than a decade.[34]

Finally, communism's potential appeal to the black masses was the major external pressure on the Association to modify its program during the early 1930's, although recent research indicates that the movement attracted only a tiny proportion of the black population during the Depression. During the first half of the 1930's, the Communists' tactics focused on denunciation of the black middle class and "bourgeois" organizations like the NAACP for their alleged alliance with white capitalists against the black masses. The Communist organ, *The New Masses*, singled out Du Bois for special condemnation, and as late as 1935 the same periodical accused Spingarn of dominating the NAACP, while Walter White and the other black officers were depicted as underlings who were merely executing his bidding. Du Bois shunned the Communists during the 1920's and 1930's because he believed the white proletariat to be as prejudiced as non-Communist whites against blacks. As early as 1930 Spingarn had warned Walter White that "now is the time to bring home the fact that we are a safer bet for the South than the Communists." [35] As will soon become apparent, Spingarn viewed the Communists as major rivals for the allegiance of the black masses.

Despite mounting pressures for modification of the Association's historic program and the overt willingness which Spingarn was to display toward effecting a stronger economic program for the NAACP, a deep and unbridgeable gulf separated him from men of the ideological bent of Abram Harris and Du Bois. Simply stated, the fervent cravings of his colleagues for an economic program could never fully capture Spingarn's imagination; he was firmly convinced that the major problems confronting the world and the Negro were political and not economic in orientation. In a series of lectures delivered in early 1931, at New York's New School for Social Research, Spingarn summarized his philosophy:

> . . . I think that though the whole world is talking of nothing but economics and the most popular theory of today is that the old political methods must be dropped and we must adopt economic methods, I shall attempt to show you . . . that all our problems are rather political than economic and that even in Russia not an economic but a great political experiment is being carried on of which the economic is merely one of the many materials. And I am inclined to believe although this seems absolutely opposed to the whole current of our thought that there is going to be a revival of the concept of political

idealism; that is, the concept that politics, the government of men, is the central problem of practical life.[36]

At the same time, Spingarn rejected economic determinism on the grounds that there were no "causes" in history. If one were told that a certain act was the cause of a war, he explained, then one must ask what caused the act, and on and on *ad infinitum.* The only truth which one could grasp centered in the issues involved in the phenomenon at hand and its ramifications for the future. Nor could there be any set interpretation or philosophy of history, insisted Spingarn, for man's will was the guiding force in all history, and to adopt a hard and fast philosophy or interpretation would circumscribe the breadth and unpredictability of man's will.[37]

Spingarn interpreted even communism within a political rather than an economic framework. The production and distribution of wealth under any system was only a part of the larger political process, he argued; whatever the economic system, there would always arise the question of who should govern and execute the economic program. The only new feature of the Russian experiment was the furnishing of capital by the state rather than the individual. Thus, Russia was currently conducting one of the world's greatest political experiments, Spingarn contended.[38]

American blacks were issued a special warning not to view communism as the harbinger of a utopian society in which all men would be equal. Rather, the masses must do the bidding of a small minority, and if communism ever prevailed in the United States, the minority in control would be "the Georgia crackers and labor leaders who hate Negroes, and who say, like the Russians, you can have equality if you are like us—and like us would mean being white." Whatever the political system, Spingarn concluded, there would always be a need for an organization like the NAACP, for rights could not be attained by sitting back passively.[39]

Spingarn's interpretation of the Senate's rejection in 1930 of Judge John J. Parker, whom President Hoover nominated

as a justice of the Supreme Court, demonstrated how emphatically he emphasized the political nature of the problems
confronting blacks. Parker, a North Carolinian, had been
quoted ten years earlier as saying that the Negro's participation in politics was "a source of evil and danger." Similarly,
the judge had alienated organized labor by upholding the use
of injunctions to prevent union organizers from enlisting
workers who had signed "yellow-dog" contracts. Through
the combined and sustained propaganda and publicity efforts
of the NAACP and the American Federation of Labor, not
only was Parker rejected by the Senate but the Association,
working through its branches, marshaled sufficient black
votes and public sentiment to defeat the re-election bids of
two senators who had strongly backed Parker. It was the
most impressive demonstration yet witnessed of black Americans' united political strength.[40]

Commenting on the victory in an address delivered at the
NAACP annual mass meeting in January 1931, Spingarn insisted that "it is a mistake to think that plutocracy is the
chief danger of American democracy"; rather, the major danger was "caste, a far more insidious enemy and a far more un-
shakable master than money, which to a certain extent is
within the reach of all men." The nation currently was engaged in a "neck and neck race between Indian caste and our
historic democracy," he charged, and the Negro's defeat of
Parker had demonstrated that the black man, for evil or
good, had taken a stand against caste and in favor of integration into "the complete mass of American democracy." [41]

Thus, Spingarn responded harshly to those who would have
the Association abandon its historic primary goal of attaining
the Negro's civil and political equality. Addressing the 1930
NAACP Annual Conference, he issued the following warning:

> There are some who believe that the hope of the South-
> ern Negro lies in allying himself with the poor whites
> against the wealthy white classes of the South; there are
> others who think that the Negro race as a whole should
> make common cause with the white liberal and the

white radical. I bring a warning against this false hope
and shallow doctrine.[42]

In phrases which attested to his belief in rugged individual-
ism, Spingarn maintained that the black race would never fit
into any single class; rather, it would contain rich and poor,
liberals and conservatives, men of inferior ability and men of
superior ability. The Negro merely wanted an equal chance
to share in American democracy and an equal opportunity "to
share in that aristocracy of ability and leadership which
every democracy must build up."[43] Spingarn was reaffirming
his belief that the existing American system was worth sharing in; waiting in the wings were others, like Abram Harris,
who questioned the basic nature of that system. Never could
the twain meet.

Yet even as Spingarn so ardently defended his belief in the
viability of noneconomic liberalism and the validity of the
Association's primary goal of equal citizenship rights for
blacks, he was obliged to admit that the outlook for a solution
to the race problem was growing dimmer, not brighter. He
had been expounding the doctrine of racial equality to both
whites and blacks for more than twenty years. He had never
seriously wavered in his belief that appeals to the traditional
American principles of justice and fair play would topple the
walls of prejudice. In 1913 he had optimistically prophesied
that the black man would enjoy equality "in this generation."
But by 1932 the confidence of an earlier day had bowed to
reality and Spingarn publicly admitted that racial equality in
America was still no more than a dream shared by a handful
of people. In 1932 he confided to Herbert Seligmann, the
NAACP Director of Publicity, that a speech on racial equality
that he, Spingarn, was preparing largely represented an appeal to "white idealism" more than to black aspirations
"which after all can hardly stir white people." He pon-
dered whether whites, in the midst of the Depression, would
even listen to an appeal for racial equality. But, asked
Spingarn rhetorically, "is it not worth trying if only because
it does not merely repeat the popular talk about economics,

proletariat, and international color problems?"[44] At the same time, however, Du Bois and other blacks were wondering how long unsuccessful appeals to white idealism could be expected to hold the allegiance of the black masses.

A leader who is truly adept in the execution of his role realizes that, regardless of his personal beliefs, he cannot refuse to respond to appreciable external or intraorganizational pressures for redefinition of the polity's purpose or role. To remain static in the wake of such pressures would entail risking a decrease in membership, estrangement of the larger community, and a concomitant decline in the organization's stability. Confronted with this dilemma, Spingarn displayed one of his strongest attributes as an institutional leader: a keen sensitivity to shifting currents of thought and, more important, a willingness to explore new programs, even those that were diametrically opposed to his personal inclinations.

Undoubtedly it was Spingarn's increasing awareness of the limited success which thus far had attended the struggle for racial equality, coupled with the mounting pressures for reappraisal of the Association's historic program, which occasioned a slightly more radical tinge in his rhetoric, beginning in late 1932. His defense of the Association's historic program of equal citizenship rights through protest, agitation, and legal redress remained as staunch as ever; but those who listened carefully to his pronouncements could perceive an increased receptiveness to the doctrines of change. Addressing the NAACP annual mass meeting of 1932, Spingarn defended the American system as superior to those of Asia, Russia, and Africa for the attainment of minority rights. But in tones reminiscent of the fiery New Abolitionism of an earlier day, he added:

> I say we have fought for these rights [of the Negro] under the American system, but I want to say that this Association does not intend to defend any system. It is solely for the purpose of defending colored people in their rights. And though we in our Association represent

every shade of political and economic and social opinion,
if the American system will not give those rights we are
willing to try any other system that will give those
rights. . . .[45]

This same ambivalence of Spingarn's—holding to the old
doctrine while reaching out to grasp new ones—was apparent
in "Racial Equality," a speech delivered before the NAACP Annual Conference of 1932 and later widely distributed as a
pamphlet of the same title. He reaffirmed his long-held belief
that "the Negro cannot gain his rightful place in the sun of
American life until he has won the battle for Racial Equality,"
but he hastened to assure his listeners that the NAACP was
aware of the pressing economic problems of the day and
would develop a new economic program.[46]

In early 1932 Spingarn took the first step toward an extensive reappraisal of the NAACP's historic purpose and role,
the first since the organization's inception in 1909. In a confidential statement to the Committee on Administration, he
wrote:

> When we started in 1910 and for a considerable number
> of years thereafter we had all the young colored intellec-
> tuals with us; now we have few or none with us. Our
> programme needs reconsidering, revamping; our affili-
> ations may need realigning. Has the time come for a new
> Amenia Conference? [47]

At the April 1932 Board Meeting, the Directors authorized
Spingarn (in his capacity as Board Chairman) to appoint a
committee to formulate a new economic program for the
NAACP. However, at the May 1932 Board Meeting, Spingarn
again urged that an Amenia Conference be convened to supplement the efforts of the Board's committee.[48]

Thus, Spingarn gradually committed himself and the Association to at least a modicum of change toward a new economic orientation. Yet it was apparent that many underlying
problems threatened his success. He was a member of an
older generation—fifty-seven years old in 1932—yet he must

internalize and implement the aspirations of a younger and relatively more militant generation. He was a white liberal steeped in the tradition of noneconomic liberalism, yet he must speak to the needs of blacks, many of whom had discarded that brand of liberalism as obsolete. He was the white president of a black organization during a period when black Americans increasingly were perceiving and seeking control of their destiny and their institutions. In short, Spingarn was to become entrapped in a game of catch-up rather than innovation, in a ceaseless effort to interpret blacks' aspirations and then to translate them into a reality that would not compromise his own principles. Like the frenzied Alice in Wonderland, Spingarn often would be obliged to run twice as fast just to stay in the same place.

Spingarn's persistent call for a second Amenia Conference was the most obvious symptom of the sense of urgency which the forces of change engendered within him. He suggested that the second Conference, like the first Amenia Conference of 1916, be held at Troutbeck, in the summer of 1932. However, unlike the 1916 meeting, which largely had attracted older leaders of the race and which had sought to effect a consensus in support of the Association's traditional purpose and role, the second Conference was to be convened for the express purpose of reappraising and even criticizing the very basis of the consensus which had derived from the 1916 gathering.[49]

Spingarn exerted considerable effort to ensure that the Conference would not be a farce; that the conferees would be untrammeled in their discussions and criticisms, regardless of how favorable or unfavorable their conclusions might be. Only the most promising young blacks of the day were to be invited—"younger men who have finished their training and begun their careers and yet are still thinking"—and Spingarn strongly urged that members of the Board of Directors and officials of the Association "including myself would drop in almost as spectators and not too long or too often." In an attempt to ensure that the Conference would largely reflect the aspirations of blacks, Spingarn insisted that "no white people should be included [as participants]." [50] For the Abolitionist the game of catch-up had begun in earnest.

Nevertheless, the initial attempt to convene a second Amenia Conference ended in failure. Spingarn was willing to host the gathering, bear the expenses, and have the invitations dispatched under his letterhead but, with his usual disdain for routine and details, he insisted that "someone else" must assume the many responsibilities involved in convening such a meeting. He warned that the Conference would entail much work and expense and urged that the NAACP office staff not undertake the project unless they were "enthusiastic" about it and would begin to master the details immediately. Although Walter White assured Spingarn that the Conference would "mean so much to the Association," a general passing of the buck ensued among members of the office staff. Roy Wilkins complained to White that everybody in the office had departed for summer vacations without having made any Conference preparations and that he, Wilkins, did not "feel equal to the responsibility of proceeding with plans on my own initiative." Apparently White also planned to take his vacation before plans for the Conference were completed, for Wilkins suggested that the project might be postponed, if not altogether abandoned, until "after you [White] return August 1." Du Bois expressed surprise when, in mid-July, he learned that invitations to the meeting had not been mailed, and he, too, observed that it was probably too late to convene an August Conference unless the invitations were dispatched within the next two days (by July 15). [51]

Shortly afterward the NAACP executives, in consultation with Spingarn, decided to postpone the Amenia Conference until the summer of 1933. The official explanation that was issued to the public blamed the postponement on the Depression and "other reasons" and the need for more time to work out the details of the meeting. [52]

In December 1932, less than five months after the abortive attempt to convene a second Amenia Conference, Spingarn broached to a few intimate friends the possibility of his resignation from the NAACP presidency. He confidentially inquired "whether now is the time to make a member of the colored race head of the NAACP," insisting that "it would serve as a most significant symbol of progress, a milestone in the history of the race." [53] Exactly what prompted his decision is not clear, but it is likely that the seeming lack of cooperation of the office staff in planning the Amenia Conference, general despondency over the Depression, and, perhaps, doubts as to the white leadership's continuing effectiveness in the wake of increasing black militancy weighed heavily upon his mind. Spingarn's emphasis upon the desirability of a black successor betrayed his awareness and sensitivity regarding the issue of balancing white and black control of the organization.

Spingarn was dissuaded from resigning by "colored friends" who were "unanimously and vehemently" opposed to the idea, despite his insistence that he would continue his labors for the Association regardless of who was selected as his successor. Du Bois especially urged Spingarn to reconsider his decision to resign, insisting that the current period of stress, retrenchment, and criticism was the wrong time (from the standpoint of public opinion) for the NAACP to make a change of presidents. Significantly, however, Du Bois agreed with his white friend that the time was indeed ripe for a Negro head of the Association and, in addition to submitting the names of several potential black candidates, he observed that it would be a fine gesture for Spingarn to step aside when prosperity returned and there was a reasonable excuse for doing so.[54]

Yet even as Spingarn entertained thoughts of resigning, he continued to urge with renewed vigor the convening of a second Amenia Conference. Throughout December 1932, he contacted the Association's officials, inquiring whether a Conference was desirable and urging that preparations begin as early as possible. His persistence, coupled with the general tone of his letters, denoted an air of urgency.[55]

But it soon became apparent that there was no more enthusiasm within the NAACP administrative hierarchy for this second attempt at a second Amenia Conference than there had been for Spingarn's proposed 1932 meeting. "Some member, or members" of the Board of Directors told Spingarn that Walter White was not "particularly keen" about the project, an accusation that Spingarn initially believed, but the truth of which White emphatically denied. Rather, the Secretary blamed any seeming hesitation on his part on his preoccupation with numerous routine office tasks. Similarly, the Board of Directors displayed a singular dearth of enthusiasm for the Conference; the months of January and February 1933 passed without the Directors' official endorsement of a summer meeting.[56]

Indeed, the NAACP Board of Directors increasingly was becoming a factor to be reckoned with in regard to the swirling currents of unrest which seemingly surrounded the Association on every side. As Du Bois aptly and disapprovingly observed, even the black Board members were largely middle-class individuals who, fully as much as their white counterparts, were firmly convinced that the black man's attainment of full civil and political rights—the historic primary goal of the Association—must take precedence over any program of black economic uplift.[57] In short, like Spingarn, the majority of both the black and white NAACP Board members were noneconomic liberals. As will be discussed in a later chapter of this study, Isadore Martin, a Philadelphia real estate agent who amassed the best attendance record of any black Board member during the period 1926–1932, preferred to see the Association pass out of existence rather than substantially alter its historic role. Martin's adamancy was equaled by that of Mary White Ovington, who consistently refused even to discuss the possibility of altering the NAACP's historic purpose and role. More important, new and often younger blacks who served on the Board or the office staff during the 1930's—including Walter White, Roy Wilkins, and Louis T. Wright—usually proved as adamant as their older colleagues in upholding the Association's traditional historic program.[58] Undoubtedly they were largely convinced of the validity of the organization's historic program and, therefore, were not particularly enthusiastic about the convening of a

Conference that might, and perhaps could even be expected to, criticize the organization's program.

In essence, the NAACP had institutionalized in the truest sense of the term, including the hardening of goals and values that so often attends institutionalization. In the midst of demands for change during the 1930's, its personnel sought not merely the polity's survival; rather, they attempted the virtually impossible feat of ensuring the organization's survival without altering appreciably its historic values. Such rigidity boded ill for the future.

Upon discovering that he was making little or no headway toward garnering support for the convening of an Amenia Conference, Spingarn resigned from the NAACP presidency and Board chairmanship in March 1933. It is impossible to determine whether his resignation was designed to galvanize the Board to action on the convening of an Amenia Conference, or whether he sincerely intended to relinquish permanently his posts in the organization. The former motive is well within the realm of possibility, for the interpersonal relationships within the administrative hierarchy had grown so strong that the mere act of submitting one's resignation had become virtually a formalized means of inducing the Board to assume a solicitous stance. It will be recalled that throughout the organization's history Villard, Spingarn, and Du Bois not infrequently had (usually with success) employed the threat of resignation as a means of bringing the Board to heel.[59]

In his official letter of resignation, Spingarn offered no explanation other than he no longer felt able to continue in his current posts. He urged the Board to begin an immediate search for his successor, insisting that "under no circumstances" would he accept re-election at the expiration of his current terms (December 1933). But Spingarn confided his true feelings to Mary White Ovington. He insisted that he simply had lost interest in the Association as it was currently being run. He was dissatisfied with the "spirit" that prevailed in the organization, maintaining that "I do not feel like allowing my name to be used to represent that spirit." In the beginning the Associations had had a program which was "thrilling" and "revolutionary" for its day; a program which had provided at least a little hope of solving the "whole problem." "Now we have only [legal] cases, no programme, and no hope," Spingarn lamented. He explained that if he were a lawyer like his brother Arthur, he undoubtedly would find something interesting and difficult in every legal case and, therefore, would not miss the "cement" of a program. As it was, he was not interested in a succession of legal cases.[60]

Spingarn charged that every effort he had made to give new hope to the Association's program had "been ignored or thwarted by the Secretary or by the Board," obviously with reference to the rumor of White's not being "keen" on the Amenia Conference idea and the Board's delay in endorsing the meeting. Spingarn hastened to add that he was not criticizing anyone except himself. If an overwhelming segment of the Board or the membership "sympathized with my attitude," he confided, he could view the whole situation in a different light. Finally, he reminded Miss Ovington that the reason why so many of the Association's branches were "moribund" was because they had emphasized dramatic cases rather than programs; they had viewed a program as if it were "an academic thesis instead of an instrument of hope and enthusiasm!" [61]

In a confidential letter to his friend James Weldon Johnson, Spingarn further elaborated his reasons for resigning. He had been "dissatisfied" for "some time" with the way in which the NAACP was being run. He viewed the attempt of the Board and the "Staff" to thwart his proposal for a new program as a personal affront, a manifestation of their lack of confidence in him. Under the circumstances, concluded Spingarn, "I think someone who has the undivided confidence of the Board or the membership should take my place as President and Chairman." But he also assured Johnson that he would never desert the Association and the cause for which it stood, "not until I am dead." [62] Thus, as had been the case on two previous occasions, in 1915 and in 1918, Spingarn resigned when he could not induce the Board to endorse a course of action that he strongly favored.

On the other hand, many of Spingarn's observations about the Association's program were valid. When the organization was founded in 1909, its primary goal of attaining the black man's full civil rights and effecting his total integration into the larger society was indeed revolutionary. In addition, the crusading zeal that had emanated from the fiery New Abolition campaigns had fortified the more routine phases of the program with an intangible idealism—a "cement" as Spingarn would term it—which perhaps had been capable of capturing men's imaginations and maybe even their hearts. But after about 1919, as the process of institutionalization set in, the Association became the victim of what administrative specialists term "the retreat to technology." [63] The purpose and role which the organization had adopted in 1909 underwent no appreciable reappraisal or updating. The hiring of a cadre of full-time, professional line officers during the post-World War I period made for increased efficiency, but there was also an almost undefinable, but no less real, decline in the fervor and crusading zeal which had characterized the New Abolition of a day not long past. More important, the Association began to develop set patterns of tactical response to problems that confronted it: when a lynching occurred, an investigator was dispatched and the usual protest and publicity ensued; when discrimination occurred in violation of the law, the Legal Department swung into action; where congressional legislation was concerned, lobbying and letters of protest to congressmen were the prescribed responses. In essence, by the end of the 1920's the purpose, role, tactics, and responses of the NAACP had become so well defined that the organization could operate from day to day virtually without guidance from the top-level leadership. The problem of executing routine duties almost drove James Weldon Johnson, the Executive Secretary during the 1920's, to a nervous breakdown; but the fundamental questions of what shall we *do* and what shall *be*—questions with which any polity which is constantly evolving must deal—had been answered long in advance.

There was also some truth in Spingarn's charge that the Association's program had become centered in a "succession of [legal] cases." While major agitation and protest campaigns against lynching, discrimination, and the exclusion of blacks from labor unions met with limited success or outright failure, the Legal Department during the 1920's and 1930's amassed victory after victory before the Supreme Court in addition to less spectacular victories in the lower courts. Indeed, it is not an exaggeration to say that the NAACP's national prestige derived largely from the phenomenal successes of the legal-redress phase of its work. Yet for a man like Spingarn, to whom physical activity and the idealism of the cause at hand were so important, there could be little solace in the intricate and detailed paper work of the attorney's trade.

Walter White professed to be utterly "stunned" by Spingarn's resignation, pondering whether the President's dissatisfaction with the way in which the office was being run accounted for his action. He insisted that the "affection and gratitude" with which American blacks regarded Spingarn made it impossible for his resignation not to be detrimental to the Association during the current critical period, and charged that the NAACP's enemies would attribute the resignation to "all manner of motives." White concluded that there could be no worse time for Spingarn to resign.[64]

White followed up this initial letter to Spingarn with a series of behind-the-scenes moves, all aimed at having the resignation retracted. He asked James Weldon Johnson to write Spingarn, and he urged Johnson to attend the April Board Meeting because "a word from you in person to Joel would have, I know, tremendous effect." In the meantime, White arranged a conference with Spingarn; their meeting consumed the "entire afternoon." Apparently Spingarn gave White a somewhat different version of his reasons for resigning than he had given Johnson and Ovington, for White concluded from the meeting that Spingarn's resignation was due to his personal discouragement and his doubt that "any problem, national, world, racial, financial or otherwise, can be solved." However, at the end of the conference, Spingarn assured White that he did not wish to harm the Association; that he was not above changing his mind if he could be shown that he had made the wrong decision; that he was "open" to the conviction that he should continue as President and Board Chairman. Immediately after the conference, Spingarn sent White a follow-up note designed to "make my position clear." "Nothing short of an overwhelming expression of confidence and of desire to have me stay on the part of the Board or of the membership" would induce withdrawal of the resignation.[65]

The debate over Spingarn's resignation wore on through April, May, and early June. The Board appointed a committee chaired by James Weldon Johnson to consult with Spingarn, and each committee member wrote the President, requesting that he reconsider his decision. Still other appeals came from a biracial assortment of Board members and friends of Spingarn, all of whom expressed two conclusions: that Spingarn's courage, devotion, and idealism could not be replaced; that his resignation would render immeasurable harm to the Association. At the June Board Meeting, the Directors passed a resolution stating that it would be a "calamity" for the Association to lose its President "at this time"; that "certain factions" would spread rumors that the NAACP was on its "last legs"; that Spingarn had the total support of the Board, officers, members, and branches; that the NAACP's success during the current troubled period depended, in large measure, upon the ideals, experience, wise counsel, and executive ability of its President. The resolution concluded with an expression of the Board's "sincere wish" that Spingarn would rescind his resignation.[66]

After several weeks of deliberation, Spingarn concluded that "in view of the unanimous sentiment expressed that my resignation . . . would be a serious detriment to the Association," there was no alternative to retaining his posts. "It will be a great comfort to me to know that I have the confidence of the Board and the membership during this period," [67] he wrote.

If Spingarn's resignation was designed to galvanize the Board to action on the convening of a second Amenia Conference, he had accomplished his purpose. Shortly after receiving the resignation, the Directors authorized the convening of a second Amenia Conference to be held under the auspices of the Association, "provided however that the Association is involved in no expense in connection with the Conference." The Board ruled that the participants need not be in sympathy with the NAACP's program, and specified that the Conference was to have no formal connection with the Association.[68]

Because Spingarn was able to provide overnight accommodations at Troutbeck for only twenty-five to thirty persons, extreme care was exercised in ferreting out the most desirable conferees from among the numerous young blacks who were eligible to participate. Du Bois prepared a circular letter, which was sent to "persons all over the United States," requesting that they send in the names of individuals whom they knew or of whom they had heard and who they felt should participate in the meeting. It was explained that the typical conferee should be an independent thinker of strong, honest character, "not men who have just finished school, but rather those who have been out a few years, and yet who are not fixed in their ideas." The numerous names garnered from this nationwide appeal were then examined "with a fine tooth comb" by the Spingarn brothers, Roy Wilkins, and White, after which the four men agreed unanimously on twenty-seven persons. Du Bois, who had begun his teaching duties at Atlanta University, was sent the list of twenty-seven names, plus a second list of fourteen names, with the understanding that he would select eight conferees from the latter list.[69]

Spingarn's personal suggestions of potential conferees reveal much about the trend of his thinking. All the persons he listed—including Robert R. Moton, Booker T. Washington's successor as head of Tuskegee Institute; Mordecai Johnson, Howard University's president; and Robert Abbott, editor of the Chicago *Defender*—had been actively demanding full citizenship rights for blacks and could therefore be classified as progressive thinkers in regard to the Negro question.[70] On the other hand, none of the persons suggested by Spingarn was associated with the current economic "radicalism" of the day. Indeed, in comparison to men of the ideological bent of Harris and Du Bois, Spingarn's choices could be classified as spokesmen of conservative Negro thought whose ideological approach to civil rights approximated the noneconomic liberalism of the Association's traditional leadership. Exactly what criterion Spingarn used in making his selections is not clear. Perhaps he was seeking to ensure that moderate views were given expression at the Conference. Perhaps others had already suggested the names of whatever "radicals" he might have favored. Perhaps his selections betrayed a lingering dedication to his own and the Association's traditional approach to the Negro problem.

The thirty-three persons who were finally selected to attend the Conference represented a broad spectrum of thought and a diversity of backgrounds. Probably the most "radical," in terms of their critical attitude toward the Association's historic program and tactics, were Abram Harris and Du Bois. Since 1928 Harris had tenaciously sustained a crusade for the unity of white and black labor against the capitalist class as the surest means to black uplift; Du Bois had already begun to seriously embrace the idea of black voluntary segregation and self-help as the key to the race's uplift. A large number of the young conferees, many of whom were destined to attain national prominence in their respective fields, were professors at Howard University in the District of Columbia. In addition to Harris, the Howard contingent included Ralph Bunche, later to attain worldwide acclaim for his work in the field of international relations; Rayford Logan, destined to emerge as a nationally known historian; E. Franklin Frazier, who earned national recognition as a sociologist; and Charles Houston, later to become Dean of Howard's Law School and one of the Association's chief counsels. Included among the other participants were Elmer A. Carter, editor of the Urban League's official organ, *Opportunity;* Louis L. Redding, a Wilmington, Delaware, attorney and civil rights activist; and Harry W. Greene, Director of the School of Education, West Virginia State College. In addition to Du Bois, the Association was represented by Roy Wilkins and Walter White. Du Bois recalled in his autobiography that at least one Communist was numbered among the conferees.[71]

In the final analysis, the Conference participants were educated, middle-class (or potentially middle-class) individuals: all but one were college graduates; three held the degree of doctor of philosophy. Writing seven years after the Conference had been convened, Du Bois recalled that the participants, "old and young . . . felt that too much in the past we had been thinking of the exceptional folk, the Talented Tenth, the well-to-do; that we must now turn our attention toward the welfare and social uplift of the masses." [72] But in reality it was representatives of the "Talented Tenth" who convened at second Amenia.

According to a pre-Conference memorandum dispatched by Spingarn, the avowed purpose of the meeting was to ascertain the goals of the young, educated Negro in regard to occupation and income, racial organization, and interracial cooperation. The conferees were asked to think of these broad topics within the context of the current world depression and the race problems which existed in Africa, India, Germany, and the United States. Spingarn posed the question of whether it would be possible to "work out a practical series of next steps to which we could get the adherence and immediate cooperation of a majority of the young educated Negroes?" Obviously reflecting some personal concern regarding the future role of whites like himself in the civil rights struggle, Spingarn candidly asked the conferees, "What part in such a programme should white friends and sympathizers be asked to share?" [73] It is, perhaps, significant that not once in the memorandum were the black masses mentioned.

A tentative outline of the Conference program prepared by Du Bois called upon the participants to consider every facet of the race problem, especially the weaknesses and accomplishments of existing programs and potential new programs.

Listed for consideration were socialism, communism, voluntary and involuntary segregation, and dispersion in the sense of loss of black identity. Du Bois, with his long-standing interest in Pan Africanism and a world view of the race problem, requested that the conferees think in terms of the relationship of the American Negro to his counterpart in Africa, the West Indies, and South America and that they examine the American Negro's relationship to Asiatics as well as to the white race. The conferees were to devote special attention to current difficulties in the realms of employment possibilities, income and expenses, opportunities and hindrances in social work, teaching, business and trades, and religious work. Finally, the participants were urged to consider the problems associated with emigration, revolt, and revolution.[74]

The Conference's findings dealt a summary blow to both the historic tactics and program of the Association. Although the conferees courteously disclaimed any intention of disparaging the "older type of leadership," nevertheless, they concluded that in an era of shifting social, political, and economic values, there was need of a leadership which could integrate the Negro's peculiar problems within the larger national issues. There was the distinct implication that the current leadership could not accomplish this end.[75]

In phrases that must have pleased those of Abram Harris' bent, the conferees concluded that "the primary problem is economic." The entire system of private ownership and private profit, was open to serious question, for it had failed to equalize consumption and production. The Negro especially had been burdened with weak purchasing power due to low wages accruing from his traditionally inferior status in the labor market. The federal government (the New Deal) was seeking to effect a consumption-production balance through increased wages, shortened working hours, control of labor and commodity markets, and a general co-partnership between capital, labor, and government. But the findings concluded that if the Negro were not given equal consideration under this program, it could not succeed in effectively restoring economic stability.

The Amenia conferees blamed much of the Negro's dire economic plight on the historic failure of black labor to make common cause with its white counterpart. Not only had black labor been the most exploited sector of the labor force but both black leaders and black labor itself had failed to recognize the significance of this exploitation within the economic order. Consequently, no philosophy or technique designed to change the historic status of black labor had been developed; nor did it seem likely that current government programs would effect this change. On the contrary, there were indications that current programs would perpetuate the existing status of the Negro, resulting in low purchasing power which, in turn, would present a constant threat to the security and standards of the white worker. The conferees concluded that "the welfare of white and black labor are [sic] one and inseparable and that the existing agencies working among and for Negroes have conspicuously failed in facing a necessary alignment of black and white labor."

Yet the conferees warned that Negro labor's salvation could never be realized within the existing labor movement, which was based on craft autonomy and a separatism designed primarily to control wages and jobs for the minority of skilled white workers. Thus, a new movement was needed—one that would organize skilled and unskilled, whites and blacks. Unlike the traditional labor movement, the new movement must be both politically and economically oriented as a means of effecting necessary social legislation, including workmen's compensation, regulations of woman and child labor, and unemployment insurance. These social reforms might "go to the extent of change in the form of government itself."

The conferees considered three alternatives to the current system of government: fascism, communism, reformed democracy. Fascism was rejected summarily on the grounds that it would "crystallize the Negro's position at the bottom of the social structure." Communism was termed "impossible" without a major transformation in the "psychology and the attitude of white workers on the race question and a change in the Negro's conception of himself as a worker." Therefore, through a process of elimination, the conferees endorsed reformed democracy, with the implication that the changes being wrought by the New Deal represented the reform. But the participants warned that the rights of blacks could not be safeguarded by "paternalism in Government"; rather, that the Negro must be represented on all boards and field staffs of agencies seeking to control agriculture and industry.

Finally, the conferees called upon Negroes of all classes to unite on behalf of black uplift. It was conceded that the cooperation of whites was needed for the realization of the larger aims encompassed within the findings, but blacks were reminded that it was their responsibility to take the initative in developing and executing the program the conferees had proposed. Increased economic independence of blacks was indispensable; the black church, school, and similar agencies working on behalf of black uplift could help in drawing the race together, but the educated black must take the first step toward bridging the gulf between himself and the masses.

Although the day-to-day proceedings of the Conference were kept secret in the interest of free discussion, some additional insight as to what transpired can be gleaned from the correspondence and recollections of the participants. Louis L. Redding suggested that his fellow participants were not as radical as the findings would seem to indicate. Less than two weeks after the Conference, Redding wrote as follows:

> As the discussions progressed, it seemed that there was a recession from the notion of impending change in our order. It appeared that the conferees did not want a change, that they were much more interested in protecting their personal security as individuals in the existing order. This, of course, inhibited any real contemplation of the condition of the great Negro mass.[76]

Redding's observations would appear to be substantiated by those of Ralph J. Bunche. Writing seven years after the second Amenia Conference, Bunche observed:

On the whole this Conference had no great significance.
Certainly not the significance which Dr. Du Bois has attributed to the 1916 Conference at Amenia. Some features
of the Conference are worth noting, however. First of all,
there was a wide diversity of opinion and point of view
manifested by the young Negroes. . . . There was much
talk about leaders but a discouraging lack of any evidence of any clear thinking and courageous approach to
the Negro problem . . .[77]

According to Redding, four major ideas emerged from the
Conference, all predicated on the pre-eminence of the existing political and economic order in America. First, E. Franklin
Frazier advanced the idea of a spirit of black nationalism as
an inescapable necessity in light of the pressures exerted upon
the Negro. Second, Roy Wilkins, the chief exponent of the
"Negro bloc" idea, cited the need for a "fluid body of informed opinion" among blacks. Third, Charles H. Houston
favored Negroes' participation in all political parties, presumably in lieu of the formation of a black third party or the
race's alliance with one particular party. Fourth, Emmett E.
Dorsey stressed the idea that any economic program which
blacks embraced must be viewed as but a means to the
broader long-range goal of the Negro's full integration into
American society. Redding, too, concluded that "the broad
objective of the whole program, it seems to me, would be the
integration of Negroes fully into every sphere of American
life on a basis of absolute equality. . . ."[78] If, in fact, these
were among the major ideas expressed at the Conference, it is
not clear why they were not afforded more prominence in
the official Conference findings which were released to the
public.

Taken as a whole, the results of the Conference were not
wholly satisfactory to anyone. Spingarn was amenable to
the suggestion that black labor should become more closely
affiliated with the general labor movement (although he
displayed no inclination to make this the Association's primary
goal), but he was greatly disappointed because the conferees

had failed to provide a concrete plan for implementing their conclusions. Abram Harris retorted that it was the duty of the Association's administrators, and not of the conferees, to work out the details for implementing the new programs. At the same time, Mary White Ovington concluded, with almost a sigh of relief, that with the exception of a few Communist overtones, the conferees' conclusions did not conflict with the NAACP's historic program.[79]

But perhaps no one was more disappointed with the Amenia Conference than Du Bois! In exprsssing his disillusionment, he wrote:

> I was disappointed. I had hoped for such insistence upon the compelling importance of the economic factor that this would lead to a project for a planned program for using the racial segregation, which was at present inevitable, in order that the laboring masses might be able to have built beneath them a strong foundation for self-support and social uplift; and while this fundamental economic process was going on, we could, from a haven of economic security, continue even more effectively than ever to agitate for the utter erasure of the color line.[80]

Consequently, before any action could be taken toward implementing the findings of the Amenia Conference, Du Bois seized the attention of the Association and, indeed, of the entire black community with a program all his own. Whereas Abram Harris and the Amenia conferees had projected a program whose ultimate goal was integration of blacks, through an alliance with white labor, into the larger socio-economic system, Du Bois looked beyond to what he believed to be the greener pastures of black voluntary segregation. The Amenia conferees called upon the Association to alter its historic *role;* Du Bois called for the much more difficult feat of altering its historic *purpose.*

7

THE ABOLITIONIST AS TACTICIAN: ALL COHERENCE IS GONE

Du Bois' open advocacy of voluntary segregation, beginning in January 1934, raised what proved to be the complex issue of the Association's stand regarding recognition of the validity of segregation in certain "practical exigencies." Unable to accept Du Bois' chauvinism, yet unwilling to endorse the Board of Directors' adamant stand against recognition of segregation in any form, the Spingarn brothers pitted their strength against both the Board and Du Bois. At the same time, Du Bois had concluded that not only must the Association adopt a new economic program in keeping with changing times but that it must also revise its administrative structure so as to afford the masses a significant, if not the controlling, voice in the organization's administration. Spingarn's seeming unwillingness to effect these reforms, coupled with Du Bois' public attacks upon the officials of the Association for their failure to adopt his plan, placed an unprecedented strain on the two men's personal relationship and resulted in Du Bois' resignation from the NAACP.

THE NATURE OF SEGREGATION

Du Bois made the final plunge into open advocacy of voluntary segregation in a one-page editorial in the January 1934 issue of the *Crisis*.[1] Historically the black man's greatest gains had resulted from working by and for himself in his own institutions, contended the Editor; therefore there should be no objection to the black church, the black school, and similar agencies as long as they were provided with equal facilities and, for example in the case of black neighborhoods, whites were not barred from dwelling there. During the current depression, blacks should demand their fair share of federal relief appropriations but, at the same time, they should form their own agricultural communes. Du Bois made it explicitly clear that blacks must embrace segregation out of necessity rather than choice. "In the long run the greatest human development will come from the widest individual contact," he conceded, "but this is now difficult because of petty prejudice, deliberate and almost criminal propaganda and various survivals from prehistoric heathenism." [2] Nevertheless, the fact that the NAACP's historic primary goal was the total and immediate integration of blacks into the larger society insured that Du Bois' editorial would not go unchallenged.

Walter White was the first to take up the challenge. In an article intended for publication in the February *Crisis*, the Secretary argued that the acceptance of separateness by a marginal or exploited group inevitably would relegate that group to an inferior position in national and communal life. The Negro's willing acquiescence in enforced segregation would merely encourage more discrimination in the distribution of state and federal funds, although blacks would continue to be taxed as heavily as whites. The Negro and every other ethnic, racial, or religious group should be free to attend church, live, or socialize together, concluded White, but no group could afford to condone or accept enforced segregation. White sent Spingarn a copy of the article, presumably for his criticisms or suggestions.[3]

Spingarn "strongly" urged White to revise his article so as to incorporate a lengthy statement that Spingarn drafted. The subsequent importance of the statement warrants repetition in its entirety. It read as follows:

> Various interpretations have been placed upon Dr. Du Bois' editorial, a number of them erroneous and especially the one which interprets the editorial as a statement of the position of the NAACP. It may be stated definitely that the NAACP has from the date of its foundation been opposed to segregation in any form, without any reservations whatever. Dr. Du Bois' editorial is merely a personal expression on his part that the whole question of segregation should be examined and discussed anew with the idea that the NAACP may possibly wish to alter its program as the result of any new light brought out by this discussion. There can be no objection to frank and free discussion on any subject and *The Crisis* is the last place where censorship or restriction of freedom of speech should be attempted. I wish merely to call attention to the fact that the NAACP has never officially budged in its opposition to segregation and it is as strongly opposed to segregation as it ever was. Since Dr. Du Bois has expressed his personal opinion why this attitude might possibly have to be altered, I should like to give my personal opinion why I believe we should continue to maintain the same attitude that we have for nearly a quarter of a century, but I repeat that what I am about to say is merely my personal opinion just as Dr. Du Bois' editorial expressed his personal opinion.[4]

Thus, although Spingarn displayed not the slightest intention of embracing segregation, he was determined that White should not close the door to possible changes in the Association's program.

In two subsequent communications to White, one marked "confidential" and bearing the official title of Chairman of the Board, Spingarn elaborated the points he had drafted for inclusion in White's article. The Secretary was reminded that the Board of Directors "may reverse itself on any issue at any time, and cannot be committed by you or anyone else as to its future *programme*." The ideas expressed in White's reply to Du Bois had been advanced by the *Crisis* Editor thirty years earlier, Spingarn maintained, "and that is where you and I first heard of them." Spingarn assured White that he did not believe that the Board agreed with Du Bois' views, but he insisted that the Editor had a right to express his opinions if it were made clear that they were personal and not official.[5]

Turning to the question of voluntary segregation, Spingarn informed White that not only blacks but many ethnic groups, including certain Jewish factions, were embracing a mild form of separatism, that it was a modern trend. He recalled that the Amenia conferees had endorsed cultural nationalism as the most important goal of the Negro, and he assured White that this sentiment was shared by the majority of the black intelligentsia. Spingarn disclaimed any intention of having White hide his opinions, but warned the Secretary, ". . . you realize that hundreds of Negroes think you are really a white man whose natural desire is to associate with white men . . . and all I suggest is that your opposition to segregation must not seem to spring from a desire to associate with white people." This suggestion was made entirely out of "friendly regard," Spingarn assured his colleague.[6]

Spingarn also anticipated one of the major arguments which Du Bois was to utilize in future *Crisis* editorials: that the NAACP had never officially defined its position on segregation. When White suggested that the Board again define its attitude toward segregation and in "no wise change our attitude," Spingarn replied that "this creates a more difficult problem than you appear to think." The Board had authorized certain concrete steps to combat segregation, explained the Chairman of the Board, but it never had actually defined its position on the subject. The term segregation had become a shibboleth, used indiscriminately by "unthinking" people, but it would be impossible to attack segregation as an abstract concept without also attacking the Negro college, church, and similar institutions. Nor was the issue clarified by attempts merely to draw a distinction between voluntary and involuntary segregation, insisted Spingarn, for this was but another method used by "unintelligent" people to solve the dilemma, and it raised more questions than it solved. White was assured that any suggestion he offered for the Board's consideration would be welcome but that "no action of the Board at any given time can prevent a member or officer from agitating further in favor of a future change of policy." [7]

White was angered and disappointed by Spingarn's attitude. He retorted that had he wished to associate with white people, he would have passed as white long ago; friends and associates, especially the former, were selected on the basis of mutual points of interest. If the NAACP was not opposed to segregation, then he had misrepresented its policy for nearly twenty years and insisted, "I am frankly not interested in the Association unless that is its policy." This was not an ultimatum, explained White, it was merely an honest expression of opinion. Opposition to segregation was for the sake of future generations of both blacks and whites.[8]

Nevertheless, despite his curt remonstrance, White revised his article so as to incorporate, virtually verbatim, the statement Spingarn had drafted.[9]

What was rapidly becoming a mammoth debate assumed still broader dimensions when White submitted his article to Du Bois for publication in the *Crisis*. The Editor initially refused to accept the article on the grounds that no space was available in the February issue, but later refused publication on the grounds that White's article was "untrue and unfair." First, Du Bois felt that the article conveyed the impression that White's opposition to segregation represented the official position of the Association, and he curtly informed the Secretary, "You are not the Board of Directors and you have no business to speak for them." Second, Du Bois labeled as false the article's contention that the NAACP had never officially budged on segregation (a statement included at Spingarn's behest), reminding White that the NAACP had officially endorsed a segregated Negro officers' training camp in 1917.[10]

Thus, unwittingly, Du Bois was attacking White for statements that were, in part, Spingarn's. "It is rather ironical," Spingarn wrote White, "that the only passage in your article to which Dr. Du Bois objected was the passage I suggested your adding in order to make it clear that the opinions expressed both by you and by him were personal and not official!" [11]

The segregation debate wore on in succeeding issues of the *Crisis*. Du Bois pointed out (as Spingarn had anticipated) that the Association had never adopted an official stand on segregation and had never denied the "recurrent necesssity" for separate united action by Negroes for self-defense and self-development, although he conceded that separate action usually had been viewed as "a necessary evil involving often a recognition from within of the very color line which we are fighting without." But the Editor insisted that on occasion the NAACP had consciously fostered segregation citing as examples Spingarn's advocacy of a segregated Negro officers' training camp in 1917 and the Association's policy, dating from the 1920's, of encouraging bloc voting by blacks.[12]

Having been drawn into the public debate by Du Bois' reference to the segregated officers' training camp, Spingarn offered a point-by-point reply to his old friend and adversary in the March *Crisis*. The NAACP's belief in the basic wrongness of segregation superseded any written statement, wrote Spingarn: "I am thinking of a faith, a conviction, a state of mind, not an official pronouncement." Indirectly the Association had denounced segregation as early as 1911, for in its annual report of that year it had pledged to secure equality of opportunity *"everywhere,"* and equality of opportunity and segregation are incongruous concepts. Nor did Spingarn deny that on occasion the NAACP had accepted some forms of segregation, but he contended that such tacit acceptance in specific instances "does not affect our attitude toward segregation in general." Opposition to segregation as an evil must never cease; rather, one must deal with the question of "making concessions to practical exigencies." It was the age-old debate between Abolitionist and relativist, idealist and realist, agitator and statesman, doctrinaire and practical man. The question of when to condone the existence of segregation, even when recognizing it as a necessary evil, would be a most difficult one, warned Spingarn, but the question of segregation itself was neither trying nor new.[13]

At the same time, Spingarn considered whether the Association should, perhaps, reverse its historic attitude and embrace segregation as a positive good. If segregation were accepted as a positive good rather than a necessary evil, he speculated, it would raise the question of whether a young Negro would not find a Negro college more enjoyable, beneficial, and fulfilling than a white college. Spingarn explained that he was not offering solutions to these problems but merely attempting a clear and concise statement of the issues. He insisted it was imperative that the Association deal with three basic questions: (1) Should the Association cease viewing segregation as an evil, whether necessary or otherwise, and concede its possibilities of good? (2) If the Association chose to consider segregation as evil, should it oppose all forms of segregation, no matter how necessary or expedient, or should it, in special instances, recognize segregation as a necessary evil? If the latter alternative were chosen, when and how were the specific instances for accepting segregation to be selected? (3) If the NAACP were to concede that segregation was not an evil in itself but only in the way it was utilized, should segregation be embraced as a means to black cultural and social advancement, or should it be opposed in specific instances and, if so, when and how? "The second question is relatively a simple one to answer compared with the first and third," declared Spingarn, "but it would be tragic if we gave the wrong answer to any of them." [14]

The complexity of the issues which Du Bois and Spingarn had raised became even more evident when the Association's officers settled down to the task of actually defining and stating the organization's official attitude toward segregation. Walter White offered the following definition of segregation *per se:*

> Race segregation is the arbitrary and enforced setting apart on the basis of race and color, and the denial of the right to participate in public, semi-public, and quasi-public institutions and activities, whether such denial is by law or by custom.[15]

Voluntary association of blacks in churches, lodges, and social agencies was not to be considered a form of segregation. "I think we should definitely call that something else," insisted White. However, Joel and Arthur Spingarn, who believed that most black "voluntary" institutions were merely the by-products of enforced segregation, informed the Secretary that his definition of segregation was "not at all adequate." Arthur Spingarn suggested that White's statement be discussed at the next meeting of the Committee on Administration.[16]

Meanwhile Louis T. Wright had drafted a segregation resolution which declared that the Association was opposed both to race segregation—that is, arbitrary and forced separation based on race, color, or national origin—and the denial (because of race) of participation in public or quasi-public institutions and activities. The NAACP did not accept "any existing segregation or discrimination whether tacit, implied, or inferred," because to do so was in violation of the letter and spirit of the Fourteenth and Fifteenth amendments.[17] Thus, Wright's position was more extreme in its opposition to segregation than White's, for Wright inferred that voluntary separateness of blacks was undesirable and unacceptable.

Du Bois' segregation resolution was considerably at variance with those of White and Wright. The Editor conceded that the NAACP always had opposed the "underlying principle" of racial segregation and would continue to do so, but he insisted that the NAACP had recognized that when argument and appeal had proved useless or slow in combating segregation, a (minority) group like American Negroes must "associate and cooperate" for self-advancement and self-defense. Thus, the Association always had recognized and encouraged black institutions, not as a means of fostering "artificial separation" of people; rather, "with the distinct object of proving Negro efficiency . . . ability and discipline, and demonstrating how useless and wasteful race segregation is." [18] Thus, although Du Bois carefully avoided endorsing segregation as a positive good, nevertheless his position was diametrically opposed to that of Louis Wright. As Spingarn had predicted, it was the question of accepting or rejecting segregation in certain "practical exigencies" which proved the most difficult of all the issues.

Spingarn's segregation resolution occupied a medial position in relationship to those of Wright and Du Bois, although it tended more toward Du Bois' view. Spingarn urged that any resolution adopted by the Board embody the two doctrines that had characterized the Association's historic attitude toward segregation: (1) affirmation of the inherent evilness of segregation; (2) complete freedom of action in specific cases. The Board frankly should admit that "we [the Association] have tacitly accepted, and will continue to accept, certain forms of segregation," insisted Spingarn, for to deny that Negro colleges, churches, schools, and businesses were forms of segregation forced by law or custom "would simply confirm the assertions of some of our enemies . . . that when it comes to thinking we are a brainless organization." Furthermore, the resolution should make clear the NAACP's intention to develop the "genius" of the black race and to heed the Amenia conferees' call for the fostering of race consciousness. The NAACP must not encourage its members and officers to use a "Pol-parrot cry of 'no segregation'" as a substitute for real thinking in a resolution which did not reserve liberty of action. [19]

Hence, when the Board of Directors convened on April 9, 1934, for the purpose of adopting an official segregation resolution, it had three general alternatives: (1) to view all and every form of separation of the races as undesirable and unacceptable (Dr. Wright's plan); (2) to denounce segregation generally but to acknowledge it as a necessary evil in certain practical exigencies (the plan of the Spingarn brothers); (3) to view enforced segregation as an evil but to endorse some forms of voluntary segregation as a positive good (Du Bois' proposal).

As early as January 1934 Du Bois had predicted that he did not have sufficient support to have his voluntary segregation proposal adopted by a majority vote of the Board. Events were to demonstrate that he was absolutely correct. Only two Board members categorically supported his program of voluntary segregation—Abram Harris and Rachael Davis Du Bois, a white lecturer at Columbia and Temple universities who was noted for her work in connection with scientific studies of race relations and who had been recently elected to the Board at Du Bois' suggestion. At least three Board members—Mary White Ovington; Carl Murphy, editor of the Baltimore *Afro-American*; and Isadore Martin, one of the most active black Board members since 1926—not only vehemently opposed Du Bois' scheme but would be calling for his resignation within a matter of weeks. Lillian Alexander, although an ardent admirer of Du Bois and always willing to defend him from personal attack, was stalwart in her support of the Association's historic program.[20] Louis Wright's segregation resolution had already placed him on record as an implacable foe of anything that remotely smacked of segregation. Nor could Du Bois expect the Spingarn brothers to support a program which endorsed voluntary segregation as a positive good.

When the Board voted on April 9, it rejected both Du Bois' voluntary segregation program and the Spingarn brothers' segregation resolution. J. E. Spingarn did not attend the April Board meeting, having departed for a New Orleans vacation,[21] but Arthur Spingarn was present and fought for more than an hour on behalf of the brothers' proposal. "There were twelve or fourteen members of the Board present," confided Arthur Spingarn to his brother, "and I seemed to be the only one in favor of our resolution." Instead, the Board passed a "substitute" resolution—a "silly one," wrote

Arthur Spingarn—with only one opposing vote, that of Mary White Ovington.[22]

The resolution which the Board adopted was highly ambiguous, for although it explicitly denounced all forms of "enforced segregation," it did not specify whether black churches, schools, and similar institutions were to be considered forms of enforced segregation. The Board's resolution read as follows:

> The National Association for the Advancement of Colored People is opposed both to the principle and the practice of enforced segregation of human beings on the basis of race and color.
>
> Enforced segregation by its very existence carries with it the implication of a superior and inferior group and invariably results in the imposition of a lower status on the group deemed inferior. Thus, both principle and practice necessitate unyielding opposition to any and every form of enforced segregation.[23]

Hence, in the final analysis, the Board had failed to address itself to the crucial question raised by Spingarn and Du Bois: whether or not the Association would officially acknowledge the necessity for segregation in certain "practical exigencies."

J. E. Spingarn condemned the Board's resolution as being "revolutionary" and "weak." It was not always possible to precisely define enforced segregation, argued Spingarn; therefore the NAACP was committed to opposing unalterably a condition for which there was no exact definition. The South's enforced separation of the races meant that Southern black schools and colleges represented enforced segregation and must therefore be unalterably opposed by the Association. The resolution was revolutionary and weak from still another standpoint, contended Spingarn, for it expressed disapproval of only enforced segregation whereas the Association's historic attitude had been one of opposition to all segregation as an evil, although there sometimes had been a need to submit to it. Finally, Spingarn charged that the resolution was revolutionary because it obligated the NAACP to offer "unyielding" opposition to "every" form of enforced segregation. "Unless I cannot understand English," he insisted, "this means that we must oppose every institution that is segregated by force or custom, whereas in the old days we could say that their segregation was an evil but we did not have to oppose them." [24]

In essence, the Spingarn brothers were flatly overruled by the Board—one of the few such instances during their twenty-three years in the NAACP. J. E. Spingarn found himself in an especially precarious position, for although he was firmly convinced of the inadequacy of the segregation resolution, he was obliged as Chairman of the Board to implement it. Rather than oppose the Directors' will, he chose to enforce the resolution to the letter, undoubtedly in an attempt to demonstrate what he believed to be its adverse effects and thereby maneuver the Board into reconsidering its position. In his capacity as Board Chairman, Spingarn directed that no officer of the NAACP was to speak at any Negro school or college in the South until after the next Board meeting; that no monies received from such institutions be acknowledged or used until the Board gave official authorization; that communication with Southern Negro colleges and schools be held to an absolute minimum; that no NAACP meetings be held in any of the institutions in question. The Board's resolution was "silly," insisted Spingarn, but the failure to execute immediately its obvious and direct implications "would brand us as hypocrites, and that is the last thing we can afford." [25]

Spingarn's disgruntlement over the Board's resolution was rivaled only by that of Du Bois. In his autobiography, published six years after the defeat of his program of voluntary segregation, Du Bois noted:

> The Association seemed to me not only unwilling to move toward the left in its program but even stepped decidedly toward the right. And what astonished me most was that this economic reaction was voiced even more by the colored members of the Board of Directors than the white.[26]

Whereas Spingarn confined his criticisms of the Board's resolution to private communications with White, Du Bois
publicly attacked the ambiguous wording of the resolution
and the Board's alleged conservatism in the May 1934 issue
of the *Crisis*,[27] a move which, as will soon become apparent,
was to have serious, and even dire, consequences for the
Editor's relationship with the Association.

Du Bois and Spingarn's challenge of the segregation resolution left the Board no alternative but to offer an official
explanation of the April resolution. Upon Dr. Wright's motion, the Board, at its May meeting, voted the following
statement of clarification of the April resolution:

> The resolution passed at the April meeting of the
> Board in opposition to "enforced segregation" did not
> imply that we approve of other forms of segregation.
> We believe that all forms of segregation are in their
> origin, if not in their essential nature enforced. Even
> where segregation exists this does not alter our convic-
> tion that the necessity that has brought it into being is
> evil, and that this evil should be combated to the great-
> est extent possible.[28]

Thus, the Board had taken virtually the same stand in slightly
different words; the Directors still had not dealt with the
crux of the controversy: whether or not the NAACP would
officially acknowledge the necessity for segregation in "certain practical exigencies." On the other hand, the Board
had left no doubt that blacks' total integration into American
life was desired and, conversely, that Du Bois' chauvinism
was unwelcome. After five months of heated debate, the
segregation controversy touched off by Du Bois' January
editorial had come full circle.

DU BOIS: THE FINAL STRUGGLE

Du Bois' position regarding segregation was but one of
several factors that contributed to his resignation from the

NAACP and the *Crisis* in July 1934. The old enmity between Walter White and Du Bois over the administration and financing of the *Crisis* continued unabated, paralleling the debate on the nature of segregation. More important, by January 1934 Du Bois had become adamant in his demands that the NAACP completely revise its administrative structure so as to afford the rank-and-file membership a major, if not the controlling, voice in the organization's administration. The reader should keep in mind that Du Bois' demands for administrative reform, although treated separately in this study, were inextricably linked in his mind with the necessity for a new program, specifically black voluntary segregation. As he viewed it, the realization of the reforms he demanded taken as a whole, would transform the NAACP into an organization by, of, and for the black masses. But what the Editor did not fully grasp until it was too late was that the reforms he advocated threatened the continuing status, prestige, and value systems—what administrative specialists term *security*—of the incumbent, old-guard NAACP leadership. In such cases, at least some resistance to change on the part of the incumbent leadersthip is to be expected.[29]

Only the basic issues in the White-Du Bois feud need be recorded. It will be recalled that in late 1933 Du Bois had accepted a professorship at Atlanta University, although continuing to serve as Editor-in-Chief of the *Crisis*, with George Streator and Roy Wilkins serving as co-managing editors in New York. This arrangement proved totally unsatisfactory. First, Du Bois' absence from New York did little to ease the perennial tension between the *Crisis* office and the Secretary's office, for Streator, whom Du Bois considered a close friend and ally, assumed his chief's old role of attempting to prevent White from gaining control of the *Crisis*, with Du Bois charting much of the strategy from Atlanta.[30]

Second, Streator and Wilkins could not agree on the duties each was to perform as co-managing editors of the *Crisis*. From the outset Wilkins had not wanted to serve as an editor of the *Crisis*, for by December 1933 he was performing the duties of the Assistant Secretary and of three executives who had been dismissed as part of the Association's intensive retrenchment drive, and he warned that additional duties would overwork him. Specifically, Wilkins insisted that Du Bois' suggestion that he undertake the responsibility for five pages of news and pictures in each monthly issue of the *Crisis* was virtually impossible in light of his current work load. Nevertheless, the Board of Directors, which was pressed for funds with which to hire an editorial assistant, voted a small increase in Wilkins' salary and assigned him the position of co-managing editor of the *Crisis*, but without specifically defining his duties. In April 1934 Streator, who was firmly convinced that Wilkins was a close ally of Walter White, complained that the new co-managing editor's total contribution to the preparation of the *Crisis* consisted of "advice and hot air." Yet Streator warned Du Bois not to press the issue of Wilkins' work load, for this might alienate those Board members who were sympathetic toward Wilkins yet whose support was indispensable for effecting Du Bois' reform of the Association's program and administration.[31]

Third, Streator was not satisfied with his official status. Wilkins was entitled to attend Board meetings in his capacity as Assistant Secretary, but Streator was not accorded this privilege even after becoming an editor of the *Crisis*. Undoubtedly to no one's surprise, White spearheaded the drive to prevent Streator's attendance at Board meetings. The most crushing blow to Streator's ego came in January 1934 when the names of the members of the Board of the newly created Crisis Publishing Company were announced. Du Bois, Arthur Spingarn, White, Wilkins, Lillian Alexander, and Louis T. Wright were named, but not Streator. An enraged Du Bois promptly complained in a semipublic circular letter (addressed to "Friends") that his absence from New York and Streator's omission from the Board of the Crisis Publishing Company would result in virtual control of the *Crisis* by the Secretary's office. Du Bois charged that the action was but another manifestation of the NAACP's undemocratic administration, an effort to run the organization by small committees which were not answerable to any representative body of public opinion.[32]

Last, White, Du Bois, and Streator clashed over the perennial issue of the Association's financial contributions to the *Crisis*. The Secretary rarely missed an opportunity to inform anybody who was interested that the NAACP had given the *Crisis* $35,409.38 between 1929 and March 1934. White charged that Du Bois, in return, had done nothing to help the Association, and had even refused to visit the branches and engage in similar field work. Du Bois counterattacked with a statement to the Board of Directors in which he charged that the Secretary exercised a virtual "dictatorship" over the Association. White's rebuttal came in the form of his own memorandum to the Board, in which he maintained that the Board had always kept close tabs on the Secretary's office, but had permitted Du Bois a free hand in planning and disbursing the *Crisis* budget. Indeed, White suggested that several years earlier, when Du Bois had published a series of children's "Brownie Books," he had used *Crisis* funds to launch the venture but had kept the profits from the sale of the books for himself.[33] In the final analysis, White bent his efforts toward ensuring that the Association would contribute no more money to the *Crisis*.

On the other hand, Streator complained that the Association was constantly in arrears in paying the *Crisis* the $100 monthly subsidy the Board had voted. (White was the official in charge of seeing that this obligation was met.) At the same time Du Bois feared that if the *Crisis* ledgers did not show a reasonable profit, White would use this as an excuse to make trouble for Du Bois and Streator.[34]

As had been the case for several years, the Spingarns were obliged to seek a middle ground between White and Du Bois, exercising with consummate skill the art of interpersonal leadership. But one overpowering factor made this latest phase of the controversy between the two men more serious than any in the past. Du Bois was rapidly assuming the stance that he would not remain in the Association if White were retained as Secretary, having insisted as early as February 1934 that if the Association were not completely reorganized

—meaning White's dismissal—he would resign. Thus, as a potential mediator, Spingarn found himself in an impossible situation. Both Streator and Du Bois perceived that he was obsessed with the idea that the Association should be structured in accordance with recognized principles of scientific management—that is, that one central executive, the Secretary, should be responsible for supervising the other salaried workers and coordinating and executing the basic policy which the Board formulated. In fact, Streator frankly told Spingarn that the crux of the problem was Spingarn's obsession with this idea and his having closed his mind to any alternative. Du Bois and Streator did not question the merits of the principle; they merely insisted that White was the wrong man to be placed in charge of the office.[35] In sum, Du Bois was demanding that Spingarn make a final and irrevocable choice between the Secretary and the Editor.

Spingarn's position was made even more untenable by the fact that, as usual, he was not wholly in accord with all of the views and actions of either White or Du Bois. For example, Spingarn shared some of White's displeasure over the financial arrangements between the *Crisis* and the Association. He had expressed surprise in late 1933 when White supplied him with statements showing that the Association had contributed more than $30,000 to the *Crisis*, and thenceforth he had tightened the reins on the *Crisis*' financial management. In March 1934 Spingarn dispatched an official memorandum to Du Bois, calling upon the Editor to have Streator observe more businesslike practices in reporting the receipt and disbursement of *Crisis* funds and, more specifically, to have Streator submit detailed financial statements to the Board of the Crisis Publishing Company and report to the Company all business trips. Spingarn informed Du Bois that he had intended to bring this matter before the Board earlier, maintaining that "I am afraid that as Chairman of the Board I have been somewhat derelict in my duties." [36] Earlier, when White had inquired of Spingarn what action should be taken regarding paying the *Crisis* the $100 monthly subsidy—the same subsidy which Streator had complained was constantly in arrears—Spingarn instructed White to let the subsidy cancel a $300 debt which the *Crisis* office owed the Association.[37] In short, no money passed hands, although it undoubtedly was generally known that Streator was counting upon the $100 subsidy to keep the *Crisis* operating.

On the other hand, Spingarn was far from a total accord with White. As was noted earlier, they were not in agreement on the Association's stand on segregation; indeed, Spingarn's position on this all-important issue was closer to that of Du Bois. In addition, it is impossible to ascertain the lingering effects, if any, of Spingarn's earlier belief that White had thwarted the first attempt to convene the second Amenia Conference and Mary White Ovington's accusation that the Secretary was seeking to control the Association. At any rate, the two men had their share of differences after January 1934, exclusive of any earlier animosity they might have harbored. In March 1934 Streator reported to Du Bois that Spingarn had been excluded from an NAACP program in Washington, D.C., and that he blamed White. Spingarn was so infuriated, Streator maintained, that he was willing to see the Secretary summarily fired.[38]

Spingarn even became involved in the tug of war which developed between White and Du Bois regarding who should and should not be added to the Board of Directors and the staff. For example, White was anxious to have George Schuyler, a foremost advocate of black consumer cooperatives, brought into the Association's work as either a Board member or in some other official capacity. But Du Bois had been fighting for "quite some time" to keep Schuyler out of the Association on the grounds that he would do anything for money and that he could not be trusted to represent the best interests of the NAACP. Apparently Spingarn's appraisal of Schuyler more nearly approximated that of Du Bois, for Streator gleefully reported that he and Du Bois had scored a victory because Spingarn, too, was "determined" to keep Schuyler out.[39]

In still another vein, the Spingarn brothers foiled a subtle attempt by White to have the Association's news published in the Pittsburgh *Courier* rather than the *Crisis*. In early April 1934 Streator informed Spingarn that White and Wilkins were releasing news to the *Courier* in an attempt to divert the public's interest from the *Crisis*. Spingarn asked Arthur by whose authority this was being done and whether it had been approved by the Board of Directors. He suggested that Arthur Spingarn see Streator about the matter before the next Board meeting. Arthur Spingarn told Streator and Harris that White had arranged for Robert Vann, editor of the Pittsburgh *Courier*, to come to New York in order to make arrangements for the *Courier*'s publication of Association news, but that he, Arthur Spingarn, was opposed to this because he did not believe Vann trustworthy. Arthur Spingarn raised the issue at the April Board Meeting, resulting in the passage of a resolution instructing the Secretary to first submit all NAACP news to the *Crisis* office before its release to other newspapers. In addition, Streator was given the option of printing or not printing the news submitted to him.[40]

But these random concessions to Du Bois were too little, too late; the Editor had long since fixed his attention upon the broader and more complex issue of completely restructuring the Association's administrative hierarchy. As early as April 1931, Du Bois had warned his colleagues that "either the mass of those intelligently interested in our program must share in the government of the Organization, or our popular support will become so small as to hamper our resources and influence." Similarly, Du Bois in addressing the NAACP Annual Conference of 1932, prophesied that the NAACP could not much longer presume to speak for the black masses without affording the masses a major role in policy formation. One of the major criticisms leveled against the Association, he observed, centered in the fact that it was a peculiarly centralized organization, that the Board was self-perpetuating, and that the Chairman of the Board had too much power. Du Bois urged that the branches be given more power; that young people be actively enlisted for work in the Association, "for those who are in it are not going to run it very much longer"; that the organization respond to the voice of the masses.[41]

More specifically, Du Bois called for substantial changes in the structure and composition of the Board of Directors, the primary goal being the election of new and more progressive-minded Board members. He suggested that the number of NAACP Vice-Presidents—largely honorary posts—be increased indefinitely and converted into an advisory body of elder statesmen as a face-saving means of absorbing inactive Board incumbents. Du Bois listed nine Board members, including Carl Murphy, editor of the Baltimore *Afro-American* and, significantly, one of Du Bois' most severe critics, who should be kicked upstairs to the vice-presidency. He suggested ten new replacements on the Board, including Abram Harris; Rachael Davis Du Bois; Sterling Brown, a black poet and professor of English at Howard University; Charles Houston, the Dean of Howard University's Law School; and Martha Gruening, a white social worker who had displayed an active interest in the Association for many years.[42] Du Bois was convinced that the addition of these new faces on the Board of Directors would pave the way for the reforms he had envisioned in the Association's program and administration.

Spingarn gave only verbal acquiescence to Du Bois' proposals to decentralize the authority which the National Office traditionally exercised. He readily conceded that the NAACP was long overdue for democratization—"all of us have felt this for years," he wrote—but that "for some reason or other" the processes of reform had never got under way. However, as late as July 1934, Spingarn had not approved any of the many plans that had been suggested for according the branches and the membership a greater voice in the Association's administration. One plan called for the South's representation on the Board of Directors in exact proportion to its black population; Spingarn vetoed this idea because it would "completely disorganize the whole work of the Association and reverse its ideals beyond recognition." A second plan called for all elections (presumably of officers and Board members) to be conducted by the Annual Conference, in

which all members and branches of the Association participated; Spingarn objected to this plan on the grounds that
it "would mean chaos." [43] He expressed the belief that some
workable solution to the problem of democratization could
be found—but none had been found as late as July 1934.
Thus, Du Bois' plea for decentralization of the powers enjoyed by the national office bore little fruit.

On the other hand, Du Bois' plans for renovating the
Board of Directors through the addition of new and more
progressive members moved apace with Spingarn's approval
and assistance. Spingarn, no less than Du Bois, had experienced
firsthand the Board's recalcitrant stand against even the slightest change in the Association's historic program. For example,
it will be recalled that he had resigned as President of the
NAACP in 1933, partially because the Board had seemed
reluctant to convene a second Amenia Conference. Again, in
April 1934, the Board was to defy the Spingarn brothers by
taking an adamant stand against all forms of enforced segregation as opposed to the more flexible resolution favored by
the brothers. Hence, when Du Bois broached the subject
of electing new members to the Board, Spingarn agreed
that "the Board needs a 'face-lifting' and this can be done
most painlessly by gradually adding people like those whom
you suggest." Consequently, by January 1934 the Board
encompassed many new members who had been suggested
by Du Bois, including Abram Harris, Sterling Brown, and
Rachael Davis Du Bois. And, as late as April 1934, Spingarn
reiterated his belief that the best means of securing a more
enlightened program for the Association was by continuing
to add liberal-minded individuals to the Board.[44]

But as if fate had played some cruel joke, Du Bois became
entrapped in his own machinations. By April 1934 the Board
encompassed a host of new and younger members, but most
of them proved as strongly integrationist in their views as
their older colleagues on the Board. Even Abram Harris,
who staunchly supported Du Bois throughout the segregation
controversy, would reject the principle of black voluntary
segregation several months later when he was called upon

to draw up a future plan and program for the Association. Nor could Du Bois derive any comfort or hope from the second Amenia Conference, for its findings had called for the unity of white and black labor—a quite different concept from black chauvinism. In fact, Streator warned Du Bois that he could not depend upon the Amenia conferees to follow up the findings of the Conference, for many of them were in White's camp [45]—and, as White's adamant integrationist stance had demonstrated, his camp was many miles away from black chauvinism. In the final analysis, Spingarn was the only Du Bois sympathizer who was powerful enough to aid substantially in the realization of Du Bois' reforms. Indeed, Spingarn once reminded Streator that he was the only friend on the Board of Directors that Streator had.[46]

But even where Spingarn was concerned, Du Bois found himself in an impossible corner. After 1930, as the Editor's thoughts increasingly centered upon voluntary segregation and self-help for blacks, it was perhaps inevitable that he should question anew the role which white liberals—even old friends like Spingarn—were to play in this black movement. In his address to the NAACP Annual Conference of 1932, Du Bois had predicted that the Association's adoption of a new economic orientation would "find opposition in the membership . . . and among friends of the white race who are with us." (Spingarn was seated on the platform with Du Bois when this statement was uttered). The idea was still prevalent, warned the Editor, "that after all we are going to achieve our economic freedom in the United States in the way that economic emancipation has been brought in other days." [47] To those who observed closely there were unmistakable signs that Du Bois seriously questioned Spingarn's continuing power within the Association. For example, it has been noted that in 1933, when Spingarn threatened to resign the presidency, Du Bois candidly told him that it might be well for him to step aside when the time was opportune and permit a Negro to assume the presidency. Similarly, in October 1933, when Du Bois outlined his plan for altering the composition of the Board of

Directors, he had suggested that Spingarn retain the presidency of the NAACP, but had not mentioned Spingarn's retention of the powerful post of Board Chairman.[48]

Nor was Du Bois convinced that Spingarn sincerely intended to effect major reforms in the Association's program and administration despite the Abolitionist's anxiety to convene a second Amenia Conference and his verbal acquiescence in the call for a new economic program. In January 1934 Du Bois confided to Abram Harris that the greatest obstacle to be overcome in effecting a new economic program was the Spingarns' outdated economic philosophy. Similarly, Streator, too, grew impatient as Spingarn continued to veto plans for decentralization of the power of the national office. He insisted that Du Bois had overestimated Spingarn's interest in reforming the Association and warned that "after all, reform means no Spingarn." [49] In the final analysis, then, there was no room *within* the Association for Du Bois to maneuver—no place to go.

The *Crisis* became the outlet for Du Bois' wrath and frustration, an action that laid the groundwork for both a major confrontation with Spingarn and the Editor's resignation from the Association. When White replied to Du Bois' January editorial on segregation by insisting that the Association had always opposed segregation, Du Bois retorted that White's Caucasian features prevented him from understanding the Negro problem. When Spingarn upheld the Association's historic stand against segregation in a March 1934 *Crisis* article, Du Bois replied that if Spingarn was correct, then the net result had been "a little less than nothing." For good measure, Du Bois included a liberal sprinkling of criticism of the Board of Directors for its reluctance to revamp the NAACP's program.[50]

This unprecedented public criticism of the Association's officials, more than the issue of segregation *per se*, marked the beginning of the end of cordial relations between Du Bois and Spingarn. Spingarn told Streator that every light-skinned mulatto, including Du Bois' old friend John Hope, now the president of Atlanta University and Du Bois' employer, was "infuriated" by Du Bois' having called Walter White "white." In early April, immediately after Du Bois' initial attack, Spingarn sent the Editor an ultimatum that he cease publicly attacking the Association's officials. Streator warned Du Bois that Spingarn had "come out in the open" and would attempt to effect Du Bois' dismissal from the *Crisis* at the next (April 9) Board meeting. Streator further reported to his chief that "rumors" indicated that the Board must dismiss Du Bois in order to keep its self-respect in the wake of his attacks.[51]

The rumor of Spingarn's alleged plan to have Du Bois ousted spread like wildfire from Streator to Lillian Alexander and thence to other members of the Board, creating a minor tempest. Mrs. Alexander, who happened to be in Atlanta, rushed to Du Bois' side and dispatched a host of night letters to key Board members, urging that they foil Spingarn's plan. The Association could do without Spingarn more readily than it could spare Du Bois, contended Mrs. Alexander. The opposition to Du Bois was a manifestation of "jealousy," she charged, and she warned Arthur Spingarn that she intended to "fight the attempt of your Brother to oust Du Bois from the *Crisis*." Mrs. Alexander also protested to J. E. Spingarn, appealing to his sense of love for the organization. She urged Abram Harris, Du Bois' strongest supporter on the Board, to attend the April 9 meeting, promising to pay his fare to New York.[52]

There appears to have been more excitement and exaggeration than fact in the rumor which Streator and Mrs. Alexander perpetuated. Spingarn asked his brother to raise the "Du Bois incident" at the April Board meeting, but J. E. Spingarn did not attend the meeting. Instead he departed for what was ostensibly a New Orleans vacation, during which he was to rendezvous with his wife who was returning from a trip to Guatemala. However, in what was undoubtedly a move that took many by surprise, Spingarn and his wife stopped in Atlanta during their return trip to New York in order to confer with Du Bois.[53] Perhaps Mrs. Alexander's agitation had altered Spingarn's original intentions. Perhaps he could not resist a last attempt at making peace with his old friend and adversary.

And, indeed, the conference did bring peace—at least temporarily. The two men conferred very candidly in Du Bois' room for three and a half hours. Du Bois was prepared to speak his mind, even if it should precipitate a spat, but Spingarn was so pleasant and flexible that the Editor had no opportunity to vent his wrath. Spingarn insisted that he sincerely favored a reorganization of the Association and that he wanted Du Bois' help and cooperation in the venture. Du Bois suggested that Roy Wilkins should be the first one fired, to be followed by White and William Pickens (the NAACP Field Secretary and an increasingly severe critic of Du Bois). Spingarn generally agreed, but insisted that it would be difficult to dismiss White and Pickens in the midst of the Depression unless they were assured of other employment. Spingarn credited White with several important accomplishments but conceded that he was simply not the right man to hold the position of Secretary. Spingarn suggested that the quickest way to effect organizational reform lay in continuing to add young people and liberals to the Board of Directors.[54]

Du Bois left the Atlanta conference greatly pacified, although not quite convinced of Spingarn's total support. On the one hand, Du Bois felt that a basis for cooperation and understanding had been established. Shortly after the conference he told Spingarn that he, Du Bois, had all but given up hope of understanding his white friend but that he was now ready to cooperate as long as the cooperation was mutual and real. On the other hand, Du Bois confided to Streator that he was aware of Spingarn's fluctuating temperament and, therefore, was not relying solely upon his support. Nevertheless, the Editor concluded that the task awaiting Streator and himself would be eased considerably if they could have Spingarn's power and influence on their side.[55]

Nor did the Atlanta conference do anything to ease the tension between White and Du Bois. When White's sister, who resided in Atlanta, invited the Spingarns and Du Bois to dinner, Du Bois sent the Spingarns but he would not go himself.[56]

The entente was short-lived. Even as Spingarn and the Editor were reaching an accord in Atlanta, the NAACP Board of Directors, at the April 9 meeting in New York, was dealing Du Bois a measure of both victory and defeat. Isadore Martin, one of Du Bois' harshest critics, raised the issue of the Editor's recent public attacks on the Board, but Abram Harris, Rachael Davis Du Bois, and Louis T. Wright forestalled consideration by effecting adjournment. Arthur Spingarn reported to his brother that the Board did not seem to consider the matter serious. At the same time, however, the April Board meeting dealt Du Bois a severe setback, for the Directors adopted a resolution declaring its opposition to all forms of enforced segregation—a ruling that boded ill for Du Bois' black chauvinism proposal as well. Du Bois replied in the May issue of the *Crisis* with unabashed criticism of the ambiguous wording of the resolution since it did not define "enforced" segregation. At its May meeting, the Board not only reiterated its opposition to segregation in any and every form but reaffirmed that the *Crisis* was the official organ of the Association and ruled that "no salaried officer of the Association shall criticize the policy, work or officers of the Association in the pages of the *Crisis*." Any potentially critical remarks were to be submitted to the Board for approval or disapproval.[57] In short, despite the tentative agreement that Du Bois and Spingarn had effected during their Atlanta meeting, obviously they had not resolved the all-important issue of public criticism of the Association's officials. Thus, the situation in regard to this issue quickly reverted to the same point as before the conference.

Indeed, Spingarn rapidly made it clear that he had not budged from his initial opposition to public criticism of the Association's hierarchy in the pages of the *Crisis*. A visibly concerned Streator reported to his chief that Spingarn was "wrought up" by the attack on the Board in the May *Crisis*. Shortly afterward, when Roy Wilkins asked Spingarn (in his capacity as Board Chairman) for clarification of the Board's resolution banning public criticism, Spingarn informed Wilkins that the resolution was effective as of the June issue of the *Crisis* and that it was the duty of the Editor and managing editor to see that no criticism appeared and, if necessary, to delete it. If there were any uncertainty regarding what constituted "criticism," said Spingarn, then the material should be submitted to the Board of Directors or the Board of the Crisis Publishing Company for a ruling. He reminded Wilkins that the resolution prohibited criticism only by salaried officials, and instructed the Assistant Secretary to send a copy of this letter to the editors of the *Crisis* and the directors of the Crisis Publishing Company.[58]

Streator thought that he perceived a growing hostility on the part of the Spingarn brothers toward himself and Du Bois after the critical May *Crisis* editorial. Arthur Spingarn was keeping the Board of the Crisis Publishing Company "talking money" (presumably in an attempt to emphasize the *Crisis'* failure to realize a substantial profit) and, at the same time, J. E. Spingarn was giving Du Bois the "double cross," Streator warned. Spingarn had predicted that Du Bois would not "last" much longer at Atlanta University and had even begun "gossiping" about the Editor's alleged "amours." Streator concluded that "Joel is petty as hell!" and that "I am sure more than ever that Joel is an old maid and needs, besides, a nursemaid." However, Streator cautioned Du Bois against mentioning any of this information to Spingarn, for there might be a trap to see how closely Streator reported to his chief. Streator reported that Louis Wright was the only person "who can save us," but that even Wright was undecided on the choice between White and Du Bois.[59]

Meanwhile, one week before the passage of the May resolution banning public criticism of the Association and its officers, Du Bois had prepared and sent to press highly critical editorials for the June *Crisis*. The Editor telegraphed Spingarn that his resignation was now inevitable and, without awaiting a reply to the telegram, dispatched a letter to Spingarn the same day, enclosing his resignation. Du Bois assured his friend that he had no intention of creating a controversy; he merely wanted to quit and be silent. He praised the job Streator had done in editing the *Crisis* and expressed the hope that Streator would be promoted to Editor-in-Chief if the magazine were continued.[60]

In his actual letter of resignation, Du Bois summarized his differences with the Association. He could not comply with the May resolution banning criticism of the Association and its officials in the *Crisis*, although he conceded that the Board had the right and even the duty to take such action when differences of opinion threatened the organization. But he questioned the "wisdom" of drawing a distinction between criticism by salaried and unsalaried officials. Du Bois admitted that he had not always been right during his thirty-five years of work on behalf of the Negro, but he insisted that he had been sincere and that he was unwilling to be limited "at this late date" in the expression of his honest opinion. The *Crisis* had never been intended merely to express the official opinion of the Association, and he had always believed that anyone's opinion, no matter how antagonistic to his own or the Association's views, should be published there. Du Bois was unwilling to edit the *Crisis* unless this policy were continued; therefore, he resigned every position he held in the Association, to become effective immediately (May 1934).[61]

Despite their differences with Du Bois, the Spingarns made a final effort to effect a compromise which would afford the Editor at least nominal ties with the Association while, at the same time, upholding their conviction that the *Crisis* could not be utilized to publicize the internal affairs of the organization. Spingarn asked Streator not to publicize Du Bois' letter of resignation, presumably pending the next Board meeting on June 12. However, shortly before the June Board meeting, the New York press publicized the resignation, although Du Bois assured Spingarn that he had not released it. Apparently, it was the release of the resignation to the public before the Board had had an opportunity to act on it which provoked Arthur Spingarn to offer a motion at the June 12 meeting to the effect that Du Bois'

resignation be accepted. The clerk of the Board recorded in
the original set of June Board minutes that Arthur Spingarn
had offered the motion, with a seconding motion having been
made by Charles Edward Russell (one of the white liberal
founders of the organization), but that the motion had been
lost. The clerk asked J. E. Spingarn whether she should
record this motion in the official minutes.[62] Since no record
of Arthur Spingarn's having made such a motion appears in
the minutes, one may assume that Spingarn's reply was in
the negative.

Meanwhile, Arthur Spingarn's motion of June 12 led Lillian
Alexander to revive the rumor that Spingarn was attempting
to oust Du Bois, and Streator again helped her spread it.
Whereupon Spingarn went to the *Crisis* office and gave
Streator "hell" for suggesting that he would do such a thing.
Spingarn's display of anger and indignation was so convincing
that Streator conceded that "the thing is a puzzle." [63]

Whatever the case, the Spingarns continued to attempt a
compromise with Du Bois, even after the June 12 Board
meeting. Du Bois came to New York and talked at length
with the brothers, but no satisfactory arrangement was forthcoming. Spingarn suggested that Du Bois might relinquish
the editorship of the *Crisis*, but submit signed articles peri-
odically. Du Bois vetoed this proposal on the grounds that
it would appear that he was merely hanging on to the
Association and attempting to salvage his pride. Next, the
Spingarns suggested that if Du Bois were determined to
sever his connections with the *Crisis*, then he should at least
retain his membership on the Board of Directors and the
Spingarn Medal Committee. But Du Bois insisted that total
and complete separation from the Association and the *Crisis*
was the only solution. He thanked the Spingarns for all
they had done in his behalf and assured Joel Spingarn that
nothing could alter their friendship.[64]

In a second and more lengthy letter of resignation and
in communications to friends, Du Bois made a final statement of his reasons for leaving the Association. "Negative"
protest and agitation would no longer suffice for an organiza-

tion representing blacks. He had tried unsuccessfully to reform the NAACP and was withdrawing in the hope that younger men or others, in the absence of his sometimes trying personality, could bring about the necessary changes. Du Bois insisted that his differences with the Association regarding segregation was not the reason for his resignation; the segregation dispute was a minor matter. As long as White and Wilkins retained power, and as long as the Spingarns and others permitted them to do so, he could not remain in the NAACP. The Editor expressed the belief that the Spingarns were sincere in their friendship toward him, but that even present developments had not convinced them that the Association could not continue under the leadership of White and Wilkins. Finally, Du Bois reiterated his objections to the abridgment of his freedom of expression in the *Crisis* and lamented that the once great Association currently lacked executive officers who possessed either the ability or the disposition to guide the organization.[65]

At the July Board meeting, Spingarn offered a lengthy resolution that was apparently intended as a rebuttal to the charges advanced in Du Bois' letter of resignation. The Board's May resolution prohibiting criticism of the Association's officials in the *Crisis* was neither novel nor new, insisted Spingarn, for a Crisis Committee had supervised the Editor's utterances for a number of years. Du Bois had always acknowledged the Board of Directors' right to supervise his editorials, and prior to 1934 he had never suggested or stated criticism of the Association in the pages of the *Crisis*. Nor was it true that Du Bois' pleas for reform had fallen on deaf ears, maintained Spingarn, for during the preceding eighteen months he had never appeared before the Board to argue his proposals persuasively, although he should have realized that spoken argument before the body which must ultimately enact the reforms was indispensable. Yet Du Bois had attended only two Board meetings between January 1, 1933, and July 10, 1934, and he had not attended any Board meetings since September 1933. The Editor's absence in Atlanta could serve as no valid excuse, noted the resolution, for he had visited the *Crisis* office almost every month during the same period. Concluding on a somewhat softer note, the resolution stated that nothing therein was intended to imply lack of appreciation for Du Bois' services.[66]

Two days after the July Board meeting, and after Du Bois had severed all connections with the NAACP, Spingarn wrote some afterthoughts regarding the controversy to White. The Board had neglected a great deal for a number of years because of the *Crisis* problem, a problem that derived from "the powerful and peculiar personality of the Editor." Spingarn told White that he, Spingarn, had been "troubled by the state of your health and nervous system as a result of such worry," and reminded the Secretary that "no statesman or executive can survive unless he has a very bad memory for criticisms, irritations, and defeats" [67]—a peculiar statement in light of the fact that Spingarn had confided to Du Bois that White was not the right man for the post he held.

8

THE TWILIGHT OF
WHITE LIBERALISM

Ironically, a serious attempt to effect some of the reforms
which Du Bois had advocated was launched within a
matter of weeks after his departure from the NAACP. In
September 1934 a committee of the Board of Directors drafted
a "Future Plan and Program," which challenged the continuing adequacy of the noneconomic liberalism of the Association's traditional leadership—and particularly that of the
white founders—as a means of eradicating the proscriptions
confronting the race; outlined a bold new economic orientation for the NAACP; and called for a greater share of the
administrative control of the organization by the rank-and-
file membership.

The reforms proposed by the Committee on Future Plan
and Program gave rise to the most important policy decision
in the NAACP's nearly quarter-century of existence. To the
"insurgents" who drafted the Future Plan and Program, the
major issue was whether the organization's traditional leader-

ship would approve such sweeping program and structural changes, some of which clearly threatened the elite administrative status the old leadership had long enjoyed. For example, it had been the "closed corporation" aspects of the NAACP's administrative structure that had enabled a handful of individuals, like the Spingarn brothers, to wield such extensive power and influence within the organization. Conversely, inclusion of the rank-and-file in the policy-making process could be expected to circumscribe, if not destroy, the old power elite.

More important, the reforms advanced in the Future Plan and Program conjured up the fundamental question of how polities that have institutionalized—that is, whose personnel, resources, and goals have been geared for a number of years toward a specific end—react to sudden and perhaps traumatic change. For example, could the NAACP leadership, with its distinctly middle-class orientation, effectively administer a new program which heavily emphasized the masses without itself undergoing radical alterations in composition? Could the NAACP branches, which traditionally had been relatively loosely organized internally, execute competently a new program entailing specialized branch personnel and a higher degree of precision in the execution of branch activities? In the final analysis, the fundamental question was whether a polity which had institutionalized in a given structural form and role could, on relatively short notice, adapt itself to a new orientation.

HANDWRITING ON THE WALL

In June 1934, while Du Bois' resignation from the Association was being debated, Mrs. Rachael Davis Du Bois proposed that a committee be appointed to plan and study the future program of the NAACP and report its findings at the fall (September) meeting of the Board. The branches and the participants at the 1934 NAACP Annual Conference were to be invited to submit suggestions to the committee. The committee that Spingarn appointed (in his capacity as Board Chairman) represented a broad spectrum of opinion regarding the Association's historic purpose and role, and included both older and relatively recently elected Board members: Abram Harris as Chairman, Rachael Davis Du Bois, Mary White Ovington, Louis T. Wright, James Weldon Johnson, Sterling Brown.[1] Spingarn specifically instructed the Clerk of the Board to include the Board Chairman and the Secretary as ex-officio members of the committee. In addition, he sought to ensure that the committee would not include the *Crisis* in its investigation. When the clerk recorded in the July Board minutes that the name of the committee was "Committee on Plan and Program of the Association and the Future of *The Crisis*," Spingarn had the clerk change the title to "Committee on Future Plan and Program of the Association."[2]

From the outset, before the Committee on Future Plan and Program convened, Abram Harris made it clear that in his opinion the very "purpose" of the NAACP must be changed if any progress were to be made. The struggle for civil liberty and political rights was no longer adequate, he insisted, for the current problems confronting blacks were economic. Mere protest and agitation about differential wages and employment of black workers (the heart of the Association's current economic program) did not touch the real roots of the problem; rather, if the NAACP were to continue as an effective organization, it must educate the black worker and farmer as to their position in the economy and show white workers that they had a common economic interest with their black counterparts.[3] In short, Harris envisioned the Committee on Future Plan and Program as a vehicle for refining and implementing the findings of the second Amenia Conference. Harris' ideas were not radically new, for Du Bois had been calling for the unity of white and black labor since the 1920's; he had long since moved beyond to what he believed to be the more fruitful avenue of black chauvinism.

A preview of the impending struggle between the "conservatives" on the Board and the Harris "radicals" became manifest when the Committee on Future Plan and Program was confronted with the decision of where to convene its first meeting. Spingarn offered to host the Committee during the Labor Day weekend at Troutbeck, insisting that the participants could thereby escape the distractions of the office and engage in undisturbed discussions. But when White informed Harris of Spingarn's offer, Harris demurred on the grounds that "I don't see how the Committee can function while it is the guest of the Chairman of the Board." Discussions should be free and untrammeled, but in the home of the Board Chairman, some members "might not feel free to say some things that they would ordinarily say." It might be better to hold the Committee meetings in New York City despite the summer heat,[4] Harris concluded.

In fact, Harris initially planned to draft the Committee's findings unilaterally, then have the other Committee members suggest revisions. Specifically, he proposed to meet with White, Spingarn, and the other members to work out the major problems to be resolved, after which the Committee was to meet again "to consider my [Harris'] report and to work out the final draft," which would be presented to the Board of Directors.[5]

For a change, it was now Walter White's turn to play the role of interpersonal leader. He thanked Harris for candidly expressing his opinion about meeting at Spingarn's home, but assured him, "You need have [no] apprehension about perfect freedom of expression." He reminded Harris that James Weldon Johnson was ill at his home in Great Barrington, Massachusetts, and would find it easier to come to Troutbeck, while Mary White Ovington, who also resided in Great Barrington, probably could come to Amenia, but not to New York City. Besides, argued White, would not the Committee's refusal to meet at Spingarn's home "be an admission that some members of the Committee would be less outspoken and honest than they would be elsewhere?" Whereupon Harris left it to the members of the Committee to make the decision.[6]

Meanwhile, Spingarn had grown perplexed and annoyed

by the Committee's delay in responding to his invitation. He told Roy Wilkins to tell White that he, Spingarn, could not wait longer than a week for the Committee's decision since he would like to make other plans for his family during the Labor Day weekend if the group did not wish to be his guests. White wired Harris that it was his personal opinion that "out of courtesy we should accept." Again, however, Harris insisted that the members of the Committee must make the decision.[7]

In resolving the issue the Committee divided along practically the same lines as had prevailed in the recent Du Bois controversy. Mary White Ovington could come to Troutbeck but not to New York City. Rachael Davis Du Bois felt that the Committee should be able to do "concentrated thinking" in the New York office, where indispensable data were readily available, and that the group should not "bind ourselves to any set plan until we meet and see what is the best thing to do." James Weldon Johnson pleaded a prior engagement as a reason for not being able to attend the meeting, regardless of where it might be held.[8] Meanwhile, as White was awaiting the responses of the members, Spingarn, who was obviously enraged, informed Wilkins that if he, Spingarn, did not receive a reply within three days, Wilkins should inform the Committee that there would be no conference at Troutbeck.[9] After all was said and done, the meeting was held in New York City. For Spingarn, the handwriting was clearly on the wall.

From that moment, the Spingarn brothers' attitude toward the Committee on Future Plan and Program noticeably hardened. J. E. Spingarn did not attend the Committee's meetings, and informed Harris that Arthur Spingarn could not attend the Committee's first meeting because he did not plan to be in New York during the week in which it was scheduled. Similarly, Mary White Ovington washed her hands of the Committee, insisting, "I do not really belong at it [the Committee's meeting] because I feel that we have a large program as it is . . . and that our one need is money." [10]

Thus, unhampered by the presence of the old-guard leadership, Harris and his followers were free to draft a far-reaching proposal for the complete reorganization of the Association. The insurgents had won the first skirmish; but they were soon to learn that winning the war was quite a different matter.

THE ECLIPSE OF NONECONOMIC LIBERALISM

Interpreting his charge as broadly as possible, Harris subjected every aspect of the NAACP's program and administration to microscopic examination.[11] The preliminary report of the Committee on Future Plan and Program, submitted to the Board of Directors in September 1934, was prefaced by a lengthy statement emphasizing that the Association's efforts in regard to the economic uplift of blacks had been incidental to its civil liberties program, a factor attributed to the founders' faith in the tenets of eighteenth-century liberalism. The organization's program had thus been linked to the reform movements of the nineteenth and early twentieth centuries. This brand of liberalism had sought to guarantee political and economic freedom, of which the latter encompassed the individual's right to state protection in the acquisition of property and in its employment for private ends. But although democratic liberalism sought to guarantee freedom in the use of property once it had been acquired, "it did not create the conditions which made the acquisition of property open to all members of society." Initially democratic liberalism had worked, noted the report, because the frontier, with its limitless free land and natural resources, provided an escape from poverty and prevented the crystallization of social classes and the development of radical class consciousness, although the frontier had been virtually closed to the black masses. Thus, the frontier had cushioned the impact of technological and financial changes upon the worker.

But with the passing of the frontier, continued the report, that economic freedom which had been so germane to liberalism increasingly became a privilege of the few. The growth of corporate wealth, consolidation, and monopoly made the acquisition of property increasingly difficult; and since property was the basis of freedom and independence, the Negro's debased status would have been unaltered even if he had succeeded in acquiring citizenship rights and civil liberties. Consequently, blacks were relegated to the position of a landless proletariat, a reservoir of cheap labor. Because the Negro lacked equal privileges and opportunities, he was more easily exploited than the white worker. Yet events had reduced the white and black masses to a virtually identical economic position. Their identity of interest and the "bankruptcy of liberal reformism" had been most cogently manifested by the Depression of 1929 and subsequent events, during which both white and black workers had been forced to increasingly lower levels of job and income competition, thereby enabling employers to play one group off against the other. The differential wages effected by the National Recovery Administration codes represented an extension, if not crystallization, of the state of affairs which enabled employers to divide and rule; in Southern agriculture, the concentration of the landlord's power and the displacement of white and black sharecroppers and tenants further displayed the identity of interests between white and black workers.

This did not necessarily mean that the NAACP must discontinue its current efforts to obtain economic justice for blacks, continued the report, but it did mean that the Association must change its ultimate objectives in the economic realm. Rather than merely attempting to ensure that blacks received equal job opportunities, the NAACP must direct its energies toward inducing blacks to "view their special grievances as a natural part of the larger issues of American labor as a whole." Conversely, the white worker must be made to realize that his destiny and well-being were inextricably linked with those of his black counterpart; that the white worker's support of the black worker's disadvantage not only increased the historic hostility between the two groups but provided a reservoir of cheap labor which hampered the unity and organization of labor. The Association's new economic program must stress that the world which would result would be neither black nor white, but it must be attained through the solidarity of white and black labor.

Having outlined the alleged bankruptcy of the NAACP's historic program, the Committee's report called upon the organization to alter its historic role so as to emphasize the black worker and to foster unity with his white counterpart. To realize these goals, the report recommended: (1) that the NAACP establish workers' and farmers' councils in strategic agricultural and industrial areas. The councils should conduct classes in workers' education, foster the building of a labor movement which would be industrial in character, and seek to unite all labor, white and black, skilled and unskilled, agricultural and industrial; (2) that the Association seek to lay an intellectual foundation for united political action by black and white workers on the national, state, and local levels, with the aim of securing legislation dealing with such pressing problems as old-age pensions, unemployment insurance, and regulations governing the labor of women and children; (3) that the NAACP serve as a basis for national and regional labor conferences which would formulate plans for political and propagandist activities to be conducted either independently or in cooperation with other sympathetic groups; (4) that the Association actively oppose racial chauvinism in the organized labor movement as well as among all workers, while at the same time attempting to eliminate Jim-Crowism and employment and wage discrimination in local and national trade-union groups by demonstrating the disastrous effects upon both white and black labor. In communities where similar efforts were being conducted by other agencies, the local branches of the NAACP should assist the existing agencies in functioning more efficiently.

In terms of the NAACP's historic tactics, the Committee on Future Plan and Program's most radical proposal was that the organization utilize direct-action techniques to fulfill the new program rather than continuing to rely upon the traditional tactics of oral and written agitation and protest.

The workers' councils were not to be mere discussion groups; rather, "through actual participation in strikes, lockouts, and labor demonstrations [the councils] will seek to protect the interests of Negro workingmen and to promote their organization and unity with white labor." Although the establishment and administration of cooperative societies was not a primary goal of the workers' councils, they might foster such societies when deemed desirable by taking "an active part in creating the understanding and atmosphere necessary to their establishment and successful functioning."

The Future Plan and Program report also provided an extensive procedural outline for the Association's guidance in enacting the new economic program. The national office should cooperate with the branches in building up a literature adapted to the needs of workers in particular communities, but that also would permit a local worker to see the relationship between his interests and those of workers throughout the country. Much of the existing literature on cooperation, the labor movement, white and black labor competition, and industrial-agricultural problems should be simplified and reprinted in pamphlet form for use in the workers' and farmers' councils. The NAACP should undertake more systematic research and investigation in the realms of industry and agriculture, the results of which should be published from time to time in the *Crisis* and other periodicals, and especially in the form of special books and pamphlets.

More important, the report urged the NAACP to take over the work of the Joint Committee on Recovery, making its voluminous records the basis of the Association's investigation and agitation of current economic conditions. It was recommended that John P. Davis, the Joint Committee's Executive Secretary, be appointed to head the NAACP's new economic program.[12] Indeed, the report called upon the Association to relinquish immediate control of the new program to an "Advisory Committee on Economic Activities," to be composed of not less than five members, all of whom were to be distinguished in some phase of economics. The Chairman of the proposed Advisory Committee would be chosen by the

Board of Directors and he, in turn, was to appoint the other four members, subject to the Board's approval.

Finally, the report of the Committee on Future Plan and Program suggested that the successful execution of the new economic program would necessitate a measure of administrative decentralization,[13] with the obvious implication that the highly centralized authority traditionally enjoyed by the national office would have to be relinquished. The branches must be grouped geographically by regions, each of which must be provided a full-time, salaried secretary.[14] Local branches must be strengthened and provided full-time programs encompassing public lectures, forums, facilities for disseminating information on local conditions, and techniques for aiding in the formulation of cooperative societies wherever desirable.

The Committee on Future Plan and Program made no attempt to tabulate the exact costs of the new economic program, but it estimated that at least $2,500 would be added to the annual expenses of the NAACP if it decided to take over the work of the Joint Committee on Recovery and to employ the Joint Committee's Secretary, John P. Davis, to coordinate the new economic program. Although the Committee on Future Plan and Program explicitly disclaimed any responsibility for outlining means of financing the new program, it did offer the general suggestion that new costs might be met through a grant from the American Fund for Public Service, the Racham Fund, or a drive for new members.[15]

The NAACP administrators' response to the economic section of the report of the Committee on Future Plan and Program was varied and, as usual, transcended racial lines. Roy Wilkins expressed the opinion that theoretically the proposed economic program was valid; he was especially pleased with the suggestion that the Association assume control of the Joint Committee on Recovery. But in a lengthy memorandum to Walter White, Wilkins made it explicitly clear that he believed that the new economic program would be, in the long run, detrimental to the Association's cause. "I am convinced," he wrote, "that the masses of Negroes in this country are concerned with lynching, discrimination, segregation, . . . I am afraid that if we go off too heavily on a theoretic social and political and economic program, we will find that we shall have cut ourselves loose from the support of the bulk of our followers." This might not be as it should be, but the fact remained that such was the case. Furthermore, Wilkins considered the cost of the proposed economic program prohibitive, contending, "It is in this section of finances that it seems to me the Committee has failed utterly to make suggestions of any value." Whereas the Committee had estimated that the assumption of the work of the Joint Committee on Recovery would increase the NAACP's annual expenses by only $2,500, Wilkins insisted that the new costs would be a minimum of $5,000. He estimated that the cost of implementing all of the proposals in the Future Plan and Program (including those having to do with administrative reorganization which are listed below) would be at least $12,000 per year. Yet, because there was "not a single item" in the new program which would catch the fancy of the masses, there was little hope of raising thousands of dollars with which to meet the added expenses. If the Committee on Future Plan and Program had studied the history of the NAACP, concluded Wilkins, it would have found that large sums of money had been obtained only when specific cases of injustice aroused public emotion and indignation.[16]

Indeed, the question of how the new program was to be financed was afforded paramount consideration by almost all who surveyed the Future Plan and Program. Daisy Lampkin, the black Field Secretary, who was in a position to know the needs of the branches, thought that the proposed workers' councils would be especially beneficial in the South, but questioned the expense such a program would entail. Presumably because of the problem of finances, she also was "not so sure about the wisdom of taking over the work of the Joint Committee on National Recovery."[17] Similarly, Harry E. Davis, a black Cleveland attorney whom Du Bois earlier had suggested as Spingarn's successor to the NAACP presidency, considered the Future Plan and Program as merely "a

basis for the discussion of our future." Davis estimated that
the implementation of the entire program (including the
administrative reforms) would cost the Association $250,000
per year, "and this is an amount which is unthinkable at
present." [18]

Walter White expressed agreement with the broad outlines
of the new program but, as the officer who would be charged
with the responsibility of raising funds, he was especially disturbed by the question of financing. He asked Harris to ex-
plain how $2,500 could pay for John Davis' salary, additional
stenographic aid, traveling expenses, printing costs, and other
items entailed in assuming control of the Joint Committee on
Recovery. He reminded Harris that there was a strong possibility that no money could be obtained from either the
American Fund for Public Service or the Racham Fund.
Experience had demonstrated the necessity "of looking most
critically at such matters and particularly to consider also not
only whether a program is good or not, but how we are going
to be able to finance and put it over," [19] concluded White.

While some NAACP administrators focused their criticism
of the Future Plan and Program on the issue of finances,
others delved into the more complex problem of institutional
change. Charles Houston, the young black Washington attorney whom the Committee on Future Plan and Program
suggested should be employed to coordinate the Association's
legal work, and William Hastie, a member of the Board of
Directors who was destined to become the first black federal
circuit court judge, questioned the feasibility of the new economic program on the grounds that "adapting an existing
organization to such a program is very different from that of
creating a new organization around that program." The Association should expand and organize its efforts on behalf of
black economic uplift, maintained Hastie, "but it seems to me
that, for the time being at least, this will be but one aspect of
a many-sided program." If the new economic program were
launched, a full-time, professional economist must be hired
by the NAACP; Wilkins and White should not further di-
versify their activities. Betraying his personal doubts about

the mass appeal of the new economic program, Hastie concluded that the net result of any new activities should be a "long-time" program which would permit the NAACP's branches to appeal to and hold the attention of the man in the street.[20]

Isadore Martin found practically no merit in the proposed economic program. First, he warned that it would be unwise for the Association to create any new jobs at the current time because of the Depression and the organization's financial plight. More important, Martin was of the opinion that much of the work suggested in the new program was currently being done by the National Urban League. "If the work we set out to do twenty-five years ago is done—that is, if we are in a rut and can go no further—then it seems to me," said Martin, "that the only wise thing to do is either merge with the Urban League or dissolve the organization." [21] In short, Martin would rather see the NAACP pass out of existence than appreciably alter its historic role; ideologically he stood at the opposite extreme of the Harris insurgents. That such diametrically opposed views of the need for change were represented on the Board of Directors boded ill for the future.

Meanwhile, the white liberals in the administrative hierarchy largely directed their attention to the question of whether the principles of eighteenth-century liberalism upon which the Association's program rested (but which the report of the Committee on Future Plan and Program had denigrated) were, in fact, no longer valid. Joseph Prince Loud, former President of the Boston branch and a member of the Board of Directors since the NAACP's incorporation, was squarely opposed to the suggestion that the organization's historic primary goal of attaining blacks' full citizenship rights be altered. The Association's accomplishments "in the past twenty-five years have, in the main, met with my hearty approval and cooperation," maintained Loud, "but I view with alarm the proposed changes in policy from that of claiming full citizenship rights for the Negro, to one of partisan and class appeal." For members of a minority group to undertake a program like that which the Committee on Future Plan and

Program proposed "would be suicidal both for the Association and the Negro." [22]

But the staunchest defense of the brand of liberalism that
Harris and his adherents had so thoroughly excoriated came
from Mary White Ovington. She pointed out that the
NAACP had been formed for the express purpose of securing
the Negro's full civil, political, and social rights, and she insisted that "I have yet to talk to any Negro who does not
agree to this platform." It was the Negro's desire to share in
American life as fully as the white American which had
formed the basis of the NAACP's phenomenal growth. Harris
was not primarily interested in changing this goal, Ovington
correctly asserted, but merely in altering the method by which
it could be attained. Instead of having the Association continue its opposition to wage and job discrimination and anti-
Negro sentiment among white workers, Harris and his followers wanted the Association to induce Negroes to see their
peculiar grievances as a natural part of the larger American
labor movement. "I am opposed to this," insisted Ovington,
first, because such a philosophy was held by very few blacks,
but every Negro stood for the NAACP's program, at least in
his heart. Second, to change the organization's tactics and to
concede that it was wrong to work on behalf of one minority
group or race without working on behalf of all labor would
destroy the Association. Third, Ovington charged that in
reality Harris was preaching "economic determinism, the class
struggle, in politics, socialism and communism," although he
was not utilizing those terms; in regard to unionism his program was more closely aligned with that of the I.W.W. than
the A.F. of L. "This is revolutionary doctrine to which I for
one of the Board subscribe," [23] Ovington confessed, "but
those who want to bring it to the Negro will do best to bring
it through socialist or communistic organizations." If a
"middle class" organization like the NAACP were to adopt
Harris' program, she warned, "we should run ahead and
then back water when dissension came." The Association
could not afford to adopt a half-way course, for its "enemies,
especially the communists, would love to see us destroy

ourselves by adopting a program akin to theirs." [24]

Finally, Ovington insisted that first things must be first. The great nineteenth-century Abolitionist Wendell Phillips also had been asked to join the labor movement of his day, she observed, but he had refused on the grounds that chattel slavery must be destroyed before wage slavery could be abolished. Similarly, the modern Negro must battle to overcome what chattel slavery had left behind before he could enter any movement for revolutionary change. The Negro must work for his own amelioration, argued Ovington, and "even when he fails he has gained by the conflict." [25]

For Spingarn, the proposed new economic program posed one of the strongest tests of the degree of his conversion from noneconomic liberalism. As early as 1932, in his forceful "Racial Equality" speech, he had publicly placed himself on record as favoring a stronger economic orientation for the Association. The following year, in the summer of 1933, he had seized the initiative in convening a second Amenia Conference for the avowed purpose of reassessing the NAACP's historic program. Spingarn's latest pronouncement on the issue of a new economic orientation for the NAACP was contained in a letter of July 1934 to Abram Harris, in which he implied that Du Bois' pleas for the adoption of a stronger economic program might have been heeded by the Board of Directors many years previously if the Editor had but drafted and presented a detailed outline of the program he envisioned.[26] The public would soon discover how sincere and successful the Abolitionist had been in modifying the philosophy of noneconomic liberalism to which he had adhered for so many years.

Rejecting the adamant stand of Joseph Prince Loud and Mary White Ovington, Spingarn reached out to embrace at least a portion of the new economic program while, at the same time, firmly holding to what he believed to be the most cogent features of the NAACP's historic program. On a copy of the report of the Committee on Future Plan and Program which contains revisions in Spingarn's handwriting, the economic section is untouched, although extensive re-

visions appear in other parts of the document.[27] Similarly, in
addressing the NAACP Annual Conference of (June) 1935,
during which the report was under consideration for adoption
by the branches, Spingarn extolled the merits and accomplishments of the NAACP's historic program, but added:

> But, after all, the ideals that govern and have governed
> an organization for twenty-five years need some kind of
> evolution, development, change; and the NAACP is
> young enough, flexible enough, to conserve what is best
> of its old heritage and to try new methods and new
> ideals. . . . We know that the white workers of the
> United States have virtually all the rights that the
> NAACP is fighting for for colored people—the right to
> vote, lack of discrimination, no segregation; and yet the
> white workers are neither rich nor happy. They have
> equal opportunities. That gives us something to think
> about; and that is, can we persuade the white workers
> of America that the cards are stacked against them ex-
> actly as they are stacked against colored people, and
> the only hope for them is to combine with colored people
> in seeing that the cards are no longer stacked against
> them both.[28]

Whether or not Spingarn had become a sincere convert to
the concept of the unity of white and black labor as opposed
to merely expressing overt concessions to public pressure is
a moot point. That he could even mouth such words indicated that whether because of external pressure or personal
conviction, ideologically he had come a long way since the
days of the New Abolition. In comparison to the highly
traditionalist stance of Loud, Ovington, and Martin, Spingarn's position was far to the left.

On the other hand, Spingarn strongly urged that the
NAACP not go overboard with economic considerations;
rather, that it maintain its historic emphasis upon the securing
of civil and political liberties while expanding outward to
encompass the economic sphere. When John P. Davis, the
Executive Secretary of the Joint Committee on Recovery,

drafted an economically oriented syllabus for the proposed workers' classes, Spingarn questioned the competence of the average branch to interpret it and observed that there was generally too great a tendency to view everything in economic terms.[29] Although Spingarn assured the delegates at the 1935 Annual Conference that the NAACP intended to embrace a new economic orientation, he hastened to add:

> Now even if the economic problem becomes an important problem of our organization; . . . it is my feeling that there will still be need for the old role of the NAACP. I am not so sure that the socialized control of production will eat up all the hate in the hearts of men, and there will still be need for an organization that will see to it that every man receives equal rights regardless of his race, his creed or his color.[30]

Viewed from a strictly administrative standpoint, Spingarn's middle-of-the-road stance on the all-important issue of substantially altering the organization's historic program was sounder in terms of the Association's survival than either the inflexible opposition to change voiced by Loud, Ovington, and Martin, or the call for sudden and extensive change advocated by the Harris faction. To strike a delicate balance between recasting the polity's aims to a degree that will not corrupt its basic principles while, at the same time, responding sufficiently to pressures for change to ensure the organization's survival—such is the nature of effective leadership.[31]

Whereas Spingarn let the economic section of the report stand as written, he did not spare criticism of suggested changes in other aspects of the NAACP's historic program. He vetoed the report's suggestion that the Association become more directly involved in politics. Historically, the NAACP had been distinctly nonpartisan, including on its Board of Directors persons of all political persuasions, and encouraging its members to vote for candidates of either major party if the candidates displayed sympathy for blacks' interests. Thus, where the report of the Committee on Future Plan and Program called on the Association to "continue its political

agitation and lobbying in behalf of the rights of the Negro,"
Spingarn revised this passage to read: "continue its present
work in behalf of the political and other rights of the Negro."
Similarly, the report urged the NAACP to be ready "to support any third party representing the interests of American
workers as a whole and the special interests of the Negro."
Undoubtedly fearing that the phrase, "any third party," might
encompass the Communist Party, Spingarn revised this sen-
tence to read: "to support any party which at any given
time in the opinion of the Board of Directors . . . represents
the interests of American workers as a whole and the special
interests of the Negro." Finally, the report recommended that
the NAACP "continue its policy of electing to public office
persons sympathetic to the interests of Negroes until a *third*
party is formed." But in a subtle play on words, Spingarn
altered this passage to read: "continue its policy of supporting for public office, persons sympathetic to the interests
of Negroes until *such* a party is formed." [32]

Spingarn also gave close attention to that phase of the report dealing with segregated transportation. Historically, the
Association had utilized both legal action and political lobbying in an attempt to attain integrated public transportation
facilities, both intrastate and interstate. However, whether by
accident or design, the report indirectly acknowledged that
some degree of segregation in public transportation might
have to be accepted. Specifically, the report called upon the
Association to "strive to abolish Jim-Crowism in intrastate
transportation by making it uneconomic, insisting upon identical not similar conveniences *under conditions of racial
separation.*" Upholding the Association's historical position,
Spingarn revised this passage to read: "strive by all economic,
political and legal means possible to abolish Jim-Crowism in
intrastate transportation making it uneconomic, insisting upon
identical not similar accommodation *without any separation
of races.*" Finally, that section of the report dealing with
transportation accommodations recommended that the
NAACP foster socialization of the railroads; Spingarn completely deleted this passage. [33]

In addition to formulating a new economic orientation for the NAACP, the Committee on Future Plan and Program devoted the entire second half of its report to recommendations aimed at a sweeping revamping of the organization's administrative structure. Some degree of administrative reorganization was essential for the fullest realization of the economic program which the Committee had devised. But the Committee was equally as concerned with the problem of administrative reforms from the standpoint of democratizing the Association. As was noted in Chapter 3 of this study, the democratic constitutional structure of the NAACP was all but negated by the default of the membership from participation in the Annual Business meetings, the membership's failure to indulge its prerogative to independently select Board candidates, and many members' laxity in attending monthly Board meetings. As a result, by the 1920's major policy-making, for all practical purposes, had been relegated by default to a handful of Board members and the NAACP had become a closed corporation, complete with a self-perpetuating Board of Directors.

As has been noted,[34] by the early 1930's an ever-mounting chorus of voices, led by that of Du Bois, was demanding that the Board's virtually absolute control of the organization be shared with the rank-and-file membership. Yet it had been the old "closed-corporation" type arrangement of the central bureaucracy which had enabled the Spingarns and a few other Directors to wield such extensive personal and official influence over the organization. Conversely, for every additional branch or member who would be given a voice in the decision-making process, the potential ability of Spingarn and the other members of the power elite to wield influence would be diminished proportionately. In the administrative realm, the twilight of white liberalism was at hand.

The Committee on Future Plan and Program assumed the avowed task of suggesting means of diffusing power and authority within the NAACP without decreasing efficiency. First, the Committee urged that the Association's activities be divided into five distinct categories: Economic; Legal and Political; Educational; Publicity, Research and Investigations; Financial.[35] By 1920 the NAACP was employing a Chairman of the Legal Committee, a Director of Branches, and a Director of Publications and Research to supervise their respective realms, but historically such vital tasks as political lobbying, the solicitation of funds, and general publicity and educational activities had been combined under the general supervision of the Executive Secretary and his assistants. Under the plan proposed by the Committee on Future Plan and Program, the assistant secretary was to assume responsibility for all "routine" office tasks, thereby freeing the Executive Secretary to serve as coordinator of the suggested five major activities in addition to continuing his supervision of lobbying and political activities. In the first section of its report, the Committee had recommended that the new economic program be placed under the direction of a five-member team of outside experts. Thus, this vital area of the Association's program was to be removed from the Secretary's control.[36] In addition, branch activities, which traditionally had been supervised by a Director of Branches and his handful of assistants based at the national office, were to be more closely knit by dividing the branches geographically into five regions, each with a permanent supervising secretary.[37]

But it was the Committee's suggestions regarding the selection and tenure of Board members and national officers that directly affected Spingarn and the other members of the traditional power elite. In order to curb the historic self-perpetuating tendency among national officers, the Committee urged that the selection of Board members and national officers be given over to a seven-member nominating committee, consisting of four persons selected by the branches at the NAACP Annual Conferences and three persons selected by the Board.[38] It is significant that the membership, rather than the Board of Directors, was to have majority representation on the committee. Equally as important was the Committee's recommendation that the NAACP President, as well as all other national officers, be elected to terms of office of not less than two years nor more than five. Since the inception of the organization, the Board of Directors had elected the national officers, including the President, for terms of one year. However, the interpersonal relationships within the Association apparently had grown so strong that no rival candidate was presented for an office as long as the incumbent expressed a desire to retain his post. There was no instance in the NAACP's history prior to 1934 in which a major national officer—President, Board Chairman, Treasurer—relinquished his office for reasons other than death or resignation, both of which were infrequent. For example, Miss Ovington and Spingarn shared the Board Chairmanship for twenty of the twenty-three years from 1911 to 1934. Conversely, no incumbent in any of the three major national executive posts relinquished his position as a result of a strong challenge from a rival candidate.[39]

Next, the Committee on Future Plan and Program attacked the Board's practice of conducting major business with the presence or consent of only a handful of Board members. In Chapter 3 of this study it was noted that the distant location of many Board members from New York, where meetings were held, the failure of most prestigious members to attend meetings, and general laxity of attendance had narrowed the group regularly present at Board meetings to approximately eight or nine members by the 1920's. The Committee sought to remedy this situation by recommending that the NAACP constitution be amended to increase the number of Board members from forty to forty-eight, each of whom was to be elected for a four-year term, thereby causing the terms of one-fourth of the Board members to expire annually. More important, the Committee recommended that a quorum of one-fourth, or a dozen, of the forty-eight members be required at Board meetings. Undoubtedly the Committee reasoned that the eight new Board seats would serve the double purpose of affording the rank-and-file membership greater representation without the embarrassment of forcing the resignation of incumbents, as well as increasing the likelihood of a numerically larger attendance at Board meetings.

The constitutional powers of the Board Chairman and the

Board's committee system were given special consideration by Harris and his Committee. As is often the case with large-scale organizations, the NAACP conducted the bulk of its business through standing committees—e.g., Budget Committee, Nominating Committee, Crisis Committee, etc. The Chairman of the Board appointed all committees of the Board and was himself an ex-officio member of all committees. The delegates to the Annual Conference of 1919 passed a resolution calling upon the Board Chairman (then Mary White Ovington) to appoint more blacks as committee chairmen and members, a request which met with prompt compliance. Some ten years passed before Du Bois launched his first major outcry against the committee system, largely because Walter White's membership on the *Crisis* Editorial Board was objectionable to him. Also, it will be recalled that Du Bois' disgruntlement with the Budget Committee in 1931 led him, together with the majority of the salaried executives, to attack the appointive powers of the Board Chairman, an attack which was partially responsible for Miss Ovington's resignation from the Board Chairmanship in 1932.[40]

The Committee on Future Plan and Program recommended that the power to appoint committees be vested in the entire Board, rather than the Board Chairman, with the understanding that the Board might delegate this responsibility to the Chairman whenever desired. In addition, the Committee suggested that salaried officials be eligible for membership on all committees of the Board, with the exception of those committees which pertained to personnel and employment.[41]

Spingarn immediately bent his efforts toward seeing that the report of the Committee on Future Plan and Program was not foisted on the Board of Directors by the Harris sympathizers. Using his authority as Board Chairman, he specifically directed Walter White to inform Harris that no action was to be taken on the document until a copy was in the hands of every member of the Board. When, because of a "bad cold," Spingarn could not be present at a special Board meeting convened on September 25, 1934, for consideration of the report, he requested that no action be taken by the Directors until the next Board meeting. Harris merely summarized the contents of the report at the September 25 meeting, although the Board had paid his expenses to New York for the express purpose of hearing his detailed explanation of the document.

The report, as revised and adopted by the Board of Directors, was at best a compromise, providing a clear-cut victory for neither of the contending factions. Ostensibly because of limited funds, the Board voted to establish workers' education "classes" (to be conducted by the branches) in lieu of the proposed regional workers' councils, with the stipulation that the classes be designed to fulfill the same objectives as had been suggested for the councils. The Board omitted any reference to direct-action tactics like the strike, lockout, and workers' agitation as a means of furthering the interests of black labor. It was decided not to take over the work of the Joint Committee on Recovery; rather, the NAACP was to "cooperate with existing organizations," seeking the use of their records in guiding the organization's new economic program. An "efficient person" (with no specific mention of John P. Davis) was to be hired to direct the Association's economic activities as soon as finances would permit. Whereas the report of the Committee on Future Plan and Program recommended that the new economic program be placed under the direction of a team of outside experts over which the Board of Directors would have only limited control, the Board voted to place the program under its immediate direction and to utilize a five-man committee (presumably composed of outside experts) as an advisory body to the Board.[42]

In the final analysis, then, the recommendations of the Committee on Future Plan and Program in the economic sector were robbed of their most cogent aspects. Emphasis upon classes in workers' education as the chief means of unifying black labor, coupled with the prohibition on the use of the strike, lockout, and demonstrations, relegated the new economic program, in terms of tactics, to the age-old methods of the dissemination of information through the written and spoken word. On the other hand, by inducing the Board to endorse even a limited program for unifying black labor, Harris and his Committee had caused the Association to embrace a bolder economic orientation than ever before in the organization's history. More significantly, implicit in the Association's adoption of the more positive economic orientation was the admission that the organization's historic struggle for civil and political rights was no longer totally adequate.

The report's recommendations for alterations in other sectors of the NAACP's historic program were also practically emasculated by the Board. Reference to the Association's participation in a third party or to any appreciable alterations in its traditional political activities was omitted, as was any mention of socialization of the railroads. Indeed, the final report, as adopted by the Board, incorporated almost verbatim the revisions Spingarn had made in this section.[48] The report's recommendations for strengthening and extending the NAACP's educational and research programs were the only ones which passed the Directors' scrutiny substantially intact.

The administrative reforms proposed by the Committee on Future Plan and Program met an equally dire fate; the Directors revised or negated just enough of the key recommendations to permit the Board's traditional ultimate control over administration. Whereas the report had recommended that the rank-and-file membership have majority representation on the new seven-member Nominating Committee for Board and national officer candidates, the Board voted to have three members elected by the Annual Conferences and three by the Board, and to have the Board Chairman serve as the seventh member with permanent status. Hence, the Board's representatives retained the power to overrule the rank-and-file's appointees. The recommendation that the presence of one-fourth of the enlarged Board be necessary to constitute a quorum at meetings was completely ignored, although it was voted that the Board be enlarged to forty-eight members. One of the Committee's key recommendations looking toward the transfer of administrative control of the organization to the rank-and-file was that a majority vote of the members in good standing of any one of the several branches should be sufficient to amend the national constitution. The Board revised this recommendation so as to require the national Directors' approval of the branch members' proposed amendment.[44]

Spingarn made no overt attempt to block the proposals for administrative reform. On a copy of the Committee's report, with revisions in his handwriting, the section dealing with administrative reorganization was left untouched, probably because he, along with the other national administrators, was indirectly under attack. In addressing the 1935 NAACP Annual Conference, during which the revised report was under consideration by the branches' delegates, Spingarn professed to welcome democratization. He told the delegates that for twenty years the NAACP had been thinking of how the branches could be given more power over the organization's administration, but that "it is not as easy as it seems." He promised that the Association would be "gradually" democratized so that the branches would have "more and more power." [45] But even as Spingarn spoke so optimistically, he must have realized that there were no immediate prospects for the realization of his promises, since the revised report of the Committee on Future Plan and Program left ultimate control of the organization in the hands of the Board of Directors.

Thus, the Harris insurgents who had struggled so diligently to revamp the NAACP's program and administration emerged with less than a half victory on both counts. In December 1934, shortly after the Board had voted on his Committee's report, a greatly disgruntled Harris informed Walter White that his contribution had been made, other commitments made his time scarce, and that he felt he should resign his seat on the Board of Directors. The final blow to Harris' ego came a few weeks later when an official of the National Urban League inquired of Harris whether he was aware that the League recently had formulated a program of workers' councils which was almost identical to the one Harris had proposed for the NAACP. Harris assured the official that he had not been aware of the League's plans and that his program for the Association derived from theories he had been espousing since 1928.[46]

"OLD ABOLITIONISTS NEVER DIE . . ."

Ostensibly the Harris insurgents had been dealt a crushing
defeat, and the way seemed clear for the resumption of business as usual by the NAACP old-guard leadership in late
1934. But for one of such sensitive temperament as Spingarn,
apparently even ultimate victory could not entirely erase the
more unsavory aspects of the long struggles surrounding the
resignation of Du Bois and the challenge of the Harris faction.
In fact, he was so thoroughly depressed by the controversy
surrounding the Future Plan and Program that he virtually
dropped out of active participation in critical decision-
making for nearly a year after the Committee's report had
been rejected. When the NAACP Nominating Committee convened in late 1934, after the defeat of the Future Plan and
Program was assured, Spingarn insisted that he not be renominated for another term as Board Chairman. Instead, the
Committee selected Louis T. Wright, thereby affording the
organization the first black Board Chairman in its history. The
lively correspondence regarding financial policies which White
and Spingarn had maintained since 1930 also declined to a
trickle after late 1934, although the impact of the Depression
upon the Association had not yet dissipated. Similarly, in
April 1935, after four years of intensive personal interest in
the critical decisions involving the allocation of funds, Spingarn declined membership on the Budget Committee.[47]
    By the end of 1936, after a year of withdrawal, there were
unmistakable signs of Spingarn's reviving, though still limited,
interest in the NAACP, undoubtedly reflecting a general resumption of the status quo following the departures of Harris
and Du Bois. Although the powers inherent in the Board
Chairmanship had passed to Wright, the new NAACP constitution of 1936 afforded the President ex-officio membership
on all committees of the Association. Spingarn resumed his
membership on the Budget Committee and was one of the most
frequent attenders of the meetings of the Committee on Ad-

ministration until the end of 1938, when the first signs of a fatal illness (a brain tumor) brought all his activities to an abrupt halt. In addition, he remained active, until the onset of illness, in the Association's ill-fated attempt to secure a federal anti-lynching law, and did not hesitate to offer his opinion, though rather academically, on random matters which captured his attention.

But at best, Spingarn became a considerably less important figure within the Association's administrative hierarchy after 1935. White increasingly directed questions regarding policy matters to the entire Committee on Administration, which was presided over by a new Chairman, Louis T. Wright. Perhaps out of deference to Wright, Spingarn curbed whatever personal power he might still have been capable of wielding. Indeed, if an arbitrary date must be set for the passage of the "control" of the Association to blacks, it is 1935.

Yet Spingarn's decline derived from issues which antedated the struggle over the adoption of the Future Plan and Program and which were more fundamental than a mere changeover in the Board Chairmanship. For more than twenty years Spingarn had believed that appeals to the public conscience and the Negro's peaceful agitation and protest would bring racial equality in America. His personal philosophy, like that of the Association, rested on those principles of noneconomic liberalism which stressed equal civil and political rights for all under the existing socioeconomic system, and special privileges for none. During the early years it had been this philosophy that had formed the veritable genius of the Association's program and success; a philosophy so right and so fundamentally American that rich and poor, socialist and noneconomic liberal, black and white, radical and conservative —"all right thinking Americans," as Spingarn put it—could rally to its call. The program relied for success on the inherent justness of the American people.

Spingarn's dilemma derived not from the invalidity of the noneconomic liberalism which he espoused, for this philosophy could not be denounced without undermining principles on which the nation itself rested. Rather, the tragedy of Spingarn, like that of the NAACP, was rooted in the failure of the American people to fulfill the commitment to principles which they professed to hold dear. When those like Du Bois and Harris, who had grown impatient, demanded an accounting of the concrete fruits of noneconomic liberalism after a twenty-year trial, the Abolitionist, through little fault of his own, had no wholly satisfactory reply. Lack of public response had made a once daring program appear conservative and ineffective. Although Du Bois and Harris passed from the immediate scene after 1934, the speeches delivered at Annual Conferences during succeeding years by men like John P. Davis and Ralph Bunche grew more militant in their denunciation of noneconomic liberalism.

Not only changing times but age as well had begun to overtake Spingarn by the mid-1930's. In one of his last major speeches, entitled "What the NAACP Expects of Its Youth," which Spingarn delivered in 1937, when he was sixty-two, he conceded that the spotlight had all but passed from those like himself who had labored in the organization for more than twenty-five years. Almost as if attempting to justify the continuing presence of such older leaders, he recounted the fiery New Abolitionism of an earlier day, assuring his young listeners that those who had grown old had once been young and enthusiastic. "Now we need the help of all the youth," said Spingarn, "but the youth needs us; I mean it needs the great background and tradition of the NAACP." Although he conceded the necessity for militancy, he reaffirmed his belief that militancy must be exhibited in "the American way." [48]

Upon Spingarn's death in 1939, Arthur Spingarn retired as Chairman of the Legal Department in order to succeed his brother as President of the Association. However, with the powerful Board Chairmanship in the hands of Wright, the presidency reverted to the largely honorary post which it had been during the tenure of Moorfield Storey. Mrs. Spingarn was elected to fill her husband's unexpired term on the Board of Directors. The aging Mary White Ovington, the last of the triumvirate of white liberals who had remained at the center of administration after 1930, retired from her work with the Association in 1940, less than a year after Spingarn's death.

During the late 1930's black men who by then were advanced in age still sometimes reminisced in their correspondence to the national office about the fiery New Abolitionism of a day long past. Most of all, they seemed to remember the young white man who so often had become literally flush red with anger and indignation over the injustices accorded darker-skinned Americans. It was most appropriate that they should have remembered Spingarn in that particular light, for his life was a testimony of the efficacy of the liberal credo: that a man need not be black in order to become sincerely indignant about the second-class citizenship status of his neighbors. In 1940 Du Bois made the following dedication of his autobiography: "To Keep the Memory of Joel Spingarn—A Scholar and A Knight." It is not farfetched to believe that one as astute as Du Bois regarding the color line could not have been entirely mistaken.

ESSAY ON SOURCES

MANUSCRIPTS

THE PERSONAL PAPERS of J. E. Spingarn are contained in three separate collections. The J. E. Spingarn Papers in the Howard University Library pertain almost exclusively to the period prior to 1919 and deal largely with his efforts to establish a black officers' training camp during World War I. The J. E. Spingarn Collection in the New York Public Library consists of correspondence relating to Spingarn's political and academic endeavors, as well as his role as an NAACP administrator. Though small in volume, the correspondence between Spingarn and several key NAACP officials during the 1930's is indispensable for understanding the inner administrative history of the organization during the most crucial phase of the Depression. The J. E. Spingarn Papers in the James Weldon Johnson Collection in the Yale University Library consist of a file of letters between Du Bois and Spingarn and between Spingarn and Johnson. The correspondence spans the entire period from 1911 to the mid-1930's and contains a number of important letters and documents pertaining to the Association's rise that are not to be found elsewhere. The Arthur B. Spingarn Papers in the Library of Congress contain pertinent letters of J. E. Spingarn and are especially rewarding for the period after 1930.

The Files of the NAACP in the Manuscript Division of the Library of Congress are, of course, indispensable for any study of the organization or its officials. The Files—some seven hundred boxes of material to the year 1939—are divided into six major sections, all of which contain personal correspondence and documents relating to the organization's rise. Unfortunately, the papers of a given official are likely to be scattered throughout the Files, although a portion of the personal correspondence of each major officer has been sorted and chronologically arranged. The Personal Correspondence section of the Files contains key Spingarn letters spanning the first thirty years of the NAACP's history, and the Annual Conference section contains stenographic reports of most of his major speeches. The NAACP national office in New York City has given over most of the organization's files to the Library of Congress, but it has retained complete sets of the Board Minutes, the official reports of major salaried officials, and the Minutes of the Annual Meetings.

The papers of key figures within the Association's administrative hierarchy also are indispensable, especially for clarifying interpersonal relationships. By far the most revealing and rewarding are the W. E. B. Du Bois Papers, in the custody of Herbert Aptheker, New York City. A much smaller collection of Du Bois Papers in the Amistad Research Center, Fisk University, contains a handful of Spingarn letters primarily relating to the decade of the 1920's. The Oswald Garrison Villard Papers in the Houghton Library, Harvard University, reveal many of the organization's inner activities during the formative years but are of practically no use in shedding light on Spingarn's specific role. A large portion of Walter White's correspondence is included in the vast James Weldon Johnson Collection at Yale University, but copies of most of White's correspondence are in the Files of the NAACP in the Library of Congress. The Files of the NAACP are the best source for delving into the roles of major officials like May Childs Nerney, Mary White Ovington, William A. Sinclair, and Louis T. Wright, for they have no personal collections of papers. The Ray Stannard Baker Papers in the Library of Congress contain a handful of letters from Miss Ovington to Baker, but few deal directly with the NAACP's development.

The papers of other figures closely connected with the Association are disappointing, both for a study of Spingarn and the organization. Included among these are the Charles Edward Russell Papers and the Moorfield Storey Papers in the Library of Congress, and the George William Cook Papers and Archibald Grimké Papers in the Howard University Library.

Other collections that contain a handful of pertinent Spingarn letters are the Theodore Roosevelt Papers, the Leonard P. Wood Papers, the Henry L. Mencken Papers, and the John Purroy Mitchel Papers, all in the Library of Congress. The Isaac Goldberg Papers in the New York Public Library are especially helpful for understanding the issues surrounding Spingarn's dismissal from Columbia University. The Emmett J. Scott Papers in the Morgan State University Library are useful for understanding Booker T. Washington's relationship with the NAACP but contain no Spingarn letters. The Booker T. Washington Papers in the Library of Congress are indispensable for clarifying Spingarn's personal opinion of Washington and the New Abolition attacks on the black leader.

BOOKS

Important biographies and autobiographies of individuals who were prominent in the Association's administrative hierarchy include Elliott M. Rudwick, *W. E. B. Du Bois: A Study in Minority Group Leadership* (Philadelphia: University of Pennsylvania Press, 1959); Francis L. Broderick, *W. E. B. Du Bois: Negro Leader in a Time of Crisis* (Stanford, Calif.:

Stanford University Press, 1960); James Weldon Johnson, *Along This Way* (New York: The Viking Press, 1933); Walter White, *A Man Called White: The Autobiography of Walter White* (New York: The Viking Press, 1948). Insightful comments on Spingarn's social and racial philosophies, as well as the policy decisions confronting the Association, are contained in W. E. B. Du Bois' autobiography, *Dusk of Dawn: An Essay Toward an Autobiography of a Race Concept* (New York: Harcourt, Brace and World, Inc., 1940). The most convenient source for the study of Booker T. Washington's relationship with the NAACP is Hugh Hawkins, ed., *Booker T. Washington and His Critics: The Problem of Negro Leadership* (Boston: D. C. Heath and Co., 1962).

It is virtually impossible to comprehend the mechanics of a large-scale, complex organization like the NAACP without employing basic sociological theory regarding organizational structure, power sharing, and the dynamics of interpersonal relations within such large-scale polities. The most informative study of leadership is Philip Selznick, *Leadership in Administration: A Sociological Interpretation* (Evanston, Ill.: Row, Peterson Co., 1957). Invaluable insight regarding participation in voluntary associations may be gained from David. L. Sills, *The Volunteers: Means and Ends in a National Organization* (Glencoe, Ill.: The Free Press, 1957); Seymour Martin Lipset, *Political Man: The Social Bases of Politics* (Garden City, N.Y.: Doubleday, Anchor Books edition, 1963); and A. W. Gouldner, ed., *Studies in Leadership* (New York: Harper and Bros., 1950).

Several excellent works provide background material for the general racial, social, and political climate of the period. Especially helpful are C. Vann Woodward, *The Strange Career of Jim Crow* (2nd ed. rev.; New York: Oxford University Press, 1957); E. David Cronon, *Black Moses: The Story of Marcus Garvey and the Universal Negro Improvement Association* (Madison, Wis.: University of Wisconsin Press, 1955); Robert Bone, *The Negro Novel in America* (New Haven, Conn.: Yale University Press, 1958); Richard Hofstadter, *The Age of Reform: From Bryan to F.D.R.* (New

York: Vintage Books, 1960); Donald R. McCoy, *Calvin Coolidge: The Quiet President* (New York: Macmillan Co., 1967); Andrew Sinclair, *The Available Man: The Life Behind the Masks of Warren Gamaliel Harding* (New York: Macmillan Co., 1965). Arthur M. Schlesinger, Jr., *The Age of Roosevelt: The Politics of Upheaval* (Boston: Houghton Mifflin Co., 1960) provides a brief summary of the status of blacks under the New Deal.

ARTICLES AND PAMPHLETS

Important aspects of Spingarn's political and social philosophy are summarized in J. E. Spingarn and others, "Segregation—A Symposium," *Crisis,* XLI (March 1934), 79–82; and his "Politics and the Poet: A Prophecy," *Atlantic Monthly,* CLXX (November 1942), 73–78. Only one or two articles dealing specifically with Spingarn have been written, including Oswald Garrison Villard, "Issues and Men," *The Nation,* CXLIX (August 1939), 174, which is a one-page obituary; and Lewis Mumford, "Scholar and Gentleman," *Saturday Review of Literature,* CLXX (August 1939), 8–9, which also is an obituary article. The best over-all summary of Spingarn's racial philosophy is found in his "Racial Equality" (Amenia, N.Y.: Privately printed at the Troutbeck Press, 1932).

August Meier, "Toward a Reinterpretation of Booker T. Washington," *Journal of Southern History,* XXIII (May 1957), 220–27; and "Booker T. Washington and the Rise of the NAACP," *Crisis,* LXI (February 1954), 69–76, 117–23, clarify Washington's relationship with the Association.

Three important aspects of the Association's program during the pre-1930 period are treated in Professors Lightfoot, Locke, and MacLear, "Howard University in the War," *Howard University Record,* XIII (April 1919), 160–63; "The New Abolition," *Howard University Journal,* X (February 14, 1913), 5; W. E. B. Du Bois, *The Amenia Conference: An Historic Gathering* (Amenia, N.Y.: Privately printed at the Troutbeck Press, 1925). The NAACP *Annual Reports* and the organization's house organ, *Crisis*, deal with every major aspect of the Association's administration and development.

UNPUBLISHED MATERIAL

The Files of the NAACP contain a wealth of information in the form of unpublished speeches of officials, reports of officers, and findings of committees. Spingarn's major speeches, most of which are contained in the Annual Conference section of the Files, are indispensable for tracing the evolution of his thought. Especially revealing are "The Second Quarter Century of the NAACP" (address delivered before the NAACP Annual Conference, St. Louis, Missouri, June 25, 1935); and "The Colored Soldier in France" (speech delivered before the NAACP Annual Conference, Cleveland, Ohio, June 1919). His "Literature and the New Era" (lecture delivered at the New School for Social Research, New York City, February 18, 1931) is one of the most important sources for an understanding of his attitude toward the economic problems growing out of the Depression. (A copy of this lecture is in the New York Public Library.)

NEWSPAPERS

The handy index to the New York *Times* makes this great paper useful throughout the period. Spingarn's dismissal from Columbia University in 1911 received extensive coverage in the Boston *Evening Transcript*, the New York *Times*, and the New York *Post*. The J. E. Spingarn Collection in the New York Public Library contains numerous clippings from papers of the Amenia, New York, vicinity, including the Poughkeepsie *Eagle*, the Poughkeepsie *Sunday Star*, and the Bronx Borough *Record and Times*. Some fourteen boxes of clippings from sundry papers are included in the Files of the NAACP. These cover almost every conceivable subject, but are not arranged either chronologically or alphabetically.

Three black newspapers are indispensable for the period from 1910 to 1920: the Cleveland *Gazette*, the New York *Age*, and the Washington *Bee*. Spingarn rarely received individual treatment in the black press, but important events in the Association's rise, especially during the period after 1930, are treated in the Baltimore *Afro-American*, the Pittsburgh *Courier*, and the New York *Amsterdam News*.

NOTES

CHAPTER 1: INTRODUCTION

[1] Interview with Mrs. J. E. Spingarn, New York City, June 19, 1968. This and succeeding paragraphs dealing with Spingarn's family background and early life are based largely upon this interview with Mrs. Spingarn and family records in her possession.

[2] *Ibid.;* interview with Arthur Barnett Spingarn, New York City, December 27, 1968. At the time of his death in November 1916, Elias Spingarn's estate totaled $228,156. New York *Times*, April 1, 1919.

[3] Interview with Mrs. J. E. Spingarn, New York City, June 19, 1968; Spingarn, "Literature and the New Era" (lecture delivered at the New School for Social Research, New York City, February 18, 1931), copy in the J. E. Spingarn Collection (New York Public Library; hereafter cited as the Spingarn Collection); Spingarn to [Oswald Garrison] Villard, December 21, 1929, Oswald Garrison Villard Papers (Houghton Library, Harvard University; hereafter cited as the Villard Papers). Arthur Spingarn's undergraduate and law degrees also were received from Columbia University. Interview with Mrs. J. E. Spingarn, New York City, June 19, 1968.

[4] *Ibid.;* Lewis Mumford, "Scholar and Gentleman," *Saturday Review of Literature*, XX (August 1939), 8; Spingarn, "Some Busy Years," n.d. [1920], Spingarn Collection; New York *Times*, July 27, 1939. Clippings and reviews of Spingarn's major published works are in the Spingarn Collection. It was also during this formative period, in 1905, that Spingarn married Amy Einstein, daughter of a wealthy Jewish businessman and the sister of one of Spingarn's Columbia classmates. Mrs. Spingarn's first American ancestor is reputed to have been a drummer boy who followed Lafayette to America and who served in the Revolution. On the strength of this family legend she joined the Daughters of the American Revolution, but relinquished her membership when the organization refused the use of its hall to Marian Anderson, the black contralto, in 1939. Four children were born to the Spingarns: two sons, Edward and Stephen; and two daughters, Hope and Honor. Interview with Mrs. J. E. Spingarn, New York City, June 19, 1968.

[5] Spingarn, "Literature and the New Era"; Mumford, "Scholar and Gentleman," 8; statement, n.n., n.d., enclosed in Spingarn to Isaac Goldberg, February 9, 1933, Isaac Goldberg Papers (New York Public Library; hereafter cited as the Goldberg Papers).

[6] Mumford, "Scholar and Gentleman," 8; statement, n.n., n.d., Spingarn Collection; statement, n.n., n.d., enclosed in Spingarn to Isaac Goldberg, February 9, 1933; Spingarn to Goldberg, May 24, 1926, Goldberg Papers.

[7] Richard Hofstadter and Walter P. Metzger, *The Development of Academic Freedom in the United States* (New York: Alfred A. Knopf, 1955), Chaps. V, VI.

[8] Spingarn to William Howard Taft, n.d. [1913], rough draft, Spingarn Collection; Spingarn, letter to the editor, Boston *Evening Transcript*, December 19, 1900.

[9] *Columbia Spectator* (Columbia University school newspaper), April 12, 1907, October 14, 1907, clippings, Spingarn Collection; New York *Times*, January 25, 1910; New York *Sun*, January 25, 1910; New York *Herald Tribune*, January 25, 1910; Boston *Evening Transcript*, March 11, 1911; statement enclosed in Spingarn to Isaac Goldberg, February 9, 1933, Goldberg Papers. Pertinent correspondence between Spingarn and Butler regarding this matter is reproduced in S[pingarn], "Columbia's Journalistic Ethics" (printed circular marked "confidential within Columbia University"), n.d. [1911], Spingarn Collection.

[10] Statement partially drafted in Spingarn's handwriting, n.n., n.d., Spingarn Collection; statement enclosed in Spingarn to Isaac Goldberg, February 9, 1933, Goldberg Papers; New York *Times*, September 4, 1908, March 10, 1911, March 26, 1911; New York *Sun*, March 25, 1911. Spingarn was but the latest of several widely acclaimed professors who had resigned under pressure or been fired from Columbia since the turn of the century. These and similar cases in other universities and colleges across the nation were manifestations of the professoriates' struggle for academic freedom and a voice in university administration, culminating in the establishment of the American Association of University Professors in 1914. See Hofstadter and Metzger, *The Development of Academic Freedom, passim.* Peck received financial assistance from Spingarn for a brief period after the former's dismissal from Columbia, but committed suicide in 1915. Greatly disturbed by the incident, Spingarn devoted the following verse to Peck, Butler, and the seven-hundred-member Columbia faculty:

> This is the man they condemn, this
>   is the man they defile,
> But by all the gods of justice, not
>   his the craft and guile.
> For another poisoned his honor, and
>   all the rest stood still
> Seven hundred rats obeyed a fox's
>   will;
> Another cast him out, another
>   struck him dead,
> But never a word of protest the seven
>   hundred said.

Quoted in Harold D. Careu, "Spingarn's Poems Reveal Spirit of Social Crusader," Pasadena (California) *Star-News*, September 20, 1924, clipping, Spingarn Collection.

[11] Statement enclosed in Spingarn to Isaac Goldberg, February 9, 1933, Goldberg Papers; Spingarn to Walter White, September 24, 1936, NAACP Administrative Files, C-227 (Manuscript Division, Library of Congress; hereafter cited as the NAACP Adm. Files).

[12] Spingarn to Isaac Goldberg, May 24, 1926, Goldberg Papers.

[13] Quoted in Spingarn, "Politics and the Poet: A Prophesy," *Atlantic Monthly*, CLXX (November 1942), 75.

[14] *Ibid.*

[15] Spingarn to George E. Woodberry, n.d. [1899], rough draft, Spingarn Collection; interview with Mrs. J. E. Spingarn, New York City, June 19, 1968.

[16] Spingarn, "Literature and the New Era."

[17] Amenia *Times*, August 20, 1910, clipping, Spingarn Collection; New York *Times*, October 23, 1908. For a discussion of the progressive movement and its philosophy see Richard Hofstadter, *The Age of Reform: From Bryan to F.D.R.* (New York: Vintage Books, 1960), pp. 5–6, *et passim.*

[18] New York *Evening Post*, December 5, 1901.

[19] *Columbia Spectator*, October 14, 1908; Bronx Borough *Record and Times*, October 4, 1908, October 20, 1908; New York *Sun*, September 30, 1908; New York *Evening Post*, September 28, 1908. Richard W. Lawrence to Spingarn, November 7, 1908; Spingarn to Joseph A. Goulden (Democratic candidate), November 4, 1908, copy, Spingarn Collection. Spingarn appears to have been the first member of the American generation of Spingarns to endorse the Republican Party, thereby departing from the Democratic loyalty of his father. Interview with Arthur Barnett Spingarn, New York City, December 27, 1968. In his campaign Spingarn received the personal endorsement of Theodore Roosevelt, Secretary of State Elihu Root, and Secretary of Commerce Oscar Strauss. New York *Times*, October 20, 1908; Elihu Root to Spingarn, October 9, 1908, letter published in New York *Times*, October 18, 1908; Oscar Strauss to Spingarn, October 7, 1908, letter published in New York *Times*, October 18, 1908; *North Side News*, October 16, 1908, clipping, Spingarn Collection. Remaining an ardent Rooseveltian Progressive after his defeat in 1908, Spingarn helped organize the first Progressive Party in Dutchess County, was a founder of the national Progressive (Bull Moose) Party (1912), and was elected a delegate to the Progressive Party's national conventions in both 1912 and 1916. See, for example, Spingarn to Theodore Roosevelt, April 29, 1911, January 9, 1913; Spingarn to Frank Harper, April 17, 1914, the Papers of Theodore Roosevelt (Manuscript Division, Library of Congress; hereafter cited as the Papers of Theodore Roosevelt); Spingarn, "Some Busy Years," n.d. [1920]; Poughkeepsie *Eagle*, October 27, 1914, clipping; *Knickerbocker Press* [Albany, New York], March 11, 1916, clipping, Spingarn Collection.

[20] See *infra*, Chap. 2.

[21] See *infra*, Chap. 3.

[22] Speech of Mr. J. E. Spingarn at Banquet Honoring Dr. W. E. B. Du Bois (delivered at Atlanta University, Atlanta, Georgia, February 23, 1938), copy in NAACP Adm. Files, C-429.

[23] "Extract From the Programme of the Amenia Field Day," August

20, 1910; Spingarn to Theodore Roosevelt, April 29, 1911, Papers of Theodore Roosevelt. Spingarn claimed to have gotten the idea for the festivals from Theodore Roosevelt's Country Life Commission, but it is probable that he was also influenced by the significance of sports in bridging the communications and social gaps between gentlemen and commoners in England. Describing a trip he had taken to England in the summer of 1909, he observed that the aristocracy and plebes met with a truer democracy than in America, largely due to the media of poetry and sports, which both groups shared. *Columbia Spectator,* January 12, 1910, clipping, Spingarn Collection; Spingarn to Theodore Roosevelt, April 29, 1911, Papers of Theodore Roosevelt.

[24] Spingarn to Theodore Roosevelt, March 11, 1913, Papers of Theodore Roosevelt; "Women and Democracy," speech quoted in Poughkeepsie *Eagle,* n.d. [fall 1913], clipping, Spingarn Collection; New York *Tribune,* December 4, 1914; "Report of the Chairman of the Board, Dr. Spingarn," in Minutes of the NAACP Annual Meeting, 1916, NAACP National Office (New York City).

[25] Spingarn to Isaac Goldberg, February 9, 1933, Goldberg Papers; *Crisis,* XL (September 1939), 269. Sundry medals and awards which Spingarn received for his collection of clematis are in the Spingarn Collection.

[26] Seymour Martin Lipset, *Political Man: The Social Bases of Politics* (Garden City, N.Y.: Doubleday, Anchor Books, 1963), pp. 318–20 *et passim.*

[27] *Ibid.;* David Donald, *Lincoln Reconsidered* (New York: Alfred A. Knopf, 1955), pp. 33–34.

[28] Statement, n.n., n.d., Spingarn Collection.

[29] Lewis Mumford, Introduction to Spingarn, "Politics and the Poet: A Prophesy," 74.

CHAPTER 2: REINCARNATION OF THE ABOLITIONISTS

[1] For accounts of the founding of the NAACP, see Charles Flint Kellogg, *NAACP: A History of the National Association for the Advancement of Colored People* (Baltimore: The Johns Hopkins Press, 1967), I, 9 ff.; Mary White Ovington, *The Walls Came Tumbling Down* (New York: Harcourt, Brace and World, Inc., 1947); Jack Abramowitz, "Origins of the NAACP," *Social Education,* XV (January 1951), 21–23.

[2] For a discussion of the racial conditions which fostered the rise of the NAACP, see Rayford W. Logan, *The Negro in American Life and Thought: The Nadir, 1877–1901* (New York: Dial Press, Inc., 1954); C. Vann Woodward, *Origins of the New South 1877–1913* (Baton Rouge, La.: Louisiana State University Press, 1951); Stanley P. Hirshon, *Farewell to the Bloody Shirt: Northern Republicans and the Southern Negro, 1877–1893* (Bloomington, Ind.: University of Indiana Press, 1962).

[3] Logan, *The Negro in American Life and Thought, passim;* Minutes of the Meetings of the NAACP Board of Directors, March 7, 1911

(Manuscript Division, Library of Congress; hereafter cited as NAACP Board Minutes); J. E. Spingarn, "Memorandum," January 21, 1913; Franklin D. Roosevelt to Spingarn, January 22, 1913; Spingarn to May Childs Nerney, January 24, 1913; Spingarn and Oswald Garrison Villard to Hon. Herbert C. Ring, February 17, 1915, NAACP Adm. Files; Cleveland *Gazette*, January 23, 1915, January 30, 1915.

⁴ For a survey of Democratic and Republican attitudes toward the Negro, see Arthur S. Link, ed., "Correspondence Relating to the Progressive Party's 'Lily White' Policy in 1912," *Journal of Southern History*, X (November 1944), 480–90; Arthur S. Link, *Wilson: The New Freedom* (Princeton, N.J.: Princeton University Press, 1956); NAACP Board Minutes, 1912–15, *passim*.

⁵ Booker T. Washington, "The Atlanta Exposition Address," in Hugh Hawkins, ed., *Booker T. Washington and His Critics* (Boston: D. C. Heath Co., 1962), pp. 10–20. August Meier has shown that Washington's conservatism was more apparent than real. The Negro leader worked quietly behind the scenes in opposition to disfranchisement and other forms of discrimination. See August Meier, "Toward a Reinterpretation of Booker T. Washington," *Journal of Southern History*, XXIII (May 1957), 220–27. Several white liberals, including Oswald Garrison Villard, who initially supported Washington later switched their allegiance to the more militant NAACP. For Washington's influence upon the rise of the NAACP see August Meier, "Booker T. Washington and the Rise of the NAACP," *Crisis*, LXI (February 1954), 69–76, 117–23.

⁶ Kellogg, *NAACP*, pp. 9–16.

⁷ *Ibid.*; Mary White Ovington to Spingarn, April 5, 1918, J. E. Spingarn Collection (New York Public Library; hereafter cited as the Spingarn Collection); Ovington to the Chairman of the Board [Spingarn], September 23, 1934, NAACP Board of Directors Files, A-29 (Manuscript Division, Library of Congress; hereafter cited as NAACP Board of Directors Files); Charles E. Russell to Moorfield Storey, May 20, 1921, NAACP Adm. Files, C-74. The tenets of the NAACP's initial program are set forth in "'The Call': A Lincoln Emancipation Conference," Oswald Garrison Villard Papers (Houghton Library, Harvard University; hereafter cited as the Villard Papers).

⁸ National Negro Conference, Minutes, December 13, 1909, in NAACP Board Minutes; Report of the Chairman of the Board, NAACP Annual Meeting, January 1916, in NAACP Board Minutes; [James Weldon Johnson] to Moorfield Storey, April 5, 1927, copy, NAACP National Office (New York City); Philip Selznick, *Leadership in Administration: A Sociological Interpretation* (Evanston, Ill.: Row, Peterson and Co., 1957), *passim*.

⁹ See Kellogg, *NAACP*, Chaps. I, II.

¹⁰ *Crisis*, I (November 1910), 14; "Stenographic Report of the Address of Mr. J. E. Spingarn Before the Twentieth Annual Mass Meeting of the National Association . . . ," January 4, 1931, NAACP Board of Directors Files, A-24; Ida Wells-Barnett to Spingarn, October 19, 1910, quoted in Oswald Garrison Villard to Spingarn, n.d. [October 1910]; Ida Wells-Barnett to Spingarn, April 21, 1911; Edward H. Wright to Spingarn, October 17, 1910, J. E. Spingarn Papers (Howard University; hereafter cited as the Spingarn Papers); Allen H. Spear, *Black Chicago:*

The Making of a Negro Ghetto, 1890–1920 (Chicago: University of Chicago Press, 1967), p. 106.

[11] Oswald Garrison Villard to Spingarn, October 19, 1910, Spingarn Papers (Howard University); Executive Committee Minutes, November 29, 1910, in NAACP Board Minutes. Arthur Spingarn did not become a member of either the Executive Committee or the first NAACP Board of Directors which supplanted the Committee in 1912. When J. E. Spingarn became Chairman of the local New York branch of the Association in 1911, Arthur Spingarn aided him in the branch's legal work. In 1913 Arthur Spingarn replaced his law partner, Charles Studin, as Chairman of the NAACP Legal Committee. Interview with Arthur B. Spingarn, New York City, December 27, 1968. In contrast to his brother, Arthur Spingarn was an introvert, rarely making public addresses—the NAACP Files contain only two major speeches for his more than twenty-year career with the Association. On one occasion, after Arthur Spingarn had been affiliated with the NAACP for nearly twenty years, Mary White Ovington observed of him that he "is so quiet and says so little I do not suppose any of you [in the audience] have the least idea of what he does for us." Ovington, "Twenty Years of the NAACP" (speech delivered at the Twentieth Annual Conference of the National Association . . . , Cleveland, Ohio, June 26, 1929), NAACP Annual Conference Files, B-8 (Manuscript Division, Library of Congress; hereafter cited as the NAACP Annual Conference Files).

[12] Executive Committee Minutes, March 7, 1911, in NAACP Board Minutes; NAACP, *Third Annual Report 1913* (January 1914), pp. 24–25.

[13] NAACP Board Minutes, April 4, 1912; New York *Evening Post*, January 23, 1912, January 26, 1912; Ludline Saunders (secretary to Spingarn) to Arthur B. Spingarn, July 2, 1912; Spingarn to Arthur Spingarn, July 4, 1912, Arthur B. Spingarn Papers, Box #1 (Manuscript Division, Library of Congress; hereafter cited as the Arthur B. Spingarn Papers).

[14] Spingarn to Mrs. J. E. Spingarn, n.d., [1916], rough draft, Spingarn Collection.

[15] [May Childs Nerney] to Florence Kelley, November 18, 1913, copy, NAACP Adm. Files, C-70.

[16] Oswald Garrison Villard to Francis Jackson Garrison, September 30, 1909; Garrison to Villard, January 22, 1911, April 7, 1911, Oswald Garrison Villard Papers (Houghton Library, Harvard University; hereafter cited as the Villard Papers); "Notes on Branches for Dr. Spingarn," n.d. [1914], NAACP Adm. Files, C-70.

[17] Seymour Martin Lipset, *Political Man: The Social Bases of Politics* (Garden City, N.Y.: Doubleday, Anchor Books, 1963), pp. 187–88.

[18] NAACP Annual Meeting, Minutes, January 1916, NAACP National Office (New York City); "Notes on Branches for Dr. Spingarn," n.d. [1914]; [May Childs Nerney] to Mrs. Butler R. Wilson, October 13, 1914, copy, NAACP Adm. Files, C-70; New York *Age*, February 26, 1914; March 5, 1914; Washington *Bee*, January 24, 1914; February 28, 1914; Chicago *Broad-Ax*, n.d. [1914], clipping, Spingarn Collection.

[19] "Notes on Branches for Dr. Spingarn," n.d. [1914]; [May Childs Nerney] to Spingarn, January 20, 1914, copy, NAACP Adm. Files, C-70;

Dr. H. J. Nichols, Report, NAACP Sixth Annual Conference, May 1914; Spingarn, Remarks, NAACP Sixth Annual Conference, May 1914, NAACP Annual Conference Files, B-1.

[20] For a discussion of the relationship of the Association's branches to the parent body, see *infra*, Chap. 2, pp. 48–59. For a more detailed discussion of the controversy that arose in the Washington branch see *infra*, Chap. 2, pp. 60–61.

[21] Mary White Ovington, "Ten Years of the NAACP, 1909–19."

[22] [Spingarn] to [May Childs Nerney], December 15, 1912, copy, Spingarn Papers (Howard University); W. E. B. Du Bois, *Dusk of Dawn: An Essay Toward an Autobiography of a Race Concept* (New York: Harcourt, Brace and World, Inc., 1940), pp. 233–34; Baltimore *Afro-American Ledger*, April 5, 1913.

[23] Spingarn volunteered to undertake the New Abolition tours at his own expense, but with the understanding that they were to be under the auspices of the NAACP. The first tour of January 1913 was repeated in 1914 and in 1915, taking him to more than twenty different cities, including Chicago, Detroit, St. Paul, Minneapolis, Denver, Pittsburgh, Kansas City, and St. Louis. "Memorandum From Dr. Spingarn to Miss Nerney," n.d. [1914]; "Notes on Branches for Dr. Spingarn," n.d. [1914]; NAACP Adm. Files, C-70; statement, n.n., n.d. [1914]; "Spingarn Trip," n.d. [January 1915], NAACP Adm. Files, C-75.

[24] Spingarn, letter to the editor, *Ohio State Journal* [Columbus], January 14, 1915, clipping, Spingarn Collection; New York *Evening Post*, March 13, 1914; Spingarn, "Remarks," NAACP Sixth Annual Conference, May 1914, NAACP Annual Conference Files, B-1; Bishop John Hurst to Spingarn, May 11, 1914, Spingarn Papers (Howard University); "Introductory Remarks of J. E. Spingarn . . . Before the Twenty-third Annual Conference of the NAACP . . . ," May 3, 1932, copy, NAACP Annual Conference Files, B-8.

[25] Baltimore *Afro-American Ledger*, April 5, 1913, clipping; New York *Evening Post*, March 13, 1914, clipping, Spingarn Collection; "Introductory Remarks of Mr. J. E. Spingarn . . . Before the Twenty-third Annual Conference of the NAACP . . . ," May 3, 1932, copy, NAACP Annual Conference Files, B-8; Du Bois, *Dusk of Dawn*, pp. 238–39.

[26] Chicago *Record-Herald*, January 16, 1914, clipping, NAACP Adm. Files, C-144; *The Freeman* [Indianapolis, Ind.], January 17, 1914; NAACP press release, n.d. [1914], in NAACP Adm. Files, Spingarn Lecture Tour (special folder).

[27] NAACP Board Minutes, March 11, 1913: "NAACP Women's Committee Honors Walter White . . . ," NAACP press release, May 17, 1929, NAACP Adm. Files, C-426; Spingarn to James Weldon Johnson, June 27, 1912, NAACP Adm. Files, C-76. In his will Spingarn bequeathed the NAACP $20,000 in order that the Spingarn Medal might be perpetuated indefinitely. If the Association should pass out of existence, the medal is to be administered by the President of Howard University, or the senior professor of literature at Howard University, or the President of Fisk University, in successive order of preference as their names are listed. This section of Spingarn's will is enclosed in Arthur Spingarn to Walter White, August 21, 1939, NAACP Adm. Files (uncatalogued material).

²⁸ Spingarn to Walter White, March 8, 1923; [White] to Spingarn, March 13, 1923, copy, NAACP Board of Directors Files, A-19.

²⁹ Solomon P. Hood to Spingarn, January 6, 1913, Spingarn Papers (Howard University); Quincy, Illinois, *Herald,* January 6, 1914; Spingarn to May Childs Nerney, January 13, 1914, NAACP Adm. Files, C-75.

³⁰ Lewis Hartz, *The Liberal Tradition in America: An Interpretation of American Political Thought Since the Revolution* (New York: Harcourt, Brace and World, 1955), p. 237.

³¹ Spingarn to Booker T. Washington, February 25, 1913, Spingarn Papers (Howard University); Spingarn to Du Bois, January 11, 1914, W. E. B. Du Bois Papers (in the custody of Herbert Aptheker, New York City; hereafter cited as the Du Bois Papers); "The New Abolition," *Howard University Journal,* X (February 1914), 5; New York *Evening Post,* March 13, 1914. In 1908, while still a professor at Columbia, Spingarn had sent the first of what was destined to become a small annual contribution to Tuskegee in response to an appeal from "one of Mr. Washington's exponents." At that time he had questioned the "propriety" of portions of Washington's program, especially "as it applies to the suffrage of the colored people." [Spingarn] to Emmett J. Scott (secretary to Booker T. Washington), December 3, 1908, rough draft, Spingarn Collection; Scott to Spingarn, December 7, 1908; Spingarn to Washington, February 25, 1913, Spingarn Papers (Howard University); Spingarn to Washington, December 24, 1909; February 14, 1912; Washington to Spingarn, February 17, 1912, Papers of Booker T. Washington (Manuscript Division, Library of Congress; hereafter cited as the Washington Papers).

³² Oswald Garrison Villard to Francis Jackson Garrison, March 1, 1914, Villard Papers. Villard, who had been a Washington supporter before switching his allegiance to the NAACP, was earnestly cooperating with Washington as late as 1913 in planning a conference of small black industrial schools. Kellogg, *NAACP,* pp. 84–85. Villard to Francis Jackson Garrison, March 31, 1913, Villard Papers; New York *Age,* February 26, 1914, March 5, 1914, March 1, 1917; Washington *Bee,* January 24, 1914, February 28, 1914; Chicago *Broad-Ax,* n.d. [1914], clippings, Spingarn Collection; Cleveland *Gazette,* January 24, 1914, January 31, 1914, January 23, 1915. Harry C. Smith, editor of the *Gazette,* always had been independent of Washington. Francis L. Broderick, *W. E. B. DuBois: Negro Leader in a Time of Crisis* (Stanford, Calif.: Stanford University Press, 1959), p. 114.

³³ Spingarn to Du Bois, January 11, 1914, January 18, 1914, January 20, 1914, Du Bois Papers. A draft of Spingarn's St. Louis speech is in the Spingarn Collection.

³⁴ Spingarn to Booker T. Washington, May 18, 1914, Papers of Booker T. Washington; Spingarn, "Remarks," NAACP Sixth Annual Conference, May 1914, NAACP Annual Conference Files, B-1.

³⁵ [May Childs Nerney] to Mrs. Butler R. Wilson, December 29, 1914, December 23, 1914; "Memorandum from Dr. Spingarn to Miss Nerney," n.d. [1913]; [Nerney], "Memo for Dr. Spingarn," December 2, 1914; "Notes on Branches for Dr. Spingarn," n.d. [1914]; Nerney, "To the Chairman of the Spingarn Meetings," January 7, 1915, NAACP Adm.

Files, C-70; *Crisis,* VII (March 1914), 249; statement, n.n., n.d. [1914], NAACP Adm. Files, C-75.

[36] "Spingarn Trip—Committees and Supplementary Data," n.d. [1915], NAACP Adm. Files, C-75; "Tests of Democracy," NAACP press release, January 1915, NAACP Adm. Files, Spingarn Lecture Tour (special folder); Detroit *Times,* January 4, 1914.

[37] Dr. H. J. Nichols to May Childs Nerney, January 16, 1914; Robert W. Bagnall to Nerney, January 12, 1914, NAACP Adm. Files, Spingarn Lecture Tour (special folder); Charles T. Hallinan, "Report," NAACP Annual Conference Files, B-1; Monty Gregory to Spingarn, February 15, 1913, February 17, 1913; Spingarn to Du Bois, February 19, 1913; D[u Bois], "Memorandum for Miss Nerney," April 1, 1913, NAACP Branch Files, G-39 (hereafter cited as NAACP Branch Files).

[38] Columbus, Ohio, *Journal,* January 13, 1915; Dayton, Ohio, *Journal,* January 15, 1915; Dayton, Ohio, *Herald,* January 15, 1915; Wilmington, Delaware, *Journal,* November 23, 1914, clipping, Spingarn Collection; Spingarn to Du Bois, n.d. [January 1914], written on letter from Robert E. Simon to Spingarn, January 26, 1914, Du Bois Papers.

[39] NAACP Board Minutes, January 6, 1914, February 3, 1914, July 7, 1914; Cleveland *Gazette,* July 11, 1914; Louisville *Evening Post,* July 6, 1914; Louisville *Courier Journal,* July 6, 1914.

[40] *Guinn* v. *United States* (1915), 238 U.S. 347; *Buchanan* v. *Warley* (1917), 245 U.S. 60.

[41] J. E. Randolph (director of printing and engraving) to May Childs Nerney, July 29, 1913; Oswald Garrison Villard to "Friends," August 18, 1913, circular letter; Moorfield Storey, Du Bois, Villard to [Woodrow Wilson], August 15, 1913, copy, NAACP Adm. Files, C-411; Woodrow Wilson to Villard, July 23, 1913; Villard to Francis Jackson Garrison, November 5, 1913, Villard Papers; ——Wilson and James C. Waters to Spingarn, August 5, 1914, NAACP Adm. Files (uncatalogued material); NAACP Board Minutes, June 5, 1914, July 7, 1914, August 4, 1914.

[42] [May Childs Nerney] to Florence Kelley, September 18, 1913, copy, NAACP Adm. Files, C-70; [Nerney] to W. L. Stoddard, November 12, 1913, copy; November 14, 1913, copy; [Nerney] to Archibald Grimké, November 15, 1913, copy; "Memo for Dr. Spingarn from Miss Nerney," December 1, 1913, NAACP Adm. Files, C-412; Cleveland *Gazette,* January 24, 1914; Chicago *Daily News,* n.d. [January 1914], clipping, NAACP Adm. Files, C-441; [Spingarn] to Woodrow Wilson, November 20, 1914, rough draft, Spingarn Collection; Spingarn to Wilson, March 23, 1915, copy, NAACP Adm. Files (uncatalogued material); Spingarn, letter to the editor, Chicago *Post,* November 13, 1914.

[43] J. F. Tumulty (secretary to President Wilson) to Spingarn, March 25, 1915; J. A. McIlhenny (president of the Civil Service Commission) to Spingarn, April 6, 1915, NAACP Adm. Files (uncatalogued material); S[pingarn] to [May Childs Nerney], n.d. [February 1915], written on back of letter from N[erney] to Spingarn, February 24, 1915, NAACP Adm. Files, C-272; National Association . . . , *Ninth Annual Report 1918* (January 1919), pp. 44–45; NAACP Board Minutes, November 12, 1917, June 11, 1928, October 8, 1928.

[44] Wilmington, Delaware, *Journal,* November 23, 1914.

[45] Jessie Fauset to Spingarn, October 9, 1913; Spingarn to Fauset, October 28, 1913, Spingarn Papers (Howard University); Spingarn, "Remarks," NAACP Sixth Annual Conference, May 1914, NAACP Annual Conference Files, B-1.

[46] Quoted in [May Childs Nerney] to Oswald Garrison Villard, March 9, 1915, copy, NAACP Adm. Files, C-70.

[47] [Spingarn] to John Purroy Mitchel (Mayor of New York City), April 1, 1915, copy, NAACP Adm. Files, C-300; NAACP Board Minutes, September 13, 1915; [May Childs Nerney] to Oswald Garrison Villard, March 9, 1915, copy, NAACP Adm. Files, C-70. The film's most objectionable aspects in Spingarn's estimation included a rape scene depicting Gus, a black, pursuing a white girl, and another scene in which a mulatto politician was attempting to force marriage upon the daughter of his white benefactor. [Spingarn] to John Purroy Mitchel, April 1, 1915, copy, NAACP Adm. Files, C-300.

[48] "Report of the Chairman of the Board, Dr. Spingarn," NAACP Annual Meeting, Minutes, January 1916, NAACP National Office (New York City).

[49] S[pingarn] to May Childs Nerney, n.d. [March 1915], written on letter from Charles S. MacFarland to Spingarn, March 24, 1915; [Nerney] to Charles MacFarland, March 26, 1915, copy; Lester F. Scott to Spingarn, April 12, 1915; Nerney to Butler R. Wilson, April 5, 1915, copy; Spingarn, Villard, Du Bois and others to John Purroy Mitchel, March 19, 1915, copy; S[pingarn] to Mitchel, April 1, 1915, copy; Nerney to R. C. Wendell, March 26, 1915, copy; [Nerney] to George E. Wibecan, March 29, 1915, copy; [Nerney] to Mitchel, April 1, 1915, copy; Spingarn to Nerney, May 17, 1915, telegram; April 20, 1915; [Nerney] to Joseph Prince Loud, May 6, 1915, copy; Mary White Ovington to ——, n.d. [June 1915], copy of circular, NAACP Adm. Files, C-300; Spingarn to W. D. McGuire, February 24, 1915, copy; W. D. McGuire to Spingarn, February 27, 1915; [Nerney] to D. W. Griffith, February 25, 1915, copy; "Memo for Miss Nerney from Dr. Spingarn," March 2, 1915; Villard, Spingarn, Du Bois, and others to Mitchel, March 19, 1915, copy; Spingarn, Villard, Du Bois, and others to George H. Ball, March 12, 1915, NAACP Adm. Files, C-299.

[50] May Childs Nerney to Joseph Prince Loud, May 6, 1915; Spingarn to Nerney, May 17, 1915, telegram, NAACP Adm. Files, C-300.

[51] Cleveland *Gazette*, January 24, 1914; *McCabe* v. *Atchison Topeka and Santa Fe Railroad Co.* (1914) 235 U.S. 151; *Crisis*, IX (January 1915), 133, 137.

[52] Spingarn to Mrs. J. E. Spingarn, December 30, 1914, Spingarn Collection; Spingarn to Arthur Barnett Spingarn, December 16, 1914, Arthur Barnett Spingarn Papers.

[53] Spingarn to Amy (Mrs. J. E.) Spingarn, December 31, 1914, Arthur Barnett Spingarn Papers.

[54] Spingarn to ——, n.d [1913], Spingarn Papers (Howard University); Spingarn to Walter White, February 25, 1923, NAACP Board of Directors Files, A-19. Numerous clippings and notations pertaining to Southern feuds that occurred near the turn of the century are in Spingarn's scrapbook in the Spingarn Collection.

[55] Spingarn, "Racial Equality" (Amenia, N.Y.: A pamphlet, privately

printed at the Troutbeck Press, 1932).

[56] Omaha, Nebraska, *News*, January 22, 1915; "Report of the Chairman of the Board, Dr. Spingarn," NAACP Annual Meeting, Minutes, January 1916, NAACP National Office (New York City); "The New Abolition," 5; Spingarn, "The Colored Soldier in France" (speech delivered before the NAACP Annual Conference, Cleveland, Ohio, June 23, 1919), NAACP Annual Conference Files, B-3.

[57] National Association . . . , *Third Annual Report, 1912* (January 1913), p. 17; John Hope to Spingarn, December 20, 1912, February 28, 1913; James H. Dillard to Spingarn, November 20, 1916; H. L. McCrorey to Spingarn, November 29, 1916; Spingarn to George E. Haynes, April 22, 1912; George E. Haynes to Spingarn, May 4, 1912; J. E. McCulloth to Spingarn, January 9, 1917; Nashville *Tennessean and American*, May 3, 1912, clipping, Spingarn Papers (Howard University); *The Tar Heel* (North Carolina University school newspaper), November 25, 1916, clipping; Columbia, South Carolina, *State*, November 23, 1916, clipping; Spingarn to Mary White Ovington, January 4, 1916, Spingarn Collection; NAACP Board Minutes, December 11, 1916.

[58] Mary N. Moorer to Spingarn, February 2, 1912; W. K. Tate to Spingarn, March 9, 1915, March 15, 1915, Spingarn Papers (Howard University); Spingarn to Du Bois, January 17, 1913, Du Bois Papers.

[59] Statement, n.n., n.d., partially drafted in Spingarn's handwriting, Spingarn Papers (Howard University); C. Vann Woodward, "The Atlanta Compromise," in Hugh Hawkins, ed., *Booker T. Washington and His Critics*, p. 99.

[60] NAACP Board Minutes, 1912–1918, *passim*; Albert W. Gilchrist to Spingarn, June 6, 1911, Spingarn Papers (Howard University); M. Churchill to John R. Shillady, June 3, 1918; Spingarn to Moorfield Storey, June 18, 1918; "Unfinished Draft of Brief on Constitutionality of Proposed Substitute [for Dyer Bill (H.R. 112790)]," enclosed in Spingarn to Moorfield Storey, June 18, 1918, in the Papers of Moorfield Storey, Box #2 (Manuscript Division, Library of Congress); Moorfield Storey to Walter White, July 11, 1918, enclosed in John R. Shillady to Spingarn, August 5, 1918; Walter White to Spingarn, August 7, 1918, in Spingarn Collection.

[61] NAACP Board Minutes, February 14, 1916, April 10, 1916; Spingarn to John R. Shillady, September 29, 1919, NAACP Adm. Files, C-76; Spingarn to [Chapin] Brinsmade, n.d. [August 1914] written on back of letter from Chapin Brinsmade to Spingarn, August 25, 1914, NAACP Adm. Files, C-357; James Oppenheim, "The Lynching of Robert Johnson," *Independent*, LXXIII (October 10, 1912), 823–27; May Childs Nerney to Spingarn, October 15, 1912; Royal Freeman Nash to Spingarn, January 23, 1916, Spingarn Papers (Howard University).

[62] Spingarn and Oswald Garrison Villard, "To Members and Friends," July 15, 1916, circular, NAACP Adm. Files, C-205. Peabody later changed his offer to $1,000 contingent upon the Association's ability to raise an additional $9,000. *Ibid.* S[pingarn] to R[oy] N[ash], n.d. [October 1916] written on letter from Moorfield Storey to Roy Nash, October 17, 1916; W[illiam] O. Scroggs to Spingarn, August 20, 1916, NAACP Adm. Files, C-205; National Association . . . , *Ninth Annual Report, 1918* (January 1910), pp. 25–33; NAACP Board Minutes, December 9,

1918; Robert K. Murray, *Red Scare: A Study in National Hysteria, 1919–1920* (Minneapolis: University of Minnesota Press, 1955), pp. 178–80.

[63] Du Bois, "Memorandum to the Chairman of the Board, the Treasurer and the Secretary," December 14, 1915, James Weldon Johnson Collection (Yale University).

[64] *Ibid.;* R[obert] R. Moton to Spingarn, July 22, 1916; [Spingarn] to R[oy] N[ash], notation on letter from Moton to Spingarn, July 22, 1916; Motron [sic] to Spingarn, August 24, 1916, telegram, Spingarn Papers (Howard University); Du Bois, *The Amenia Conference: An Historic Gathering* (Amenia, N.Y.: Privately printed at the Troutbeck Press, 1925), p. 10.

[65] Statement, n.n., n.d. [1916], Spingarn Papers (Howard University); Du Bois, *The Amenia Conference,* p. 10.

[66] *Ibid.,* pp. 14–15.

[67] See *infra,* Chap. 4, pp. 108–109.

[68] See "Excerpts from Constitution Adopted at Annual Meeting of 1915 Feb[ruary] 12," in Spingarn Collection; see also the successive constitutions of the NAACP in the NAACP Adm. Files, C-428. The annual business meeting should not be confused with the Annual Conference of the NAACP. The latter retains the power to make suggestions to the Board and offer resolutions but, unlike the annual business meeting, its decision is not binding.

[69] Lipset, *Political Man,* pp. 411–12.

[70] Minutes, including attendance, of annual meetings are scattered throughout the NAACP Board of Directors Files, A-1 through A-29. An additional set of these records is included in the NAACP Board Minutes in the NAACP National Office, New York City.

[71] See representative samples of minutes of the annual meetings of the 1920's in the NAACP Board of Directors Files, A-23 and A-24. See also the minutes of the NAACP annual meetings of 1930, 1931, 1932, 1933, and 1934 in the NAACP Board of Directors Files, A-24.

[72] See the successive constitutions of the NAACP in the NAACP Adm. Files, C-428. The NAACP constitution of 1936 increased the quorum at annual meetings from fifteen to twenty-five. "Constitution of the National Association for the Advancement of Colored People (As Revised and Ratified by the Board of Directors, June 22, 1936)," in the NAACP National Office (New York City).

[73] Monthly Board attendance of each Director is conveniently listed at the beginning of the Minutes of each Board meeting. See the NAACP Board Minutes (Library of Congress).

[74] See *infra,* Chap. 7, pp. 186–216.

[75] Lipset, *Political Man,* pp. 405 ff. See also Bernard Barber, "Participation and Mass Apathy in Associations," in A. W. Gouldner, ed., *Studies in Leadership* (New York: Harper and Bros., 1950).

[76] The slates of candidates presented by the Board's Nominating Committee to the entire Board appear annually, but at random, in the NAACP Board Minutes. The slates of candidates presented to, and voted on by, the annual meetings appear in the minutes of the annual meetings in the NAACP Board of Directors Files, A-1 through A-29.

[77] "Constitution of the National Association for the Advancement of Colored People (As Revised and Ratified by the Board of Directors,

June 22, 1936)," in the NAACP National Office (New York City).

[78] NAACP By-Laws, NAACP Adm. Files, C-428; NAACP Annual Meeting Minutes, January 1919; "Constitution of the National Association for the Advancement of Colored People (As Revised and Ratified by the Board of Directors, June 22, 1936)," NAACP National Office (New York City).

[79] Biographical sketches and clippings relating to a majority of the Board members are scattered throughout the Board of Directors' Files. Information in this and the succeeding paragraph is derived from this data.

[80] See, for example, NAACP Board Minutes, September 9, 1918.

[81] See the individual Board members' attendance records at the beginning of each monthly Board meeting minutes; Charles Nagel to John R. Shillady, May 5, 1919; November 26, 1919; Arthur Spingarn to Mary White Ovington, November 21, 1919; Charles Nagel to Ovington, December 10, 1919, NAACP Board of Directors Files, A-19; J. Max Barber to Ovington, April 18, 1923; letter quoted in NAACP Board Minutes.

[82] See, for example, [Abram L.] Harris to Walter [White], May 7, 1934, NAACP Board of Directors Files, A-22. The Board departed from its tradition of holding meetings only in New York City in July 1920 when, following the Los Angeles Annual Conference, it convened an informal Board meeting for the benefit of California Board members who were unable to attend the regular New York meetings. NAACP Board Minutes, July 16, 1928.

[83] [Spingarn] to Mary White Ovington, n.d. [1911], rough draft partially corrected in Spingarn's handwriting, Spingarn Collection.

[84] See the individual Board members' attendance records at the beginning of each monthly Board meeting minutes. Portions of Miss Wald's letter of resignation are quoted in NAACP Board Minutes, February 14, 1921.

[85] Selznick, *Leadership in Administration, passim.*

[86] Any serious consideration of the small group of white liberals who were most active during the NAACP's formative years must entail brief mention of Paul Kennaday. An 1895 graduate of the Yale Law School, Kennaday became so interested in social problems that he abandoned his law practice shortly after the turn of the century in order to devote full time to settlement-house work. He was one of the first Americans to urge a national crusade against tuberculosis, and was instrumental in fostering the passage of the first workmen's compensation law. New York *Herald Tribune*, May 5, 1929. Kennaday remained one of the most active members of the Association until his death in 1929, although, for reasons which are not clear, he never wielded the administrative influence of Villard, Spingarn, or Ovington. See NAACP Board Minutes, *passim.*

[87] The major top-level nonsalaried officers chosen were Moorfield Storey, President; Villard, Chairman of the Board; Mary White Ovington, Secretary; Walter Sachs, Treasurer. NAACP Board Minutes, February 6, 1912.

[88] Ovington to Spingarn, December 20, 1915, Spingarn Collection.

[89] Lipset, *Political Man*, pp. 196–98; interview with Arthur B. Spingarn, New York City, December 27, 1968.

[90] See the successive constitutions of the NAACP in the NAACP Adm. Files, C-428. Data concerning branch operations is scattered throughout the extensive Branch Files in the Library of Congress. Conclusions presented in this paragraph regarding the branches are derived from an examination of the Branch Files.

[91] See Selznick, *Leadership in Administration*, Chap. IV.

[92] See the extensive correspondence between the national office and the branches in the NAACP Branch Files.

[93] Prior to 1914 Spingarn had served as Chairman of the New York Vigilance Committee and had been appointed Chairman of the Crisis Committee and the Committee on Branches, the latter two being sub-committees of the Board of Directors.

[94] Selznick, *Leadership in Administration*, pp. 27–28.

[95] [May Childs Nerney] to Spingarn, July 7, 1913; [Mary White] O[vington] to Spingarn, July 29, 1913, NAACP Branch Files, G-34; Boston *Guardian*, June 21, 1913.

[96] NAACP Board Minutes, August 5, 1913.

[97] Selznick, *Leadership in Administration*, pp. 93–94.

[98] Francis L. Broderick, *W. E. B. DuBois: Negro Leader in a Time of Crisis* (Stanford, Calif.: Stanford University Press, 1959); Elliott M. Rudwick, *W. E. B. Du Bois: A Study in Minority Group Leadership* (Philadelphia: University of Pennsylvania Press, 1960).

[99] Du Bois to Spingarn, October 28, 1914, Johnson Collection (Yale University).

[100] *Ibid.;* Du Bois, "Memorandum to the Crisis Committee," January 9, 1929, NAACP Adm. Files, C-162.

[101] Du Bois to Spingarn, November 29, 1910, Johnson Collection (Yale University). This letter acknowledges the loss of Spingarn's initial letter to Du Bois, dated April 5, 1910, for several months before it eventually came to Du Bois' attention.

[102] "Speech of Mr. J. E. Spingarn at Banquet Honoring Dr. W. E. B. Du Bois," Atlanta University, February 23, 1938 (marked "Confidential —Not for Publication"), in NAACP Adm. Files, C-429. In this speech Spingarn stated that his letter to Du Bois regarding the operation of the Heart of Hope Club was his first contact with the black leader. In speaking of the Ph.D., Spingarn said: "We had both gone through the most virulent of all diseases, the Ph.D. disease which, like small-pox, leaves you a cripple for life, but, if you do recover, you are immune for life." *Ibid.* "Stenographic Report of the Address of Mr. J. E. Spingarn Before the Twentieth Annual Mass Meeting of the National Association . . . ," January 4, 1931, NAACP Board of Directors Files, A-24.

[103] Du Bois to Spingarn, February 14, 1925, September 20, 1933, September 10, 1935, Johnson Collection (Yale University).

[104] Du Bois to Spingarn, February 1, 1926, March 27, 1926, Johnson Collection; Spingarn to Du Bois, March 24, 1926, W. E. B. Du Bois Papers (Amistad Research Center, Fisk University).

[105] Du Bois to Spingarn, October 28, 1914, Johnson Collection; V[illard] to [Francis Jackson Garrison], February 11, 1913, Villard Papers.

[106] Du Bois, *Dusk of Dawn*, p. 228; Spingarn to Du Bois, March 11, 1914, December 18, 1914, Du Bois Papers (in the custody of Herbert

Aptheker, New York City); Spingarn to Du Bois, October 24, 1914, Johnson Collection; Oswald Garrison Villard to Spingarn, March 20, 1913, Villard Papers.

[107] Broderick, *W. E. B. Du Bois*, pp. 101–03; NAACP Annual Meeting, Minutes, January 1916, in NAACP National Office (New York City); Du Bois, *Dusk of Dawn*, pp. 290–91. For a discussion of Spingarn's economic philosophy see *infra*, Chap. VI.

[108] Villard to Francis Jackson Garrison, October 23, 1913, Villard Papers; S[pingarn] to [May Childs Nerney], written on bottom of letter from M[ay] C[hilds] N[erney] to Spingarn, December 10, 1914, NAACP Adm. Files, C-70.

[109] Kellogg, *NAACP*, pp. 84–85; Villard to Francis Jackson Garrison, March 1, 1914, March 31, 1914, Villard Papers; Spingarn to Du Bois, January 11, 1914, Du Bois Papers (in the custody of Herbert Aptheker, New York City).

[110] "The New Abolition," Howard University *Journal*, X (February 14, 1913), 5; [Villard] to Francis Jackson Garrison, February 13, 1912, Villard Papers; notation in Spingarn's handwriting on letter from Villard to Spingarn, December 14, 1915, Spingarn Collection.

[111] Du Bois, "Memorandum for Mr. Villard," March 18, 1913; Du Bois, "Memorandum to Mr. J. E. Spingarn, Mr. Arthur Spingarn and Miss Ovington," n.d. [1913], Johnson Collection; [Villard] to Spingarn, March 20, 1913, copy, Villard Papers.

[112] "Memorandum," May 18, 1934, in NAACP Adm. Files, C-287. This memorandum records a statement dictated by phone from Spingarn to Walter White in answer to inquiries from the NAACP branches regarding differences between Du Bois and the Association in 1934.

[113] Quoted in Boston *Guardian*, September 12, 1914, clipping, Spingarn Collection.

[114] Spingarn, "Comments," opening session, Sixth Annual Conference of the NAACP, May 1914, NAACP Annual Conference Files B-1.

[115] See *infra*, Chap. 6, pp. 178–185.

[116] Selznick, *Leadership in Administration*, pp. 90 ff.; Spingarn to William Pickens, n.d. [March 1917], letter quoted in Washington *Bee*, March 17, 1917. For a discussion of Spingarn's administrative influence after 1930, see *infra*, Chaps. 6, 7.

[117] W. S. Scarborough to Spingarn, September 18, 1914, Spingarn Papers (Howard University); Spingarn to Du Bois, October 15, 1914; [Du Bois] to Spingarn, October 23, 1914, Du Bois Papers (in the custody of Herbert Aptheker, New York City).

[118] Spingarn to W. S. Scarborough, September 19, 1914, Spingarn Papers (Howard University); Spingarn to Du Bois, October 15, 1914; [Du Bois] to Spingarn, October 23, 1914, copy, Du Bois Papers (in the custody of Herbert Aptheker, New York City).

[119] Spingarn to Du Bois, December 18, 1914; [Du Bois] to Spingarn, December 21, 1914, copy; [Spingarn] to ——, December 22, 1914, copy, Du Bois Papers (in the custody of Herbert Aptheker, New York City).

[120] Spingarn to Du Bois, September 28, 1914, Du Bois Papers (in the custody of Herbert Aptheker, New York City). Spingarn conceded, "I agree with you [Du Bois] that it is not quite fair to impose on you the chief burden in any plan for economizing." *Ibid.*

[121] Spingarn to Du Bois, October 22, 1914; [Du Bois] to Spingarn, October 23, 1914, copy, Du Bois Papers (in the custody of Herbert Aptheker, New York City).

[122] Du Bois to Spingarn, October 23, 1914, Johnson Collection.

[123] Spingarn to Du Bois, October 24, 1914, Johnson Collection.

[124] *Ibid.*

[125] *Ibid.*

[126] Du Bois to Spingarn, October 28, 1914, Johnson Collection.

[127] Mary White Ovington to Spingarn, November 4, 1914; November 7, 1914, Spingarn Papers (Howard University); Du Bois "Memorandum to Mr. Spingarn and Mr. Villard," November 10, 1914, Johnson Collection.

[128] NAACP Board Minutes, December 1, 1914.

[129] *Ibid.*

[130] For a discussion of the controversy over Du Bois' army commission, see *infra.* Chap. 3, pp. 98–101.

[131] *Crisis,* XI (November 1915), 25–27; [May Childs Nerney] to Spingarn, n.d. [1914], Spingarn Papers (Howard University).

[132] Spingarn, Florence Kelley, Charles Studin to [the NAACP Board of Directors], December 6, 1915, NAACP Board of Directors Files, A-1; NAACP Board Minutes, December 14, 1915.

[133] Mary White Ovington to Spingarn, December 20, 1915, Spingarn Collection; [May Childs Nerney] to Spingarn, n.d. [1915], Spingarn Papers (Howard University).

[134] Mary White Ovington to Spingarn, December 13, [1915], Spingarn Papers (Howard University); Villard to Francis Jackson Garrison, December 31, 1915, Villard Papers; Ovington to Spingarn, December 20, 1915, Spingarn Collection. This letter discusses Spingarn's plan for a black chairman, together with Ovington's reaction to the plan.

[135] Mary White Ovington to Spingarn, December 20, 1915, Spingarn Collection.

[136] William A. Sinclair to Spingarn, January 4, 1915; [May Childs] Nerney to Spingarn, n.d. [1915]; Butler Wilson to Spingarn, December 28, 1915; William Pickens to Spingarn, January 11, 1916; Joseph Prince Loud to Spingarn, December 24, 1915, Spingarn Papers (Howard University); NAACP Board Minutes, January 10, 1916.

[137] Joseph Prince Loud to Spingarn, December 24, 1915; May Childs Nerney to Spingarn, January 6, 1916, Spingarn Papers (Howard University); NAACP Annual Meeting Minutes, January 1916, NAACP National Office (New York City).

[138] John Hope to Spingarn, October 21, 1916, Spingarn Papers (Howard University); Spingarn to James Weldon Johnson, October 28, 1916; November 6, 1916, Johnson Collection. Johnson's selection was especially significant, for the Association's ability to attract him from the New York *Age,* a paper that had been closely affiliated with Booker T. Washington, was a major coup against the Washington camp.

[139] See *infra,* Chap. 7, pp. 198–216.

[140] NAACP Annual Meeting Minutes, January 1916, NAACP National Office (New York City).

CHAPTER 3: FIRST IN WAR

[1] Cleveland *Gazette,* January 23, 1915.

[2] Spingarn, "Racial Equality" (Amenia, N.Y.: A pamphlet privately printed at the Troutbeck Press, 1932).

[3] Spingarn, "Shrine," copy in J. E. Spingarn Papers (Howard University; hereafter cited as the Spingarn Papers).

[4] Spingarn to Mary White Ovington, April 17, 1917, Spingarn Papers (Howard University). Miss Ovington lamented that Spingarn was willing to give up his "rare gift of teaching audacity and disobedience to forms" in order to enter military life, where authority ruled freedom of speech and thought was suppressed. Ovington to Spingarn, July 5, 1917, August 15, [1917], Spingarn Papers (Howard University).

[5] W. E. B. Du Bois, *Dusk of Dawn: An Essay Toward An Autobiography of a Race Concept* (New York: Harcourt, Brace and World, 1940), p. 256; Spingarn to L. S. Curtis, April 11, 1917, copy, Spingarn Papers (Howard University).

[6] Spingarn, "Politics and the Poet: A Prophecy," *Atlantic Monthly,* CLXX (November 1942), 75–76.

[7] Spingarn to Theodore Roosevelt, March 3, 1917, Papers of Theodore Roosevelt, series 1, box 323 (Manuscript Division, Library of Congress; hereafter cited as the Roosevelt Papers); Poughkeepsie *Sunday Courier,* April 15, 1917; December 16, 1917, clippings, J. E. Spingarn Collection (New York Public Library; hereafter cited as the Spingarn Collection); Interview with Mrs. J. E. Spingarn, New York City, June 19, 1968.

[8] Leonard Wood to Spingarn, January 9, 1917, Spingarn Papers (Howard University).

[9] "An Open Letter from Dr. J. E. Spingarn to the Educated Colored Men of the United States," February 15, 1917, Spingarn Papers (Howard University).

[10] Washington *Bee,* March 24, 1917.

[11] Spingarn to William Pickens, March 1917, letter printed in Washington *Bee,* March 17, 1917.

[12] Washington *Bee,* March 24, 1917; [Spingarn] to Mrs. M. C. Simpson, April 25, 1917, copy, Spingarn Papers (Howard University). Isaiah J. Butler, a New York black leader, contended that the camp issue must be decided upon a "just principle" and not "spiteful vindictiveness towards the War department." Isaiah J. Butler, letter to the editor, New York *Age,* April 5, 1917.

[13] [Spingarn] to George E. Brice, April 6, 1917; Spingarn to —— Allen, April 18, 1917; [Spingarn] to W. Norman Bishop, April 6, 1917, copy, Spingarn Papers (Howard University).

[14] See *infra,* Chap. 6, pp. 179–185.

[15] [Spingarn] to Archibald R. Grimké, April 3, 1917; Spingarn to Mrs. M. C. Simpson, April 25, 1917, copy, Spingarn Papers (Howard University).

[16] Archibald Grimké to Spingarn, March 30, 1917; Spingarn to Grimké, April 3, 1917, Papers of Archibald Grimké (Howard University).

[17] Cleveland *Gazette,* March 3, 1917, March 24, 1917.

[18] *Ibid.,* April 28, 1917.

[19] Boston *Guardian,* March 24, 1917; Baltimore *Afro-American,* February 24, 1917.

[20] New York *Age,* March 1, 1917, March 22, 1917.

[21] Washington *Bee,* March 24, 1917.

[22] *Ibid.;* New York *Age,* March 15, 1917, March 22, 1917, March 29, 1917; Cleveland *Gazette,* March 24, 1917.

[23] Gilchrist Stewart to Spingarn, March 10, 1917, Spingarn Papers (Howard University).

[24] J. Q. Adams to Spingarn, n.d. [May 1917], Spingarn Papers (Howard University).

[25] George W. Crawford to Spingarn, March 3, 1917, April 7, 1917, Spingarn Papers (Howard University).

[26] Washington *Bee,* March 24, 1917; Spingarn to Hallie E. Queen, April 30, 1917, Spingarn Papers (Howard University); Spingarn to William Pickens, [March 1917], letter printed in Washington *Bee,* March 17, 1917.

[27] Cleveland *Gazette,* March 31, 1917.

[28] Charles R. Douglass, letter to the editor, Washington *Bee,* March 31, 1917; Douglass to Spingarn, March 2, 1917, Spingarn Papers (Howard University).

[29] See, for example, Dr. S. A. Askew to Spingarn, March 30, 1917; W. T. Andrews to Spingarn, March 31, 1917; W. Norman Bishop, Stewart Davis, Beal Elliott to Spingarn, April 3, 1917; Dr. G. Jarvis Bowens to Spingarn, March 28, 1917; Webster Burnett to Spingarn, March 30, 1917, Spingarn Papers (Howard University).

[30] George E. Brice to Spingarn, March 8, 1917, March 16, 1917, March 24, 1917; George William Cook to Spingarn, March 16, 1917, Spingarn Papers (Howard University). Spingarn's Howard speech is quoted in the Washington *Bee,* March 24, 1917.

[31] George E. Brice to Spingarn, March 8, 1917; R. McCants Andrews to Spingarn, March 15, 1917, Spingarn Papers (Howard University).

[32] H. B. Frissell to Spingarn, March 30, 1917; Spingarn to George E. Brice, March 31, 1917; Spingarn to Major Halstead Dorsey, March 31, 1917, Spingarn Papers (Howard University).

[33] Spingarn to Edmund Platt, April 7, 1917; Spingarn to Mary White Ovington, April 11, 1917; George William Cook to Spingarn, April 20, 1917; Spingarn to William Pickens, April 17, 1917, Spingarn Papers (Howard University).

[34] Spingarn to Major A. W. Johnston, April 19, 1917, night letter; Spingarn to Major Halstead Dorsey, April 20, 1917; Spingarn to George E. Brice, April 28, 1917; Spingarn to Mary White Ovington, April 28, 1917, Spingarn Papers (Howard University); Professors Lightfoot, Locke, and MacLear, "Howard University in the War," *Howard University Record,* XIII (April 1919), 160; NAACP Board Minutes, May 14, 1917.

[35] George William Cook to Spingarn, April 25, 1917, Spingarn Papers (Howard University); Professors Lightfoot, Locke, and MacLear, "Howard University in the War," 161–62. Howard University's efforts toward securing the camp are summarized in the New York *Globe,*

May 14, 1917, clipping, NAACP Administrative Files, C-376 (Manuscript Division, Library of Congress; hereafter cited as NAACP Adm. Files).

[36] Kelly Miller to Spingarn, May 2, 1917, Spingarn Papers (Howard University).

[37] Spingarn to George E. Brice, April 10, 1917; John Hope to Spingarn, April 5, 1917; George E. Haynes to Spingarn, April 5, 1917, Spingarn Papers (Howard University).

[38] R. R. Moton to Spingarn, April 20, 1917; Spingarn to R. R. Moton, April 20, 1917, Spingarn Papers (Howard University).

[39] Spingarn to Captain George J. Austin, May 2, 1917; Spingarn to Major Halstead Dorsey, April 20, 1917; Spingarn to R. R. Wright, April 13, 1917; Spingarn to Roscoe Conkling Bruce, April 17, 1917; Spingarn to L. S. Curtis, April 11, 1917, Spingarn Papers (Howard University).

[40] NAACP Board Minutes, May 14, 1917.

[41] Spingarn to George B. Kelley, April 13, 1917; Spingarn to Roy Nash, April 12, 1917, Spingarn Papers (Howard University).

[42] Spingarn to George William Cook, May 2, 1917, copy, Spingarn Papers (Howard University); Spingarn to Roy Nash, April 30, 1917, letter quoted in NAACP Board Minutes, May 14, 1917; Spingarn to the NAACP Board of Directors, letter quoted in NAACP Board Minutes, May 14, 1917.

[43] Ralph A. Hayes (private secretary, War Department) to Stephen M. Newman (President, Howard University), May 12, 1917; George William Cook to Spingarn, May 14, 1917, Spingarn Papers (Howard University).

[44] James Weldon Johnson to Moorfield Storey, May 27, 1917, Spingarn Papers (Howard University).

[45] Poughkeepsie *Evening Star*, April 30, 1919, clipping, Spingarn Collection; interview with Mrs. J. E. Spingarn, New York City, June 19, 1968.

[46] [Spingarn] to Roy Nash, n.d. [1917], copy; New York *Times*, n.d. [December 1917], clipping, Spingarn Collection. Troutbeck was restored shortly after Spingarn's return from the war in 1919.

[47] Poughkeepsie *Evening Star*, April 30, 1919, clipping, Spingarn Collection; W. E. B. Du Bois, "A Momentous Proposal," *Crisis*, XVI (September 1918), 125; Du Bois to John Hope, July 12, 1918, W. E. B. Du Bois Papers (in the custody of Herbert Aptheker, New York City; hereafter cited as the Du Bois Papers). Neither the files of the Intelligence Bureau nor the several collections of Spingarn Papers offer any clear explanation of the details of Spingarn's "constructive programme."

[48] Du Bois, "A Momentous Proposal," 125.

[49] *Ibid.*

[50] Du Bois to Spingarn, July 9, 1918, July 19, 1918, Johnson Collection (Yale University).

[51] Du Bois to John Hope, July 12, 1918, Du Bois Papers; NAACP Board Minutes, July 8, 1918. The fact that Du Bois was willing to join forces with the government led a large segment of the black community to label both the Editor and Spingarn as traitors to the race. See, for example, New York *News*, July 18, 1918; Washington *Bee*, July 27, 1918;

272 *Notes (pages 99–105)*

Washington *Eagle,* July 27, 1918, clippings, Johnson Collection; F. E. Young to Spingarn, August 5, 1918; "The Charges of Mr. Nevil H. Thomas," December 24, 1928, NAACP National Office (New York City).

⁵² NAACP Board Minutes, July 8, 1918.

⁵³ [Du Bois] to Spingarn, July 9, 1918, copy, Du Bois Papers.

⁵⁴ *Ibid.;* Richmond *Planet,* September 7, 1918, clipping, NAACP Adm. Files, C-435; [George William Cook] to Du Bois, July 3, 1918, copy, Papers of George William Cook (Howard University). As was usually the case in differences among Board members, both factions in the commission controversy were biracial.

⁵⁵ Du Bois to Spingarn, July 12, 1918, copy, Du Bois Papers. Widespread publicity was given to a vitriolic personal attack upon Du Bois and Spingarn by Nevil H. Thomas, a black official in the Washington, D.C., branch. See, for example, Mary White Ovington to Moorfield Storey, September 1, 1918, NAACP Adm. Files, C-237.

⁵⁶ Du Bois to John Hope, July 12, 1918, Du Bois Papers.

⁵⁷ Spingarn to Du Bois, July 16, 1918, Du Bois Papers.

⁵⁸ John Shillady to Spingarn, July 30, 1918, Johnson Collection; Shillady to Spingarn, July 27, 1918; Spingarn, "To the Members of the Board of Directors," August 6, 1918, Spingarn Collection.

⁵⁹ Du Bois, *Dusk of Dawn,* pp. 257–58.

⁶⁰ Poughkeepsie *Evening Star,* April 30, 1919, clipping, Spingarn Collection.

⁶¹ *Ibid.*

⁶² NAACP Board Minutes, December 9, 1918, March 10, 1919; Report of the Director of Publications and Research, n.d. [1919], NAACP *Crisis* Files, F-1 (Manuscript Division, Library of Congress); S[pingarn] to Du Bois, February 26, 1919; "Report of the Director of Publications and Research for December 1, 1918 to April 1, 1919," Du Bois Papers.

CHAPTER 4: LAST IN PEACE: ECLIPSE

¹ Philip Selznick, *Leadership in Administration: A Sociological Interpretation* (Evanston, Ill.: Row, Peterson and Co., 1957), pp. 5 ff.

² New York *Age,* October 4, 1919; "Tuskegee Women Increase Donation to NAACP by $25 for 1929," NAACP press release, January 11, [1929], NAACP Administrative Files (uncatalogued material, Manuscript Division, Library of Congress; hereafter cited as the NAACP Adm. Files).

³ See Robert Bone, *The Negro Novel in America* (New Haven, Conn.: Yale University Press, 1958); E. David Cronon, *Black Moses: The Story of Marcus Garvey and the Universal Negro Improvement Association* (Madison, Wis.: University of Wisconsin Press, 1955); Francis L. Broderick and August Meier, eds., *Negro Protest Thought in the Twentieth Century* (Indianapolis, Ind.: The Bobbs-Merrill Co., Inc., 1965), p. 67. (Editors' note.)

⁴ Spingarn to James Weldon Johnson, June 27, 1921, NAACP Adm. Files, C-75.

⁵ "Division of Association into Districts," n.d. [1921], NAACP Branch Files, G-222 (Manuscript Division, Library of Congress; hereafter cited as NAACP Branch Files); "Comparative Statements of July 31, 1920, and August 31, 1920," in NAACP National Office (New York City). The number of branches that the Association lists at any given time is not a valid indication of membership participation. In 1920, 191 (approximately 55 percent) of its 342 branches were totally delinquent in terms of securing new members and sending financial contributions to the national office. *Ibid.* For an example of the diversity of sources of the Association's income, see "Contributions to the Anti-Lynching Fund to Dec[ember] 31, 1919," NAACP Adm. Files, C-135.

⁶ See, for example, Mary White Ovington to Mary McMurtrie, November 25, 1925, NAACP Adm. Files, C-140; "Memorandum from Miss Randolph to Mr. White: Subject: Bequests to the NAACP," NAACP Adm. Files, C-144; Report of the Secretary to the October Meeting of the Board, 1926, NAACP National Office (New York City); NAACP Board Minutes, February 9, 1925, January 30, 1926, April 12, 1926, October 11, 1926, March 11, 1929; Johnson to Phillip G. Peabody, January 11, 1924, copy; "NAACP Wins $1,000 Offered by Phillip G. Peabody of Boston," NAACP press release, NAACP Adm. Files, C-139; "Memorandum from Miss Randolph to Mr. Johnson," January 7, 1925, NAACP Adm. Files, C-140; [James Weldon Johnson] to Samuel S. Fels, November 9, 1926, copy, NAACP Adm. Files, C-141; "Rockefeller, Jr., Gives NAACP Contribution of $500," NAACP press release, n.d. [1928], NAACP Adm. Files, C-142; Ira W. Jayne to the National Association . . . , August 6, 1928, NAACP Adm. Files, C-143; "Edsel Ford," n.d. [1932] (a listing of Ford's donations from 1924 to 1932), NAACP Adm. Files, C-152; NAACP Board Minutes May 14, 1928. The American Fund for Public Service was established by Charles Garland, a young man from Massachusetts who relinquished his inheritance of many millions of dollars for the establishment of a fund which would aid the public welfare. See NAACP Board Minutes, September 11, 1922, June 10, 1929, February 8, 1926, June 9, 1930. Despite its ability to attract new and wealthy donors, the Association's *average* gift did not exceed $1,000 annually. Branch membership fees continued as its largest source of funds.

⁷ Report of the Committee on Resolutions, NAACP Thirteenth Annual Conference, June 23, 1922, NAACP Annual Conference Files, B-5 (Manuscript Division, Library of Congress; hereafter cited as NAACP Annual Conference Files); W[illiam] English Walling to James Weldon Johnson, August 11, 1922, NAACP Adm. Files, C-76; NAACP Board Minutes, March 11, 1918, July 8, 1918, December 9, 1918, December 13, 1920, July 12, 1926, November 14, 1927, May 14, 1928, February 10, 1930, March 3, 1930, May 12, 1930; Report of the Acting Secretary to the Committee on Administration, December 16, 1929, NAACP National Office (New York City).

⁸ National Association . . . , *Tenth Annual Report, 1919* (New York, 1920), p. 91; "Address of the 17th Annual Conference," n.d. [1926]; [James Weldon Johnson] to Moorfield Storey, April 5, 1927, copy, NAACP National Office (New York City); "Resolutions," n.d. [1929], NAACP Annual Conference Files, B-6; statement enclosed in Spingarn

to John R. Shillady, March 13, 1920, NAACP Board of Directors Files, A-19 (Manuscript Division, Library of Congress; hereafter cited as NAACP Board of Directors Files).

⁹ *Moore* v. *Dempsey* (1923), 261 U.S. 86; *Nixon* v. *Herndon* (1927), 273 U.S. 536.

¹⁰ NAACP Board Minutes, *passim*.

¹¹ Mary White Ovington to Moorfield Storey, October 24, 1921, Papers of Moorfield Storey, Box #2 (Manuscript Division, Library of Congress); James Weldon Johnson to Spingarn, December 15, 1922, J. E. Spingarn Collection (New York Public Library; hereafter cited as the Spingarn Collection); NAACP Board Minutes, February 14, 1923, February 11, 1929, March 11, 1929, June 10, 1929.

¹² NAACP Board Minutes, January 14, 1918; Mary White Ovington to Spingarn, January 11, 1922; September 25, 1919, Spingarn Collection. The cadre of salaried officials was rounded out by the hirings of Walter White as Assistant Secretary (1917) and Robert W. Bagnall as Director of Branches (1919). See *infra*, Chap. 5.

¹³ NAACP Board Minutes, October 13, 1919; [Mary White Ovington] to John Haynes Holmes, April 17, 1920, copy, NAACP Board of Directors Files, A-19 (Manuscript Division, Library of Congress; hereafter cited as NAACP Board of Directors Files). Florence Kelley and Paul Kennaday attended Board meetings regularly, although they did not hold executive offices in the Association. See the clerk of the Board's tabulation of individual Board attendance, NAACP National Office (New York City).

¹⁴ *Ibid.*

¹⁵ [James Weldon Johnson] to Spingarn, January 20, 1923, copy, James Weldon Johnson Collection (Yale University; hereafter cited as the Johnson Collection); [Mary White Ovington] to Moorfield Storey, n.d. [1923], NAACP Board of Directors Files, A-19.

¹⁶ Mary White Ovington to Spingarn, December 15, 1931, Spingarn Collection.

¹⁷ Cf. Charles Flint Kellogg, *NAACP: A History of the National Association for the Advancement of Colored People* (Baltimore: The Johns Hopkins Press, 1967), pp. 291–92.

¹⁸ See, for example, NAACP Board Minutes, March 13, 1916, October 13, 1919, February 9, 1925, June 8, 1925. Other listings of those authorized to sign checks and disburse the organization's monies are found at random throughout the Board Minutes.

¹⁹ For a full account of the Pittsburgh *Courier* charges, see *infra*, Chap. 4, pp. 120–122.

²⁰ NAACP Board Minutes, February 9, 1925.

²¹ Selznick, *Leadership in Administration*, pp. 29 ff.

²² *Ibid.*, p. 92.

²³ Interview with Mrs. J. E. Spingarn, New York City, June 19, 1968; Amy Spingarn to James Weldon Johnson, December 13, 1922, Johnson Collection; Du Bois to Spingarn, December 20, 1922; George William Cook to Spingarn, August 25, 1924, Spingarn Collection; Spingarn to Mary White Ovington, December 29, 1922; Spingarn to Johnson, June 27, 1921; Spingarn to P. L. Edwards, April 19, 1921, NAACP Adm. Files, C-75; Spingarn to Johnson, July 18, 1924, May 8, 1929, NAACP

Files (uncatalogued material); Spingarn to Walter White, April 20, 1922; Robert W. Bagnall to Spingarn, June 12, 1922, June 15, 1922, NAACP Annual Conference Files, B-5; Spingarn to Johnson, May 28, 1923, NAACP Adm. Files, C-380; Spingarn to Johnson, September 4, 1923, telegram, NAACP Board of Directors Files, A-20; White to Spingarn, July 26, 1926, NAACP Adm. Files, C-77; Richetta Randolph to Arthur B. Spingarn, November 3, 1928, Arthur B. Spingarn Papers (Manuscript Division, Library of Congress; hereafter referred to as Arthur B. Spingarn Papers).

[24] Spingarn, "The Colored Soldier in France" (address delivered at the NAACP Annual Conference, Cleveland, Ohio, June 23, 1919), NAACP Annual Conference Files, B-3; Spingarn to Walter White, July 12, 1919, July 17, 1919, NAACP Adm. Files (special folder—no title); NAACP Board Minutes, September 8, 1919; George William and Coralie Cook to Spingarn, July 30, 1919; Spingarn to Hon. Charles H. Brough, November 16, 1919, Spingarn Collection; Spingarn to James Weldon Johnson, May 8, 1929, NAACP Annual Conference Files, B-7.

[25] Lewis Mumford, Introduction to Spingarn, "Politics and the Poet: A Prophecy," *Atlantic Monthly*, CLXX (November 1942), 73–74; New York *Times*, n.d. [1939], clipping, Johnson Collection.

[26] Spingarn to Harry H. Pace, October 28, 1920; Spingarn to Mary White Ovington, December 15, 1920, NAACP Board of Directors Files, A-19; Spingarn to P. L. Edwards, April 19, 1921, NAACP Adm. Files, C-75; "Minutes of the Crisis Committee Meeting," May 12, 1919, NAACP Crisis Files, F-1 (Manuscript Division, Library of Congress; hereafter cited as NAACP Crisis Files); NAACP Board Minutes, December 13, 1920.

[27] Spingarn to John R. Shillady, March 24, 1919, NAACP Adm. Files, C-75; Shillady to Spingarn, May 21, 1919, Spingarn Collection.

[28] Mumford, Introduction to Spingarn, "Politics and the Poet: A Prophecy," 74; statement, n.n., n.d. (portions drafted in Spingarn's handwriting), Spingarn Collection.

[29] See *supra*, Chap. 2, pp. 56–59.

[30] See the NAACP Financial Files (Manuscript Division, Library of Congress).

[31] [Mary White Ovington] to Spingarn, May 27, 1919, copy; November 22, 1921, copy, NAACP Adm. Files, C-70; Amy Spingarn to James Weldon Johnson, December 13, 1922, NAACP Adm. Files, C-138; Amy Spingarn to Johnson, May 23, 1923; [Johnson] to Mrs. J. E. (Amy) Spingarn, May 25, 1923, copy, NAACP Adm. Files, C-155. Spingarn later wrote Johnson requesting that the $5,000 building fund offer be considered a personal gift from Mrs. Spingarn rather than a contribution from both of them. Spingarn to Johnson, May 31, 1923, NAACP Adm. Files, C-155. Although the Board voted to accept Mrs. Spingarn's contingent offer and a building fund was launched, very little money ($100) was collected, and the project was abandoned in December 1924. NAACP Board Minutes, May 26, 1923, December 8, 1924; [Johnson] to Mrs. J. E. Spingarn, May 29, 1923, copy, NAACP Adm. Files, C-155; Spingarn to [Johnson], November 17, 1923, NAACP Adm. Files, C-139.

[32] Amy E. Spingarn to James Weldon Johnson, January 24, 1924, NAACP Adm. Files, C-139. Peabody had sent a donation of $500 to the

Association and had pledged an additional $1,000 if the NAACP could secure gifts totaling $9,000 by March 1924. Philip G. Peabody to Johnson, January 9, 1924, letter quoted in NAACP Board Minutes, January 14, 1924; "Statement from the Chairman of the Board [Ovington]," February 11, 1924, NAACP Board of Directors Files, A-20. Spingarn to Johnson, October 30, 1925, December 9, 1928; [Johnson] to Mr. and Mrs. J. E. Spingarn, November 3, 1925, copy; "J. E. Spingarn Becomes Life Member of NAACP," NAACP press release, December 14, 1928, NAACP Adm. Files, C-142; NAACP Board Minutes, December 10, 1928.

   33 [Walter White] to Spingarn, n.d. [1929]; see list of prospective contributors in Spingarn's handwriting enclosed in ibid; [White], "Memorandum for Miss Ovington," April 23, 1929; Spingarn to James Weldon Johnson, March 14, 1929, September 5, 1929; [Johnson] to Spingarn, September 6, 1929, NAACP Adm. Files, C-163; [Johnson] to Arthur B. Spingarn, September 7, 1929, copy, NAACP Adm. Files, C-144. The Spingarns also gave liberally of their funds in support of the "Harlem Renaissance" of the 1920's. Mrs. Spingarn explained that she and her husband had "long had a deep interest and faith in the contribution of the American Negro to art and literature." She sought to stimulate this contribution and, incidentally, aid the Crisis by offering a $600 annual prize, the Amy Spingarn Prize (1924–28), for the best literary entries submitted to the Crisis. Earlier, the Spingarns had helped to finance the education of Langston Hughes, one of the foremost writers of the Harlem Renaissance. Amy E. Spingarn to James Weldon Johnson, July 18, 1924, letter quoted in NAACP Board Minutes, September 9, 1924; S[pingarn] to Johnson, August 29, 1924; Johnson to Spingarn, September 17, 1924; Amy E. Spingarn to Johnson, May 7, 1925, NAACP Adm. Files (uncatalogued material); Spingarn to Du Bois, September 17, 1924, October 24, 1924, W. E. B. Du Bois Papers (Amistad Research Center, Fisk University); interview with Stephen Spingarn, Washington, D.C., December 10, 1969.

   34 Richetta Randolph to Arthur B. Spingarn, November 3, 1928, Arthur B. Spingarn Papers (Manuscript Division, Library of Congress); Spingarn, "Some Busy Years," Spingarn Collection. Mrs. Spingarn recalled that her husband avoided routine financial management of any kind, although he possessed unusual expertise in the realm of finance. Interview with Mrs. J. E. Spingarn, New York City, June 19, 1968.

   35 [James Weldon Johnson] to Spingarn, January 22, 1926, copy, NAACP Adm. Files (special correspondence).

   36 Ibid.; Statement signed James Weldon Johnson, n.d. [February 1926], NAACP Adm. Files, C-304; Spingarn to Johnson, n.d. [February 1926], letter quoted in [Richetta Randolph] to Johnson, February 15, 1926, copy; Johnson to Spingarn, February 18, 1926, copy, NAACP Adm. Files (special correspondence); see copy of resolution creating the Investment Committee attached to "Memorandum to the Secretary [from Spingarn]," January 23, 1926, NAACP Adm. Files, C-75. The Investment Committee was to be biracial. Ibid.

   37 Spingarn to James Weldon Johnson, n.d. [February 1926], letter quoted in [Richetta Randolph] to Johnson, February 15, 1926, copy; [Johnson] to Spingarn, February 18, 1926, copy, March 2, 1926, copy,

NAACP Adm. Files (special correspondence); [Johnson] to Spingarn, April 2, 1927, copy, April 7, 1927, copy; Spingarn to Johnson, April 4, 1927, NAACP Adm. Files, C-142; NAACP Board Minutes, April 11, 1927. Despite disagreements over official policy, Johnson and Spingarn enjoyed a close personal friendship that was centered in their mutual literary interests and that transcended their relationship as co-workers in the Association. Indeed, Spingarn's relationship with Johnson perhaps was warmer than that with Du Bois, for it was not plagued by the personality problem that attended almost all of Du Bois' personal relationships. See the extensive file of personal correspondence between Johnson and Spingarn in the Johnson Collection (Yale University).

[38] "NAACP Life Memberships Becoming Popular," NAACP press release, July 20, 1928; [James Weldon Johnson] to Spingarn, December 10, 1928; Spingarn to Johnson, December 9, 1928, NAACP Adm. Files, C-142; Spingarn to Johnson, December 11, 1928, NAACP Adm. Files, C-75; NAACP Board Minutes, February 14, 1927.

[39] Spingarn to James Weldon Johnson, December 11, 1928, NAACP Adm. Files, C-75; Walter White to Spingarn, February 19, 1930; Spingarn to White, February 19, 1930, written on *ibid.*; White to Arthur B. Spingarn, March 3, 1930, copy, NAACP Adm. Files, C-144; Minutes of the Committee on Administration, March 3, 1930; Report of the Acting Secretary [White] to the Committee on Administration, March 13, 1930, NAACP National Office (New York City).

[40] Pittsburgh *Courier*, October 9, 1926; NAACP Board Minutes, October 11, 1926. The *Courier* had attacked the Association's handling of funds several months earlier, in January 1926, in an article entitled "The Sweet Scandal." The paper had demanded a public accounting of thousands of dollars in donations collected by the NAACP for the legal defense of a black Detroit doctor and his family who, in the process of defending their lives and home, had slain a white member of the attacking mob. The case, which was eventually won by the Association after a protracted legal battle, cost more than $30,000 in legal fees. Although the January *Courier* article caused the NAACP office staff great consternation, it did not create much of a stir in the black community. [Mary White Ovington] to Spingarn, January 13, 1926, copy, NAACP Adm. Files, C-70; [James Weldon Johnson] to Spingarn, October 14, 1926, copy, NAACP Adm. Files, C-202.

[41] *Ibid.*; James Weldon Johnson to Spingarn, October 15, 1926, telegram, NAACP Board of Directors Files, A-20.

[42] "Statement of J. E. Spingarn, Treasurer of the NAACP," n.d. [October 1926], NAACP Adm. Files, C-201; [Walter White] to Spingarn, October 16, 1926, copy, NAACP Adm. Files, C-202.

[43] Ernest Rice McKinney, "This Week," *Pennsylvania Guard* [Pittsburgh], October 30, 1926, clipping; Chicago *Bee*, October 23, 1926; November 6, 1926; Philadelphia *Tribune*, October 30, 1926, October 23, 1926; New York *News*, November 6, 1926; Baltimore *Afro-American*, October 23, 1926; Charleston [South Carolina] *Messenger*, October 30, 1926; Richmond *Planet*, October 23, 1926, clippings, NAACP Adm. Files, C-202.

[44] *Pennsylvania Guard* [Pittsburgh], October 30, 1926, clipping; Chicago *Whip*, October 16, 1926, October 30, 1926; Cleveland *Gazette*,

October 23, 1926; Arizona *Times* [Tucson], October 15, 1926; Detroit *Owl*, November 13, 1926, clippings; "NAACP-*Courier* 'Bury the Hatchet,'" Pittsburgh *Courier*, September 14, 1929, clipping, NAACP Adm. Files, C-202.

⁴⁵ [James Weldon Johnson] to Edwin R. Embree, June 18, 1929, copy; Spingarn to the Board of Directors, July 5, 1929; Spingarn to Dr. Evan M. Evans, July 5, 1929, Johnson Collection (Yale University). Johnson never resumed his post as Executive Secretary after his leave had expired. He accepted a full-time professorship at Fisk University and maintained his ties with the Association by serving as a member of the Board of Directors until his death in 1939. See *infra*, Chap. 5, pp. 140–141, Chap. 6, pp. 174–177.

⁴⁶ "Memorandum from Miss Randolph to Mr. White," August 4, 1939. The five candidates initially considered by the Nominating Committee were William D. Guthrie, C. C. Burlinghame, George E. Vincent, James G. McDonald, and Raymond Leslie Buell. All are believed to have been whites who had never served the Association in any official capacity at the national level. None enjoyed the national prominence of Moorfield Storey. "Memorandum from the June Board Meeting—1930," NAACP Board of Directors Files, A-21; Isadore Martin to Spingarn, November 26, 1930, Spingarn Collection.

⁴⁷ *Amsterdam News*, n.d. [December 1930], clipping; "Negroes Divided on White Leader," New York *World*, December 24, 1930, clipping, NAACP Board of Directors Files, A-24; New York *Evening Journal*, January 4, 1931.

⁴⁸ Spingarn to the Board of Directors . . . , December 1, 1930, NAACP Adm. Files, C-75.

CHAPTER 5: THE ABOLITIONIST AS ADMINISTRATOR

¹ Spingarn to Walter White, October 2, 1923, NAACP Administrative Files, C-90 (Manuscript Division, Library of Congress; hereafter cited as NAACP Adm. Files).

² [Walter White] to Spingarn, October 3, 1923, NAACP Adm. Files, C-90; [White] to Spingarn, July 18, 1924, copy; September 12, 1924, copy, August 4, 1924; Spingarn to White, July 23, 1924, NAACP Adm. Files, C-91.

³ Despite its shortcomings, *The Fire in the Flint* was received favorably in both the United States and England, and was published in France and Germany in 1927. [Walter White] to Mary White Ovington, March 12, 1927, copy, NAACP Adm. Files, C-95.

⁴ Spingarn to Walter White, October 23, 1926; [White] to Spingarn, October 20, 1926, copy, October 29, 1926, copy; [White] to Mary White Ovington, March 12, 1927, copy, NAACP Adm. Files, C-95; Spingarn to White, April 1, 1929, NAACP Adm. Files, C-97; NAACP Board Minutes, March 14, 1927.

⁵ [Walter White] to Spingarn, February 16, 1932, copy, NAACP Adm. Files, C-78.

⁶ Walter White to Spingarn, April 10, 1930, Arthur B. Spingarn

Papers, Box #4 (Manuscript Division, Library of Congress; hereafter cited as the Arthur B. Spingarn Papers).

[7] S[pingarn] to Arthur [Spingarn], April 30, 1930, Arthur B. Spingarn Papers, Box #4; NAACP Board Minutes, March 9, 1931.

[8] *Ibid.*

[9] National Association for the Advancement of Colored People, "Comparative Statement: Income and Expenses for First 10 Months of 1931 and 1932," copy; statement attached to "Memorandum to Miss Black from Mr. Wilkins," August 14, 1933, NAACP Adm. Files, C-147; statement attached to "Memorandum from Mr. White to Messrs. Wilkins, Bagnall, Pickens, and Arthur Spingarn," August 17, 1932, copy, NAACP Adm. Files, C-146; Minutes of the Committee on Administration, November 18, 1929, NAACP National Office (New York City); [Walter White] to Harry E. Davis, January 4, 1933, copy, NAACP Adm. Files, C-63; [White] to Robert W. Bagnall, March 22, 1932, copy, NAACP Adm. Files, C-78; [White] to Mrs. Jacob H. Schiff, July 18, 1930, copy, NAACP Adm. Files, C-144.

[10] See *supra*, Chap. 4, pp. 105–106.

[11] [Walter White] to Herbert H. Lehman, March 16, 1933, copy, January 9, 1934, copy; [White] to William Rosenwald, February 17, 1932, copy, NAACP Adm. Files, C-78; William Rosenwald to White, April 11, 1932, NAACP Adm. Files, C-74; Philip G. Peabody to White, November 25, 1931, NAACP Adm. Files, C-145; "Memorandum from the Secretary to the Board of Directors," copy, NAACP Adm. Files, C-147.

[12] NAACP Board Minutes, June 9, 1930.

[13] Edwin R. Embree to Walter White, March 29, 1932; [White] to Spingarn, May 25, 1933, copy, NAACP Adm. Files, C-78; Nathan W. Levin to White, July 11, 1930, NAACP Adm. Files, C-158; National Association . . . , "Comparative Statement: Income and Expenses for First 10 Months of 1931 and 1932," copy, NAACP Adm. Files, C-147; "Remarks of Mr. J. E. Spingarn . . . to the Annual Business Meeting of the NAACP . . . ," January 9, 1933, NAACP Board of Directors Files, A-24 (Manuscript Division, Library of Congress; hereafter cited as NAACP Board of Directors Files).

[14] See *supra*, Chap. 4, pp. 109–112; Philip Selznick, *Leadership in Administration: A Sociological Interpretation* (Evanston, Ill.: Row, Peterson and Co., 1957), pp. 90 ff.

[15] See, for example, "Memorandum from Mr. White to Mr. Turner," March 8, 1930, NAACP Adm. Files, C-304; "Memorandum from Mr. White to Mr. Turner," March 8, 1930; [Walter White] to Spingarn, March 11, 1930, copy, NAACP Adm. Files, C-144; White to Spingarn, December 31, 1932, NAACP Adm. Files, C-78; [White] to Spingarn, October 22, 1932, copy, November 9, 1932, copy, April 10, 1935, copy; Spingarn to White, November 10, 1932; June 26, 1933, written on letter from J. W. Griggs to National Association . . . , June 16, 1933; Spingarn to White, n.d. [1935], written on letter from White to Spingarn, April 10, 1935, NAACP Adm. Files, C-294; White to Spingarn, May 29, 1933, November 17, 1933; "Memorandum from Mr. White to the Finance Committee," November 25, 1933, NAACP Adm. Files, C-295; "Memorandum Re: Telephone Conversation with Mr. J. E. Spingarn . . . ,"

November 1932, NAACP Adm. Files, C-146; [White] to Spingarn,
February 1, 1933, copy, NAACP Adm. Files, C-147.
    16 See, for example, "Note to Mr. [Arthur] Spingarn from Mr. White,"
January 14, 1933, attached to letter from Guaranty Trust Company to
[National Association . . .], January 18, 1933; [Walter White] to
Arthur B. Spingarn, January 14, 1933, copy, NAACP Adm. Files, C-295;
"Memorandum from Miss Randolph," June 9, 1931, NAACP Board of
Directors Files, A-21; White to Spingarn, June 2, 1932, copy, November
15, 1932, NAACP Board of Directors Files, A-26; White to Isadore
Martin, May 31, 1933, telegram; White to members of the Budget
Committee, June 8, 1933, copy; Spingarn to White, May 30, 1934;
Richetta Randolph to Spingarn, June 6, 1934, copy, April 17, 1935, copy,
April 24, 1936, copy; White to Spingarn, October 14, 1938, NAACP
Board of Directors Files, A-27. Spingarn declined to serve on the
Budget Committee in 1935, undoubtedly because of recent criticism of
the highly centralized control of the Association. Memorandum to
Miss Randolph from Mr. J. E. Spingarn, April 27, 1935, NAACP Board
of Directors Files, A-27. See also *infra*, Chap. VII.
    17 Du Bois, Herbert J. Seligmann, William Pickens, Robert W.
Bagnall, Roy Wilkins, "To The Board of Directors," December 21, 1931,
NAACP Board of Directors Files, A-21. No copy of White's alleged
charges to the Budget Committee has been located in any of the several
manuscript collections.
    18 Mary White Ovington to Spingarn, December 15, 1931; [Spingarn]
to Ovington, n.d. [1931], rough draft, J. E. Spingarn Collection (New
York Public Library; hereafter cited as the Spingarn Collection).
Ovington complained that she felt useless, especially because White
never asked her opinion about matters and because she was never
invited to attend committee meetings. Ovington to Spingarn, December
15, 1931, Spingarn Collection. Ovington conveyed Spingarn's suggestion
to the Nominating Committee that the Board chairmanship and presidency be held by the same person. [Ovington] to [Isadore] Martin,
December 28, 1931, NAACP Board of Directors Files, A-28. Earlier, in
1931, James Weldon Johnson had been among the persons considered
for the treasurership, but Johnson declined because of his teaching
duties at Fisk University and his distant location from the national office.
"Memorandum from Mr. [Arthur] Spingarn to Mr. White," March 15,
1931; James Weldon Johnson to Walter White, April 3, 1931, James
Weldon Johnson Collection (Yale University; hereafter cited as the
Johnson Collection).
    19 Spingarn to Arthur Spingarn, n.d. [January 1932 noted at top of
letter in pencil], Arthur B. Spingarn Papers, Box #5; Walter White to
Spingarn, January 18, 1932, copy, NAACP Adm. Files, C-78.
    20 For a discussion of the special funds, see *supra*, Chap. 4, pp. 118-119.
    21 Arthur B. Spingarn to William C. Heaton (auditor), February 27,
1930; W. C. Heaton and Company to Arthur B. Spingarn, March 4,
1930; Arthur B. Spingarn to Walter White, March 5, 1930, NAACP
Adm. Files, C-144; NAACP Board Minutes, March 10, 1930, April 14,
1930.
    22 Spingarn and Mary White Ovington to Walter White, February
12, 1932, NAACP Adm. Files, C-76; [White] to Spingarn, February 16,

1932, copy, NAACP Adm. Files, C-78; "Memorandum to Mr. [William] Pickens and Mr. [Robert W.] Bagnall from Mr. White," February 16, 1932, NAACP Adm. Files, C-146.

[23] Spingarn to Walter White, August 12, 1932, NAACP Adm. Files, C-75; [Roy Wilkins] to Arthur B. Spingarn, October 17, 1932, copy; Arthur B. Spingarn to Roy Wilkins, October 18, 1932, NAACP Adm. Files, C-146.

[24] "Confidential Memorandum Re: Status of the NAACP," November 11, 1932, (typed initials "J.E.S." at bottom), Arthur B. Spingarn Papers, Box #46; "Memorandum from Mr. Wilkins to Mr. Turner," June 14, 1932; statement, n.n., n.d. [1933], NAACP Adm. Files, C-146. The three-member Budget Committee was biracial and usually convened at least once each month. Spingarn wielded considerable influence within the group, undoubtedly because of his financial expertise.

[25] Walter White to Spingarn, June 5, 1933, Johnson Collection; Spingarn to White, June 7, 1933, NAACP Board of Directors Files, A-27. Actually, the Association stood to save closer to $750 rather than $676.50 during the year 1933 by cutting Wilkins to half-time.

[26] Walter White to Spingarn, June 8, 1933; Spingarn to White, June 9, 1933, NAACP Board of Directors Files, A-27.

[27] L. B. McLean to Spingarn, December 29, 1932, telegram; Spingarn to L. B. McLean, September 21, 1932, telegram; Vernon F. Bunce to Spingarn, December 29, 1932; Harry E. Davis to Walter White, December 30, 1932; [White] to Harry E. Davis, January 4, 1933, copy, NAACP Adm. Files, C-63; "Remarks of Mr. J. E. Spingarn, President, to the Annual Business Meeting of the NAACP in answer to the request of the New Jersey Branches that Mr. Bagnall's position with the Association . . . be reconsidered," January 9, 1933, NAACP Board of Directors Files, A-24.

[28] [Walter White] to James Weldon Johnson, January 16, 1933, copy, Johnson Collection; Spingarn, "Memorandum to Mr. White," January 19, 1933, NAACP Adm. Files, C-75; Arthur B. Spingarn to Mary White Ovington, January 13, 1933, copy, NAACP Adm. Files, C-74.

[29] "Memorandum from Mr. White to Miss Ovington, Mr. [J. E.] Spingarn," January 18, 1933, NAACP Adm. Files, C-78; Spingarn, "Memorandum to Mr. White re: His Memorandum of January 18th," January 19, 1933, NAACP Adm. Files, C-75.

[30] See *infra*, Chap. 6, pp. 159–185; Chap. 7.

[31] Spingarn to James Weldon Johnson, May 5, 1929, Johnson Collection.

[32] NAACP Board Minutes, July 14, 1930.

[33] "Memo to Miss Ovington, Mr. Johnson from Mr. White," May 18, 1923, NAACP *Crisis* Files, F-1; "Memorandum from Mr. White to Mr. Johnson," June 18, 1929; Du Bois, "Memorandum to the Committee on Management," n.d. [August 1930]; Arthur B. Spingarn to Walter White, August 19, 1930, NAACP *Crisis* Files, F-2; "Rosenwald Fund," Report of the Acting Secretary to the Committee on Administration, June 2, 1930, NAACP National Office (New York City).

[34] Du Bois to Spingarn, December 18, 1930, Johnson Collection.

[35] [Du Bois] to Spingarn, September 17, 1930, copy, Johnson Collection; Spingarn to [Walter White], December 13, 1930, copy; Du Bois to

Spingarn, December 17, 1930, NAACP *Crisis* Files, F-3.

[36] Statement, n.n., n.d. [1932], Spingarn Collection; Du Bois to Spingarn, n.d., quoted in *ibid.*; Spingarn to Du Bois, n.d., quoted in *ibid.*; [Richetta Randolph], "Memorandum," [May 10, 1932]. NAACP *Crisis* Files, F-3; Spingarn, "Memorandum to Miss Randolph," May 11, 1932, NAACP Adm. Files, C-75.

[37] Du Bois to Hazel Branch, November 12, 1933, Du Bois Papers.

[38] See *infra*, Chap. 7.

CHAPTER 6: THE ABOLITIONIST AS TACTICIAN: TO ALL THINGS A SEASON

[1] Philip Selznick, *Leadership in Administration: A Sociological Interpretation* (Evanston, Ill.: Row, Peterson and Co., 1957), pp. 82 ff.

[2] *Ibid.*

[3] *Ibid.*

[4] *Ibid.*, pp. 62–64.

[5] See Richard Hofstadter, *The Age of Reform: From Bryan to F.D.R.* (New York: Vintage Books, 1960), pp. 275 ff., 286; Arthur M. Schlesinger, Jr., *The Age of Roosevelt: The Politics of Upheaval* (Boston: Houghton Mifflin Co., 1960), pp. 427–28; Donald R. McCoy, *Calvin Coolidge: The Quiet President* (New York: Macmillan Co., 1967), pp. 125, 328–29. For Harding's general racial attitudes, see Andrew Sinclair, *The Available Man: The Life Behind the Masks of Warren Gamaliel Harding* (New York: Macmillan Co., 1965), *passim.*

[6] Schlesinger, *The Age of Roosevelt*, pp. 426–27; John D. Hicks, *Republican Ascendancy, 1921–1933* (New York: Harper & Row, 1960), p. 92; interview with Mrs. J. E. Spingarn, New York City, June 19, 1968.

[7] Schlesinger, *The Age of Roosevelt*, pp. 427–28; statement, n.n., n.d., [1932], NAACP Annual Conference Files, B-9 (Manuscript Division, Library of Congress; hereafter cited as the NAACP Annual Conference Files). Spingarn personally called on the President's secretary at the White House, requesting that Hoover address the Conference or send a representative. The President sent Secretary of the Interior Ray Lyman Wilbur. "Memorandum from Miss Randolph to Mr. White," April 25, 1932; Walter White to —— Pinkett, April 26, 1932, NAACP Annual Conference Files, B-8.

[8] Herbert Hoover to Spingarn, February 4, 1932; "Memorandum from Miss Randolph to Miss Thorpe," February 5, 1932; "J. E. Spingarn Represents NAACP at President's Hoarding Conference," NAACP press release, February 5, [1932]; Spingarn to Walter White, February 7, 1932, NAACP Administrative Files, special folder: Conference on Hoarding (Manuscript Division, Library of Congress; hereafter cited as NAACP Adm. Files); NAACP Board Minutes, February 8, 1932.

[9] [Spingarn], "Memorandum," January 21, 1913; Franklin D. Roosevelt to Spingarn, January 22, 1913; Spingarn to May Childs Nerney, January 24, 1913, NAACP Adm. Files, C-309; Roosevelt to the Adjutant General of the Army, March 13, 1917, copy; Roosevelt to Spingarn,

July 20, 1925, November 18, 1927, J. E. Spingarn Collection (New York Public Library; hereafter cited as the Spingarn Collection).

[10] Spingarn to Walter White, June 8, 1932, NAACP Adm. Files, C-75.

[11] Spingarn to Walter White, August 5, 1932, NAACP Adm. Files, C-399.

[12] [Spingarn], "Statement Submitted to Franklin D. Roosevelt Before His Election (Fall 1932)," J. E. Spingarn Papers (Howard University; hereafter cited as the Spingarn Papers). It is possible that Spingarn was assisted in drafting this statement by other NAACP officials. Haiti was one of America's Latin American protectorates where United States intervention had been liberally exercised in the past. One of the last acts of the Hoover administration had been the negotiation of a treaty with Haiti, calling for the Haitianization of the American-staffed constabulary and the withdrawal of the Marines. The NAACP had been supporting Haitian independence since the immediate post-World War I era. Julius W. Pratt, *A History of United States Foreign Policy* (Englewood Cliffs, N.J.: Prentice-Hall, Inc., 1955), pp. 182, 300, 323, 623; NAACP Board Minutes, *passim.*

[13] Schlesinger, *The Age of Roosevelt*, pp. 426 ff.

[14] See the Minutes of the Committee on Administration, NAACP National Office (New York City). Random copies of the Committee's minutes also are to be found in boxes A-26 through A-29 of the NAACP Board of Directors Files (Manuscript Division, Library of Congress; hereafter cited as NAACP Board of Directors Files).

[15] For a discussion of critical decision-making powers and routine decision-making powers of executives, see *supra*, Chap. 4, p. 112.

[16] Report of the Secretary [to the NAACP Board of Directors], September 1932; Supplementary Report, September 12, 1932, October 1932, November 1932, December 1932; Report of the Secretary [to the NAACP Board of Directors], October 1933, November 1933, August 1935, September 1935; Report of the Department of Branches [to the NAACP Board of Directors], October 1932, NAACP National Office (New York City). Detailed summaries of the Association's program during the New Deal are included in "Application of the National Association . . . to the Christian Social Justice Fund, Inc.," January 15, 1936; [Walter White] to George R. Arthur, November 22, 1932, copy, NAACP National Office (New York City).

[17] Report of the Secretary [to the NAACP Board of Directors], September 1933, October 1933, November 1933, NAACP National Office (New York City).

[18] Walter White to James Weldon Johnson, July 12, 1934, Johnson Collection (Yale University).

[19] [Walter White] to Spingarn, December 1, 1933, NAACP Adm. Files, C-207; The Writers' League Against Lynching to Hon. Hill McAlister (Governor of Tennessee), December 16, 1933, telegram; "Members of Writers' League Against Lynching who have returned authorization to affix their signatures to the open letter to Congress . . . ," April 9, 1934; "Memorandum from Miss Randolph to Miss Marshall," January 16, 1935, NAACP Adm. Files, C-208; Amy Spingarn to [White], n.d. [March 1935], NAACP Adm. Files, C-154; S[pingarn] to White, February 4, 1936, NAACP Adm. Files, C-75.

[20] "Spingarn to Speak over NBC Network Feb[ruary] 11," NAACP press release, February 2, [1934], NAACP Adm. Files, C-420; "Advance Copy of Remarks by J. E. Spingarn over WJZ on Sunday Febr[uary] 11, 1934 . . . ," February 16, [1934]; "Protest to NBC Head on Spingarn Censorship," February 16, [1934], NAACP press release; "NBC Bars Mention of Lynching in NAACP Radio Speech," February 13, [1934], NAACP press release, NAACP Adm. Files, C-280; "NAACP to Be Active in Federal Legislation," December 18, [1936], NAACP press release, NAACP Adm. Files, C-415; Spingarn to Walter White, May 7, 1935, NAACP Adm. Files, C-75; NAACP Board Minutes, December 9, 1935; S[pingarn] to White, November 7, 1936, copy, NAACP Adm. Files, C-241.

[21] Schlesinger, *The Age of Roosevelt*, pp. 425 ff; Eleanor Roosevelt to Walter White, March 19, 1936, NAACP Adm. Files, C-73; [White] to Spingarn, May 21, 1937, copy, NAACP Adm. Files, C-75.

[22] "President of NAACP to Make Eight Speeches—Has Not Endorsed Any Political Candidate for Twenty Years," n.d., [1936], NAACP press release, NAACP Adm. Files, C-392.

[23] *Ibid.*

[24] *Ibid.*

[25] "Spingarn, NAACP Head, Congratulates President," November 6, [1936], NAACP press release, NAACP Adm. Files, C-392. Since Roosevelt's personal efforts on behalf of anti-lynching legislation, segregation in education, and related race matters were not outstanding, it is likely that the black vote shifted to the Democratic party in 1936 because of the economic benefits accruing to blacks from New Deal programs.

[26] [Walter White] to William H. Hastie, December 3, 1936, copy, NAACP Board of Directors Files, A-27; Spingarn to Franklin D. Roosevelt, December 14, 1936, night letter, March 27, 1937; [White] to Spingarn, May 17, 1937, copy, NAACP Adm. Files, C-75; White to Mrs. I. H. McDuffie, April 20, 1937, NAACP Adm. Files, C-258; Eleanor Roosevelt to White, March 19, 1936, NAACP Adm. Files, C-73; interview with Mrs. J. E. Spingarn, New York City, June 19, 1968.

[27] S[pingarn] to [Walter White], January 16, 1938, NAACP Adm. Files, C-261; White to James Weldon Johnson, March 23, 1938, Johnson Collection.

[28] Spingarn to Franklin D. Roosevelt, March 27, 1937, copy, NAACP Adm. Files, C-75; [Walter White] to Spingarn, August 18, 1937, copy, NAACP Adm. Files, C-259; Spingarn and Louis T. Wright to Robert F. Wagner and Frederick Van Nuys, December 13, 1937, telegram; Louis T. Wright to Franklin D. Roosevelt, December 13, 1937, copy; "Memorandum Re: Status of Anti-Lynching," n.d. [1938], NAACP Adm. Files, C-260; NAACP Board Minutes, April 19, 1937.

[29] See the NAACP Board Minutes, 1930–1939, *passim;* Walter White, "Memorandum to the Good Will Fund," October 18, 1937, NAACP Adm. Files, C-151; Charles Houston, "To the Trustees of the American Fund for Public Service, Inc.," June 22, 1937, Johnson Collection.

[30] *Ibid.; Nixon* v. *Condon* (1932), 286 U.S. 73; *Grovey* v. *Townsend* (1935), 295 U.S. 45; *Smith* v. *Allwright* (1944), 321 U.S. 649.

[31] Du Bois, "What Is Wrong with the NAACP?" (address delivered before the NAACP Annual Conference, Washington, D.C., May 18,

1932), NAACP Annual Conference Files, B-8.

[32] [Robert W. Bagnall] to Daisy E. Lampkin, October 28, 1930, copy, NAACP Adm. Files (special correspondence—Robert W. Bagnall); NAACP Board Minutes, May 9, 1932.

[33] [Roy Wilkins] to Arthur B. Spingarn, January 16, 1933, copy, NAACP Adm. Files (special correspondence—Robert W. Bagnall); statement enclosed in Du Bois to James Weldon Johnson, December 20, 1929, NAACP Adm. Files, C-64.

[34] [Walter White] to Robert W. Bagnall, April 11, 1932, copy, NAACP Adm. Files, C-63; Spingarn to White, June 6, 1933, Johnson Collection; notation in Spingarn's handwriting on *ibid.;* [White] to Spingarn, June 22, 1933, copy, NAACP Adm. Files, C-78; Du Bois to White, June 16, 1933, NAACP Adm. Files, C-64. See also George S. Schuyler, "Consumers' Cooperation: The Negro's Economic Salvation," n.d. [1932], NAACP Annual Conference Files, B-8.

[35] See especially Wilson Record, *Race and Radicalism: The NAACP and the Communist Party in Conflict* (Ithaca, N.Y.: Cornell University Press, 1964); Francis L. Broderick, *W. E. B. DuBois: Negro Leader in a Time of Crisis* (Stanford, Calif.: Stanford University Press, 1959), pp. 144–47; Loren Miller, "How 'Left' Is the NAACP?" *The New Masses* (July 16, 1935), clipping, NAACP Adm. Files, C-442; Spingarn to Walter White, January 27, 1930, NAACP Adm. Files, C-75.

[36] Spingarn, "Literature and the New Era" (lecture delivered at the New School for Social Research, New York City, February 18, 1931), Spingarn Collection.

[37] *Ibid.*

[38] Spingarn, "Politics and the Poet: A Prophecy," *Atlantic Monthly,* CLXX (November 1942), 76.

[39] Spingarn, "Racial Equality" (Amenia, N.Y.: A pamphlet privately printed at the Troutbeck Press, 1932); "Opening Address of Mr. J. E. Spingarn, Presiding at the Annual Mass Meeting of the NAACP," January 1931, NAACP Board of Directors Files, A-24.

[40] Schlesinger, *The Age of Roosevelt,* p. 428; NAACP Board Minutes, April 14, 1930; "Report of the Acting Secretary (for the April meeting of the Board)," 1930; "Report of the Acting Secretary (for the May meeting of the Board)," 1930, NAACP National Office (New York City).

[41] "Opening Address of Mr. J. E. Spingarn, Presiding at the Annual Mass Meeting of the NAACP," January 1931, NAACP Board of Directors Files, A-24.

[42] Draft of speech with revisions in Spingarn's handwriting, n.n., n.d. [1930], Spingarn Collection.

[43] "Opening Address of Mr. J. E. Spingarn, Presiding at the Annual Mass Meeting of the NAACP," January 1931, NAACP Board of Directors Files, A-24.

[44] Chicago *Daily News,* n.d. [1914], clipping, Spingarn Collection; Spingarn, "Racial Equality"; Spingarn to Herbert J. Seligmann, May 2, 1932, NAACP Adm. Files, C-75.

[45] "Opening Address of Mr. J. E. Spingarn, Presiding at the Annual Mass Meeting of the NAACP," January 1931, NAACP Board of Directors Files, A-24.

⁴⁶ Spingarn, "Racial Equality."

⁴⁷ [Spingarn], "Information for the Committee on Administration," n.d. [February 1932], Spingarn Collection.

⁴⁸ NAACP Board Minutes, May 9, 1932; [Richetta Randolph] to Du Bois, April 19, 1932, copy, NAACP Board of Directors Files, A-24. The committee that Spingarn appointed in his capacity as Board Chairman was composed of Arthur Spingarn, Herbert J. Seligmann (Director of Publicity), and Du Bois. He suggested that an outside expert might be consulted if the committee so desired. *Ibid.*

⁴⁹ Spingarn to Walter White, June 7, 1932, NAACP Adm. Files, C-75; [Roy Wilkins] to George S. Schuyler, July 15, 1932, copy, NAACP Adm. Files (special folder—Amenia Conference; hereafter cited as Amenia Conference Folder).

⁵⁰ *Ibid.;* Spingarn to Walter White, June 7, 1932, NAACP Adm. Files, C-75; Spingarn to Roy Wilkins, June 30, 1932, Amenia Conference Folder. White entertained the idea of inviting progressive young whites to serve as conferees, but Roy Wilkins was strongly opposed on the ground that "we do not want the reactions of white people who, no matter how intelligent upon the Negro problem, offer their views in rather academic fashion." [Walter White] to Spingarn, June 9, 1932, copy; "Memorandum to Mr. White from Roy Wilkins," June 16, 1932, Amenia Conference Folder.

⁵¹ Spingarn to Walter White, June 7, 1932, NAACP Adm. Files, C-75; [White] to Spingarn, June 9, 1932, copy, NAACP Adm. Files, C-78; Spingarn to Roy Wilkins, June 30, 1932; Wilkins to White, July 1, 1932; Du Bois to Wilkins, July 12, 1932, Amenia Conference Folder.

⁵² [Robert W. Bagnall] to [the branches], July 21, 1932, copy, Amenia Conference Folder; Report of the Secretary to the Board of Directors, August 1932, NAACP National Office (New York City).

⁵³ Spingarn to James Weldon Johnson, December 6, 1932, Johnson Collection.

⁵⁴ *Ibid.;* Du Bois, "Memorandum To Mr. J. E. Spingarn," December 19, 1932, Spingarn Collection. Du Bois suggested as future black candidates for the presidency Mrs. George William Cook of Washington, D.C., widow of one of the Board's most prominent black members; Bishop John Andrew Gregg of Kansas City; and Harry E. Davis, a prominent Cleveland attorney and member of the Board of Directors. *Ibid.*

⁵⁵ See, for example, "Memorandum to Mr. White from Mr. Spingarn," December 22, 1932; "Memorandum to Mr. White and Dr. Du Bois," December 22, 1932, Amenia Conference Folder; [Walter White] to Spingarn, December 31, 1932, copy, NAACP Adm. Files, C-78.

⁵⁶ [Walter White] to James Weldon Johnson, April 3, 1933, copy, NAACP Adm. Files, C-78; Spingarn to Mary White Ovington, March 28, 1933, Spingarn Collection.

⁵⁷ Du Bois to George Streator, July 15, 1934, Du Bois Papers.

⁵⁸ See *infra,* Chap. 7, pp. 187–216.

⁵⁹ See *supra,* Chap. 2, pp. 61–80.

⁶⁰ Spingarn to the Board of Directors . . . , March 6, 1933, NAACP Adm. Files, C-75; Spingarn to Mary White Ovington, March 28, 1933, Spingarn Collection.

⁶¹ *Ibid.*

⁶² Spingarn to James Weldon Johnson, April 4, 1933, Johnson Collection. By the time this letter was written to Johnson on April 4, Spingarn and White had conferred and White had vehemently denied the rumor that he was not enthusiastic about the Amenia Conference. Spingarn's placing the blame on the "Secretary" in his March 28 letter to Ovington, as opposed to his blaming the "Staff" in his April 4 letter to Johnson, would seem to indicate that he continued to be convinced of a lack of interest in the Conference on the part of the office workers, if not of White himself. [Walter White] to Johnson, April 3, 1933, copy, NAACP Adm. Files, C-78.

⁶³ Selznick, *Leadership in Administration*, pp. 74–82. Selznick offers the following illuminating comment regarding an organization's retreat to technology: "A characteristic threat to the integration of purpose and commitment—hence to the adequate definition of institutional mission—is an excessive or premature technological orientation. This posture is marked by a concentration on ways and means. The ends of action are taken for granted, viewed as essentially problematic "givens" in organization-building and decision-making. The enterprise is conceived of as a tool whose goals are set externally. This may not raise difficulties, if tasks are narrowly and sharply defined, as in the case of a typist pool or machine records unit. At this extreme, the organization is totally absorbed in routine tasks and leadership is dispensable. However, as we move to areas where self-determination becomes increasingly important—where "initiative" must be exercised—the setting of goals loses its innocence. In particular, if a leadership acts as if it had no creative role in the formulation of ends, when in fact the situation demands such a role, it will fail, leaving a history of uncontrolled, opportunistic adaptation behind it." *Ibid.*, pp. 74–75.

⁶⁴ [Walter White] to Spingarn, March 14, 1933, copy, NAACP Adm. Files, C-78.

⁶⁵ [Walter White] to James Weldon Johnson, March 22, 1933, copy, March 25, 1933, copy, March 29, 1933, copy, NAACP Adm. Files, C-78; Spingarn to White, March 31, 1933, NAACP Adm. Files, C-75.

⁶⁶ James Weldon Johnson to Spingarn, May 26, 1933, Johnson Collection. Johnson insisted that it would be "little short of a calamity" if Spingarn should not at least complete his current term. Johnson to ——, May 12, 1933 (letter sent to all members of the Committee charged with consideration of Spingarn's resignation), Spingarn Collection. Du Bois to Johnson, May 18, 1933, NAACP Adm. Files, C-62; Louis T. Wright to Johnson, May 20, 1933, NAACP Board of Directors Files, A-21; Isadore Martin to Spingarn, March 6, 1933; Carl Murphy to Spingarn, March 21, 1933; William Pickens to Spingarn, March 21, 1933; Mary White Ovington to Spingarn, March 24, 1933, Spingarn Collection; [Walter White] to Johnson, June 1, 1933, copy, NAACP Adm. Files, C-78; Spingarn to Johnson, June 26, 1933, Johnson Collection; Johnson to Spingarn, May 26, 1933, Johnson Collection; NAACP Board Minutes, June 12, 1933. It was White's idea to have the Board draft a resolution expressing confidence in Spingarn. [White] to Johnson, June 1, 1933, copy, NAACP Adm. Files, C-78.

⁶⁷ Spingarn to James Weldon Johnson, June 26, 1933, Johnson Collection.

⁶⁸ NAACP Board Minutes, March 14, 1933. The resolution adopted by

the Board was offered by Arthur Spingarn. *Ibid.*

[69] Du Bois to Spingarn, March 14, 1933; Du Bois to ——, March 14, 1933, Spingarn Papers (Howard University); [Walter White] to Du Bois, April 8, 1933, copy, Amenia Conference Folder. At Du Bois' suggestion, all of the persons on both lists were contacted, probably in anticipation of last-minute cancellations by some of those who had accepted. Spingarn to White, April 11, 1933, Amenia Conference Files.

[70] Notations initialed "J.E.S." on bottom of letter from Du Bois to Spingarn, March 14, 1933, Spingarn Papers (Howard University). Spingarn also listed the names of several older black leaders, including Mary McCloud Bethune and Nannie Burroughs, apparently as individuals who might serve as observers, though not participants, at the Conference. *Ibid.*

[71] The list of participants discussed in the text is derived from "List of Persons Invited to the Amenia Conference, August 18–21, 1933," Amenia Conference Folder; Du Bois, *Dusk of Dawn*, pp. 299 ff. Spingarn dispatched an invitation to each member of the Board of Directors, inviting them to Troutbeck for lunch and dinner and as observers, but not participants, at the Conference. In addition, several white observers visited the meeting, including Mr. and Mrs. Lewis Mumford and a couple identified as "a federal official and his wife." "Invitation to the Amenia Conference," July 10, 1933; "Second Amenia Conference, Amenia N.Y., August 18–21, 1933," Amenia Conference Folder.

[72] Du Bois, *Dusk of Dawn*, p. 300; "Proposed Press Release from Publicity Committee of 2nd Amenia," n.d. [August 1933]; Louis L. Redding to Roy Wilkins, September 2, 1933, Amenia Conference Folder. Eleven of the thirty-three conferees were women. "Proposed Press Release from Publicity Committee of 2nd Amenia," n.d. [August 1933], Amenia Conference Folder.

[73] Spingarn, "Memorandum No. 2: To All Those Invited to the Amenia Conference, August 18–21, 1933," Johnson Collection.

[74] [Du Bois], "Important Notice, No. 3, end of July, 1933," Amenia Conference Folder.

[75] "Findings: Second Amenia Conference, Aug[ust] 18–21, 1933," corrected copy, Amenia Conference Folder. Succeeding paragraphs in the text are based on the findings of the Conference unless otherwise designated.

[76] Louis L. Redding to Roy Wilkins, September 2, 1933, Amenia Conference Folder.

[77] Ralph Bunche, "Conceptions and Ideologies of the Negro Problem" (Unpublished Carnegie-Myrdal MSS, 1940), p. 210, Schomberg Collection (New York Public Library).

[78] Louis L. Redding to Roy Wilkins, September 2, 1933, Amenia Conference Folder.

[79] Spingarn to [Mary White Ovington], n.d. [1933], Johnson Collection; Abram Harris to Spingarn, July 27, 1934, Spingarn Collection; [Ovington] to [Spingarn,] n.d. [1933], Spingarn Papers (Howard University).

[80] Du Bois, *Dusk of Dawn*, p. 301.

CHAPTER 7: THE ABOLITIONIST AS TACTICIAN: ALL COHERENCE IS GONE

[1] *Crisis,* LXI (January 1934), 20.

[2] *Ibid.*

[3] Walter White, "On Segregation," n.d. [January 1934], see successive drafts of this article in the NAACP Adm. Files, C-430; [White] to Spingarn, January 10, 1934, copy, NAACP Adm. Files, C-78.

[4] "Memorandum from Mr. J. E. Spingarn," January 10, 1934, NAACP Adm. Files, C-75.

[5] "Memorandum to the Secretary from the Chairman of the Board: *Confidential,*" January 10, 1934, NAACP Adm. Files, C-287.

[6] *Ibid.*

[7] Spingarn to Walter White, January 12, 1934, NAACP Adm. Files, C-287.

[8] [Walter White] to Spingarn, January 15, 1934, copy, NAACP Adm. Files, C-287.

[9] See J. E. Spingarn, David H. Pierce, Walter White, Leslie Pinckney Hill, and others, "Segregation—A Symposium," *Crisis,* XLI (March 1934), 80–81.

[10] Du Bois to Walter White, January 10, 1934, January 11, 1934, telegram, January 17, 1934, NAACP Adm. Files, C-287.

[11] Spingarn to Walter White, January 17, 1934, NAACP Adm. Files, C-75.

[12] *Crisis,* XLI (February 1934), 53.

[13] Spingarn and others, "Segregation—A Symposium," 79.

[14] *Ibid.*

[15] [Walter White], "Memorandum to Messrs. J. E. Spingarn, Arthur Spingarn, Roy Wilkins, Geo[rge] Schuyler, William Pickens," March 21, copy, NAACP Adm. Files, C-411.

[16] *Ibid.;* Arthur B. Spingarn to Walter White, March 22, 1934, NAACP Adm. Files, C-411.

[17] "Memorandum from Dr. Wright to Mr. White," March 23, 1934, NAACP Adm. Files, C-411.

[18] [Du Bois], [Resolution on Segregation], March 26, 1934, NAACP Adm. Files, C-411.

[19] [Spingarn], "Memorandum to the Board of Directors Concerning the Proposed Segregation Resolution," April 5, 1934; Spingarn to Arthur Spingarn, April 8, 1934, Arthur B. Spingarn Papers, Box #6.

[20] [Du Bois] to Abram Harris, January 15, 1934, copy, W. E. B. Du Bois Papers (in the custody of Herbert Aptheker, New York City; hereafter cited as the Du Bois Papers); Isadore Martin to Walter White, April 4, 1934; Carl Murphy to the Board of Directors . . . , May 17, 1934, copy, NAACP Board of Directors Files, A-22; Mary White Ovington to [the Board of Directors], May 18, 1934, copy; [Ovington] to Louis T. Wright, May 18, 1934, copy, NAACP Board of Directors Files, A-27.

[21] Spingarn's departure to New Orleans during this crucial period

represented more than a vacation. He stopped in Atlanta to confer at length with Du Bois on grave administrative problems involving the Editor and his relationship with the Association. See *infra*, Chap. 6, pp. 159–185.

[22] Arthur Spingarn to J. E. Spingarn, April 10, 1934, copy, Arthur B. Spingarn Papers, Box #6; NAACP Board Minutes, April 9, 1934. It is significant to note that the vote against the Spingarn brothers' resolution was biracial. Indeed, the resolution which the Board adopted was offered by James Marshall, a white liberal, and seconded by Louis T. Wright. *Ibid.*

[23] *Ibid.;* NAACP press release, April 13 [1934], NAACP Adm. Files, C-411.

[24] Spingarn to Walter White, April 25, 1934, May 9, 1934, NAACP Adm. Files, C-287. At Spingarn's request, White read Spingarn's letter of May to the Board of Directors at the May Board meeting. NAACP Board Minutes, May 14, 1934. White expressed "marked surprise" at Spingarn's reference to the Board's April resolution as "revolutionary." The resolution was affirmation of the goals toward which the Association was aiming and the yardstick by which its accomplishments and failures could be measured, he argued. [White] to Spingarn, May 7, 1934, copy, NAACP Adm. Files, C-287.

[25] Spingarn to Walter White, April 25, 1934, May 9, 1934, NAACP Adm. Files, C-287.

[26] Du Bois, *Dusk of Dawn*, pp. 312–13.

[27] See Du Bois' editorial in *Crisis*, XL (May 1934).

[28] NAACP Board Minutes, May 14, 1934.

[29] Seymour Martin Lipset, *Political Man: The Social Bases of Politics* (Garden City, N.Y.: Doubleday, Anchor Books, 1963), pp. 394 ff.

[30] [Du Bois] to Hazel Branch, February 28, 1934, copy; [Du Bois] to Abram Harris, January 16, 1934, copy, Du Bois Papers. The correspondence between Du Bois and Streator during the seven-month period from January to July, 1934, provides virtually an hour-by-hour description of events at the national office.

[31] Roy Wilkins, "Memorandum to Members of the Budget Committee . . . ," December 8, 1933, copy, Johnson Collection; George Streator to Du Bois, January 9, 1934, April 18, 1934, Du Bois Papers.

[32] [Walter White] to Abram Harris, July 13, 1934, copy, NAACP Board of Directors Files, A-22; George Streator to Du Bois, January 8, 1934; Du Bois to "Friends," February 5, 1934, circular letter, Du Bois Papers. It is not clear why the Board initially would not permit Streator to attend its sessions.

[33] [Walter White], "Memorandum from the Secretary Re[:] the NAACP and the *Crisis* . . . ," March 12, 1934, copy; [White] to Martha Gruening, January 10, 1934, copy, NAACP Adm. Files, C-287; George Streator to Du Bois, April 18, 1934; [Du Bois] to Streator, March 21, 1934, copy, Du Bois Papers. White told at least one interested member of the Association that "the present problem [with Du Bois and the *Crisis*] is solely and wholly a matter of finances." White to G. A. Stewart, February 27, 1934, copy, NAACP, Adm. Files, C-287.

[34] George Streator to Du Bois, April 18, 1934; [Du Bois] to Streator, March 21, 1934, copy, Du Bois Papers.

35 [Du Bois] to Maud Cuney Hare, February 2, 1934, copy; [Du Bois] to Streator, June 26, 1934, copy, Du Bois Papers; Streator to Spingarn July 5, 1934, Spingarn Collection.

36 [Walter White] to Spingarn, May 9, 1933, copy, NAACP Adm. Files, C-78; Spingarn to Du Bois, March 25, 1934, copy, NAACP Adm. Files, C-287.

37 "Memorandum to the Secretary from the Chairman [Spingarn]," January 24, 1934, NAACP Adm. Files, C-78.

38 George Streator to Du Bois, March 2, 1934, Du Bois Papers. Streator had visited Spingarn at his home and had conferred for more than six hours about the general office situation. Streator concluded that Spingarn was worried about what Du Bois intended to do. *Ibid.*

39 *Ibid.;* [Du Bois] to Rachael Davis Du Bois, March 6, 1934, copy, Du Bois Papers.

40 S[pingarn] to [Arthur Spingarn], n.d. [April 1934], enclosed in S[pingarn] to A[rthur] B. S[pingarn], April 8, 1934; [Arthur Spingarn] to J. E. Spingarn, April 10, 1934, copy, Arthur B. Spingarn Papers, Box #6; George Streator to Du Bois, April 11, 1934, Du Bois Papers; NAACP Board Minutes, April 9, 1934. Undoubtedly the Spingarns' distrust of Vann dated from 1926, when the *Courier* had accused the Association of mishandling funds and of being undemocratically administered. See *supra*, Chap. 4, Sec. 2. Arthur Spingarn concealed Streator's role in the 1934 *Courier* controversy. When Richetta Randolph, the clerk of the Board, recorded in the April minutes that Arthur Spingarn had stated that Streator had complained to him about Association news being placed in the *Courier*, Arthur Spingarn informed Miss Randolph that he had complained to Streator, rather than *vice versa*. Arthur B. Spingarn to Richetta Randolph, April 13, 1934, NAACP Adm. Files, C-287.

41 Du Bois to ——, April 6, 1931, enclosed in "Memorandum to Miss Ovington from Dr. Du Bois," April 6, 1931, NAACP *Crisis* Files, F-3 (Manuscript Division, Library of Congress; hereafter cited as NAACP Crisis Files); Du Bois, "What Is Wrong with the NAACP?" (address delivered before the NAACP Annual Conference, Washington, D.C., May 18, 1932), NAACP Annual Conference Files, B-8.

42 Du Bois to Spingarn, October 16, 1933, Johnson Collection. White and Arthur Spingarn had been interested in securing Charles Houston as a member of the Board since the spring of 1933. At Arthur Spingarn's suggestion, White had discussed the matter tentatively with Houston at that time. [White] to Arthur Spingarn, September 21, 1933, copy, NAACP Adm. Files, C-78.

43 Spingarn to Du Bois, October 23, 1933, Johnson Collection; Spingarn to Walter White, July 20, 1934, NAACP Adm. Files, C-75. Spingarn's reluctance to embrace change probably was partially motivated by fear of Communist infiltration of independent branches and, perhaps, natural reluctance on his part to relinquish the power he wielded.

44 Spingarn to Du Bois, October 23, 1933, Johnson Collection; [Du Bois] to George Streator, May 2, 1934, copy, Du Bois Papers. Spingarn advised Du Bois that it would not be wise to have too many vice-presidents. See notation in Spingarn's handwriting on letter from Du Bois to Spingarn, October 16, 1933, Johnson Collection.

[45] George Streator to Du Bois, February 7, 1934, Du Bois Papers.

[46] George Streator to Du Bois, June 22, 1934, Du Bois Papers.

[47] Du Bois, "What Is Wrong with the NAACP?"

[48] Du Bois to Spingarn, October 16, 1933, Johnson Collection.

[49] Du Bois to Abram Harris, January 16, 1934; George Streator to Du Bois, May 11, 1934, Du Bois Papers.

[50] See editorials by Du Bois in the *Crisis*, XLI (April 1934), XLI (May 1934).

[51] George Streator to Du Bois, April 2, 1934, telegram, May 16 [1934], Du Bois Papers. No copy of Spingarn's alleged ultimatum has been located in any of the several manuscript collections.

[52] Lillian Alexander to Louis T. Wright, April 3, 1934, night letter; Lillian Alexander to Rachael Davis Du Bois, April 3, 1934, night letter; Lillian Alexander to Arthur Spingarn, April 3, 1934, night letter; Lillian Alexander to J. E. Spingarn, April 3, 1934, night letter, Du Bois Papers.

[53] [Spingarn] to [Arthur Spingarn], n.d. [April 1934], enclosed in S[pingarn] to A[rthur] B. Spingarn, April 8, 1934, Arthur B. Spingarn Papers, Box #6; [Du Bois] to Streator, April 14, 1934, copy, Du Bois Papers.

[54] [Du Bois] to George Streator, May 2, 1934, copy, Du Bois Papers.

[55] Du Bois to Spingarn, April 21, 1934, Johnson Collection; Du Bois to Streator, May 2, 1934, Du Bois Papers.

[56] *Ibid.*

[57] [Arthur Spingarn] to J. E. Spingarn, April 10, 1934, copy, Arthur B. Spingarn Papers, Box #6; NAACP Board Minutes, April 9, 1934, May 14, 1934.

[58] George Streator to Du Bois, May 9, 1934; Spingarn to Roy Wilkins, May 16, 1934, copy, Du Bois Papers.

[59] [George] S[treator] to Du Bois, May 16 [1934]; May 11, 1934, Du Bois Papers.

[60] Du Bois to Spingarn, May 21, 1934, telegram, May 21, 1934, Johnson Collection.

[61] Du Bois to the Board of Directors . . . , May 21, 1934, Johnson Collection.

[62] George Streator to Du Bois, June 12, 1934, Du Bois Papers; Roy Wilkins to White, June 8, 1934, NAACP Adm. Files, C-105; Du Bois to Spingarn, June 11, 1934, Johnson Collection; [Richetta Randolph] to Spingarn, June 12, 1934, copy, NAACP Board of Directors Files, A-22.

[63] George Streator to Du Bois, June 28, 1934, Du Bois Papers.

[64] "Memorandum to President Hope from Dr. Du Bois," June 11, 1934, Du Bois Papers; Du Bois to Spingarn, June 25, 1934, Johnson Collection.

[65] See Du Bois to the Board of Directors . . . , June 1, 1934; [Du Bois] to Streator, June 26, 1934, copy; Du Bois to the Board of Directors . . . , June 26, 1934, Du Bois Papers.

[66] NAACP Board Minutes, July 10, 1934.

[67] Spingarn to Walter White, July 12, 1934, NAACP Adm. Files, C-105,

CHAPTER 8: THE TWILIGHT OF WHITE LIBERALISM

[1] NAACP Board Minutes, June 11, 1934, July 9, 1934; Spingarn to Walter White, July 12, 1934, NAACP Adm. Files, C-105 (Manuscript Division, Library of Congress; hereafter cited as NAACP Adm. Files). Abram Harris all but forced his selection as Committee Chairman, offering to come to New York and draw up a program for the Association if the national office would pay his expenses. See, for example, [White] to Abram Harris, July 20, 1934, copy, NAACP Board of Directors Files, A-29 (Manuscript Division, Library of Congress; hereafter cited as NAACP Board of Directors Files).

[2] NAACP Board Minutes, September 10, 1934.

[3] Abram L. Harris to Walter White, July 11, 1934, NAACP Board of Directors Files, A-22.

[4] [Walter White] to Abram L. Harris, July 20, 1934, copy; [Harris] to White, July 28, 1934, NAACP Board of Directors Files, A-29.

[5] *Ibid.* In the final arrangement, the Committee divided into small subcommittees, each of which undertook the study and revision of specific areas of the Association's program—economic, educational, political, etc. The subcommittees, in turn, utilized the advice and suggestions of outside resource persons, including Charles Houston and Ralph Bunche. Abram L. Harris to Arthur B. Spingarn, August 28, 1934; Harris to Ralph Bunche, August 28, 1934; "Memorandum to Mr. Wilkins from Mr. White," August 30, 1934; Harris to the Board of Directors . . . , September 6, 1934, NAACP Board of Directors Files, A-29.

[6] [Walter White] to Abram L. Harris, July 30, 1934, copy; Harris to [White], August 4, 1934, August 16, 1934, telegram, NAACP Board of Directors Files, A-29.

[7] "Memorandum to Miss Randolph from Mr. Wilkins," August 16, 1934; [Walter White], "To the Committee on Plan and Program for the NAACP . . . ," August 16, 1934, copy; White to Abram Harris, August 16, 1934, telegram; Harris to White, August 16, 1934, telegram, NAACP Adm. Files, A-29.

[8] [Mary White Ovington] to Walter White, August 17, 1934, telegram; [White] to Spingarn, August 22, 1934, copy; [James Weldon Johnson] to [White], August 18 [1934], NAACP Board of Directors Files, A-29.

[9] Spingarn to Roy Wilkins, August 18, 1934, NAACP Board of Directors Files, A-29.

[10] Abram Harris to Arthur Spingarn, August 28, 1934; Mary White Ovington to [Walter White], September 2 [1934], NAACP Board of Directors Files, A-29.

[11] Unless otherwise designated, succeeding paragraphs are based on the "Preliminary Report of the Committee on Future Plan and Program of the NAACP," n.d. [September 1934], NAACP Board of Directors Files, A-29.

[12] Of decidedly Marxist leaning, John P. Davis later became Executive Secretary of the National Negro Congress, a left-wing organization aimed at uniting and coordinating the efforts of existing civil rights organiza-

tions. It is highly probable that Davis' eventual rejection by the Association as head of the organization's new economic program largely was due to his political philosophy. See Francis L. Broderick and August Meier, eds., *Negro Protest Thought in the Twentieth Century* (Indianapolis, Ind.: Bobbs-Merrill Co., Inc., 1965), pp. 179–80. (Editor's note.)

[13] For a discussion of the national office's control of the branches, see *supra*, Chap. 2, pp. 48–59.

[14] "Preliminary Report of the Committee on Future Plan and Program of the NAACP," n.d. [September 1934], NAACP Board of Directors Files, A-29.

[15] *Ibid.;* Abram L. Harris to Spingarn, September 21, 1934, NAACP Board of Directors Files, A-29. The Racham Fund, like the American Fund for Public Service, was one of several philanthropic foundations designed to aid human betterment through extending grants and loans to organizations and groups engaged in this field of endeavor.

[16] "Memorandum to Mr. White from Mr. Wilkins. . . ," September 19, 1934, copy, NAACP Board of Directors Files, A-29.

[17] Daisy [Lampkin] to Walter White, September 22, 1934, NAACP Board of Directors Files, A-29.

[18] Harry E. Davis to Walter White, September 21, 1934, NAACP Board of Directors Files, A-29.

[19] [Walter White] to Abram L. Harris, September 14, 1934, copy, NAACP Board of Directors Files, A-20; [White] to Harris, July 13, 1934, copy, October 11, 1934, copy, NAACP Board of Directors Files, A-22. In 1940 Ralph Bunche strongly criticized the NAACP for not having implemented the economic program advanced by the Committee on Future Plan and Program. But Bunche did not address himself to either the question of the organization's ability to adapt to the new role or the problem of finances. Ralph J. Bunche, "Extended Memorandum on the Programs, Ideologies, Tactics and Achievements of Negro Betterment and Interracial Organizations" (typescript, 1940), pp. 144 ff., Schomberg Collection (New York Public Library).

[20] William H. Hastie to Walter White, September 24, 1934, NAACP Board of Directors Files, A-29.

[21] Isadore Martin to Spingarn, September 24, 1934, NAACP Board of Directors Files, A-29.

[22] Joseph Prince Loud to Walter White, September 22, 1934, NAACP Board of Directors Files, A-29.

[23] Mary White Ovington to the Chairman of the Board [Spingarn], September 23, 1934, NAACP Board of Directors Files, A-29. Miss Ovington had been an avowed Socialist long before her affiliation with the NAACP.

[24] *Ibid.*

[25] *Ibid.*

[26] Abram Harris to Spingarn, July 27, 1934, Spingarn Collection. This letter discusses Spingarn's statement regarding the acceptance of Du Bois' economic proposals.

[27] See the "Preliminary Report of the Committee on Future Plan and Program of the NAACP," n.d. [September 1934] as revised in Spingarn's handwriting, NAACP Board of Directors Files, A-29.

[28] Spingarn, "The Second Quarter Century of the NAACP" (address

delivered before the Twenty-sixth Annual Conference of the NAACP, St. Louis, Missouri, June 25, 1935), NAACP Annual Conference Files, B-11.

[29] [Walter White] to Spingarn, October 1, 1934; Spingarn to White, October 3, 1935, NAACP Adm. Files, C-293.

[30] Spingarn, "The Second Quarter Century of the NAACP."

[31] For a discussion of the functions of leadership, see *supra,* Chap. 6.

[32] See the "Preliminary Report of the Committee on Future Plan and Program of the NAACP," n.d. [September 1934] as revised in Spingarn's handwriting, NAACP Board of Directors Files, A-29.

[33] *Ibid.*

[34] See *supra,* Chap. 6, pp. 180–185.

[35] "Preliminary Report of the Committee on Future Plan and Program of the NAACP," n.d. [September 1934]. Unless otherwise designated, the recommendations of the Committee on Future Plan and Program, as discussed in succeeding paragraphs, are derived from this report.

[36] For a fuller discussion of the evolution of the Executive Secretary's role, see *supra,* Chap. 4, pp. 109–112.

[37] For a summary of the branches' relationship to the national office, see *supra,* Chap. 2, pp. 48–59.

[38] The report does not indicate whether the final selection of Board candidates was to be the work of the Annual Conference or the Annual Business Meeting, the latter being the body which historically had elected Board members to office. For the powers of the Annual Business Meeting, see *supra,* Chap. 2, pp. 49–52.

[39] See the minutes of the Annual Business Meetings appended to the NAACP Board Minutes (Manuscript Division, Library of Congress).

[40] See *supra,* Chap. 5, pp. 132–134.

[41] The Board had never permitted salaried executives to serve on committees of the Board, even though a given salaried executive might possess the greatest amount of firsthand knowledge regarding the work with which the committee was concerned. For example, the Director of Branches or Field Secretary did not serve on the Committee on Branches.

[42] See the "Report of the Committee on Future Plan and Program of the NAACP" as revised and adopted by the Board of Directors, enclosed in "Memorandum to the Delegates to the Twenty-sixth Annual Conference, NAACP . . . ," June 14, 1935, NAACP Board of Directors Files, A-29.

[43] Cf. *ibid.* with the "Preliminary Report of the Committee on Future Plan and Program of the NAACP," n.d. [September 1934] as revised in Spingarn's handwriting, both in the NAACP Board of Directors Files, A-29.

[44] See the "Report of the Committee on Future Plan and Program of the NAACP" as revised and adopted by the Board of Directors, enclosed in "Memorandum to the Delegates to the Twenty-sixth Annual Conference, NAACP . . . ," June 14, 1935, NAACP Board of Directors Files, A-29.

[45] Spingarn, "The Second Quarter Century of the NAACP."

[46] [Abram Harris] to White, December 27, 1934; and [Abram Harris] to T. Arnold Hill, January 2, 1935, carbon; both in NAACP Board of Directors Files, A-29.

[47] James Weldon Johnson to the Board of Directors . . . , November 12, 1934, NAACP Board of Directors Files, A-28; memorandum to Miss Richetta Randolph from Mr. J. E. Spingarn, April 27, 1935, NAACP Board of Directors Files, A-27.

[48] Address delivered before the Twenty-eighth Annual Conference of the NAACP, Detroit, Michigan, July 1, 1937, NAACP Annual Conference Files, B-14.

INDEX

Spingarn (*continued*)

201–3, 207–16, 245; and economic program for NAACP, 146, 163–64, 168, 208, 231–34; education of, 4–5; and faith in justness of American people, 23, 29, 32–34, 41–43, 45, 153–54, 166, 243–44; and financial contributions to NAACP, 56, 69, 103, 116–17; financial expertise of, 57, 114, 117–20, 132–38, 242; as a horticulturalist, 3, 12, 13; as interpersonal leader, 59–61, 78, 139, 167, 201; joined NAACP, 20–21; as a literary critic, 3, 5–6, 13, 32, 42, 127–28; and lynching, 33, 44–46, 153–54, 156–57, 253; militancy of, 29, 66, 113, 167–68, 244; New Abolition campaign of, 11, 23, 26–47, 56, 66, 85, 105, 109, 175, 244, 245; and noneconomic liberalism, 13–15, 28, 29, 65, 146, 160, 166, 169, 172, 179, 231, 243–44; opposed to Washington, 29–32, 36, 47, 66, 85; patriotism of, 82–83, 166; philosophy of, 9–10, 14, 243; as a poet, 3, 5, 82–83, 115; and politics, 3, 11, 13, 28, 147, 155–56; as President of NAACP, 69, 123–24, 125, 130, 139, 169, 170–71, 173–77, 205–6, 210, 241, 242; as a publisher, 3, 115, 117, 126; and F. D. Roosevelt, 84, 148–49, 150, 151, 154–56; and segregated training for black officers, 30, 81, 84–97, 191; and segregation, 30, 33–37, 39–40, 85, 191–93, 208; and segregation, voluntary, 188, 192–97, 203, 206; social conscience of, 10–11, 12, 13, 15; as a soldier, 3, 11, 80, 81, 83–84, 96, 97–102, 112; as a teacher, 3, 5, 7, 9, 13; as Treasurer of NAACP, 110, 114,

Spingarn (*continued*)

117–22, 132, 140; and Villard, 65–68; and White, 126–30, 188–90, 203, 216; and white leadership of NAACP, 68–69, 77–80, 171; as a writer, 3, 5, 9, 115. *See also* NAACP; Negroes

Spingarn, Mrs. Joel E. (Amy), 64, 97, 116–17, 147, 154, 209, 244

Spingarn Medal, 28, 104, 122

Springfield, Ill., 17, 18

Sterne, Elaine, 39

Stewart, Gilchrist, 90

Stolberg, Benjamin, 154

Storey, Moorfield, 55, 57–58, 77, 107, 110, 123, 126, 244

Streator, George, 143, 199, 200–4 *passim*, 207, 208, 209, 210, 211, 212, 213, 214

Taft, William Howard, 44, 94

Tate, Allen, 6

Thirteenth Amendment, 42

Toledo, Ohio, 52

Trotter, William Monroe, 18, 37, 47, 60

Troutbeck (home of Spingarn), 11–12, 97–98; conferences at, 12, 47–48, 169, 178, 220–21

"Troutbeck Leaflets," 63

Tuskegee Institute, 30, 94, 104

United States Supreme Court, 35, 108, 158–59, 160, 176

University Commission on the Southern Race Question, 43

University of Cincinnati, 32

University of Maryland, 158

University of North Carolina, 42

University of Pittsburgh, 32

University of South Carolina, 42

Vann, Robert L., 120, 204

Villard, Oswald Garrison, 18, 20, 21, 23, 29, 30, 36, 39, 47, 55, 56,

B. Joyce Ross received her A.B. from Clark College in Atlanta, Georgia, and her Ph.D. from American University in Washington, D.C. Professor Ross has taught at South Carolina State College, Howard University, and Kent State University and is currently teaching history at Stanford University. J. E. Spingarn and the Rise of the NAACP *is Professor Ross's first book.*